THE BOYS OF THE SUMMER OF '48

by

—— Russell Schneider ——

SPORTS PUBLISHING INC.
CHAMPAIGN, ILLINOIS

Editor: Susan M. McKinney
Book design: Michelle R. Dressen
Book layout: Jennifer L. Polson, Susan M. McKinney
Dustjacket design: Julie L. Denzer

ISBN: 1-57167-179-x
Library of Congress Number: 98-84788

Printed in the United States.

SPORTS PUBLISHING INC.
http://www.SportsPublishing.com

This book is dedicated to the men who live within its pages, and also to my wife Kay, for her love, encouragement, understanding and help; to my family, whose love and patience provided me with the incentive and opportunity to pursue my career interests; and to the loyal baseball fans of Cleveland, who deserve many more World Championship teams.

Russell Schneider

CONTENTS

ACKNOWLEDGMENTS

Many people contributed to this book, beginning, of course, with the surviving members of *The Boys of the Summer of '48*: Gene Bearden, Ray Boone, Lou Boudreau, Allie Clark, Larry Doby, Bob Feller, Steve Gromek, Mel Harder, Bob Kennedy, Bob Lemon, Ray Murray, Eddie Robinson and Al Rosen.

Heartfelt appreciation is extended to Joe Simenic, an exceptional baseball researcher and dear friend; to Kay Schneider, a wonderful wife, an excellent reader, editor and critic, and to sportswriter Hal Lebovitz, a mentor, advisor and valued friend.

Special thanks to those who worked for the Cleveland Indians in 1948: groundskeeper Marshall Bossard, former catcher Hank Ruszkowski, public relations director Marsh Samuel, business manager Rudie Schaffer, and batboy Billy Sheridan; to members of the families of the players and employees of the Indians organization in 1948: Mike Hegan (whose father was catcher Jim Hegan), and Fred Weisman (whose father was trainer Lefty Weisman); and to Morris Eckhouse, executive director of the Society for American Baseball Research, and his staff.

Also providing assistance with their recollection of that wonderful season a half century ago were the following members of the 1948 Boston Red Sox: second baseman Bobby Doerr, pitcher Denny Galehouse, pitcher Mel Parnell, third baseman Johnny Pesky, and catcher Birdie Tebbetts; as well as pitcher Johnny Sain of the 1948 Boston Braves; employees of the Red Sox in 1948; visiting team batboy Donald Fitzpatrick; and visiting team clubhouse attendant Vince Orlando; and current Red Sox public relations director Dick Bresciani.

Numerous books also were of significant help: *Covering All The Bases*, by Lou Boudreau with Russell Schneider (Sagamore, 1993); *The Cleveland Indians Encyclopedia*, by Russell Schneider (Temple, 1996); *The Baseball Encyclopedia*, edited by Rick Wolff (MacMillan, 1990); *The Ballplayers*, by Mike Shatszkin and Jim Charlton (Arbor House, 1990); *Veeck As In Wreck*, by Bill Veeck with Ed Linn (Signet, 1962); *The Hustler's Handbook*, by Bill Veeck with Ed Linn (Fireside, 1965), Hank Greenberg, *The Story of My Life*, by Hank Greenberg with Ira Berkow (Times Books, 1989); and *Bill Veeck: A Baseball Legend*, by Gerald Eskenazi (McGraw-Hill, 1988).

Thanks also for the use of many of the photographs in this book to the Cleveland Indians, *The Plain Dealer* of Cleveland, the *Cleveland Press* collection at Cleveland State University, Jet Media, publisher of *Indians Ink*, the Baseball Hall of Fame, Lou Boudreau's collection, Mel Harder's collection, and Larry Binz of the *Helena Daily World*.

FOREWORD

by Hal Lebovitz

In *The Boys of the Summer of '48*, Russell Schneider, a meticulous researcher and chronicler, has fashioned a treasure chest filled with anecdotes, remarkable characters, drama and the story of Cleveland's most exciting season in its long, illustrious baseball history. Plus this bonus: interviews with all the remaining members of that World Championship team, a championship which has eluded the Indians in these subsequent 50 years.

To put that season in perspective for readers under 50, it was like the tense, heart-pounding playoffs of October 1997, with so many late-inning thrills and chills, except that this was the way it was from April through September in 1948. With a happier ending.

For me, Schneider's treasure chest unlocked so many personal memories, gems from that time when I was on the sports staff of the late *Cleveland News*.

The immediate flashback was to the historic playoff game, when the Indians, after finishing in a tie with the Boston Red Sox, had to go the Fenway Park for the scary confrontation that would decide which team would play the Boston Braves in the World Series.

One game. Just one game. One game: the climax to a season that had captivated all of us from the day it began. It was as though the entire city was holding its collective breath.

The *News* had three editions in those days, one that hit the streets shortly before noon, a home edition which locked up about 1 p.m. and was delivered to subscribers' doorsteps in the late afternoon, and the Five O'Clock Final, sold on street corners and drug stores with all the latest in news and sports.

The sports pieces invariably made Page One and on this day, for the playoff game, Page One had been blocked out to provide all the details and the giant headline, since the game figured to be over by edition time, we would hold the presses until it was.

Ed McAuley, our baseball writer, was in Fenway Park and he was sending up the play-by-play via Western Union ticker.

My job was to rewrite the ticker, embellish the details, add color and try to put the reader on the scene.

Fellow reporters, eager for the details, too, hung around the sports department and to this day rib me about my abnormal behavior.

In the first inning, manager Lou Boudreau, the team's inspirational leader, hit a home run into the Green Monster's screen. They tell me I was whooping it up as I wrote, and that my fingers flew jubilantly across the typewriter's keys. Then the Red Sox tied it and I seemed to freeze, unable to find the words to describe the horror.

It was not until the fourth inning, when Ken Keltner hit a three-run homer, that I perked up and began to pound out copy and send it to the composing room. And after that, as the Indians' lead increased and the game finally ended with that cherished 8-3 victory, they say I was humming and typing happy copy like a joyful lunatic.

I'll take their word for it because I do remember being on the brink of the dark precipice one moment, then to be saved and carried into the sunlight.

Now this isn't the way an objective reporter should behave—and that's the point: None of us, not even the most cynical and critical sportswriters, of which we had a few in Cleveland then, could divorce ourselves from our deep feelings for this team.

It was a blend of such interesting, unusual and friendly personalities, not a single one who was adversarial to the media, or who had an ego that was greater than the whole. You had to like them. You had to root for them, even if there's supposed to be no cheering in the press box.

This is why, as Schneider recounts, that Boudreau, late in September when the race was chokingly tight, asked the writers if it would be all right to close the clubhouse to the media after games, and the writers went along without a single protest.

Unquestionably the chief character—until he brought in Satchel Paige—was Bill Veeck, the principal owner and CEO of the team, a personality from his blond burrhead to the bottom of his wooden leg. He knew how to play the media and the fans, provide headlines and keep baseball on the front page.

He constantly seemed to be in motion—hopping around town, from street corner to bar to all areas of the Stadium, talking with fans and writers and conjuring up promotions—and one had to wonder where his indefatigable energy came from. He would close the Theatrical Grill on Short Vincent Avenue, or one of his other favorite watering spots, buying drinks for customers, writers and anybody else who might wander in.

I wondered: Did the guy ever sleep? One evening I found out. Hoping to spend some time with him one-on-one in an effort to do an introspective on this dynamo, I offered to drive Veeck to his speaking engagement in a small town in central Ohio. He would go anywhere to sell his Indians and, of course tickets. I figured we'd have plenty to talk about on the two-hour drive.

I picked him up at his Stadium office. He gave me his big smile and said, "Do you mind if I take a nap?" and promptly fell asleep. I woke him up when we arrived. He charmed the crowd that filled the small party room, shook hands with everyone, told several old baseball stories at which his audience laughed uproariously. Then we got into my car and he immediately fell into a sound sleep again. I dropped him off at the Theatrical Grill about 1 a.m., and he stayed there until closing.

So much for the story I had hoped to write, and so much for the myth about the man who never slept.

There were two other daily newspapers in Cleveland then, the morning *Plain Dealer*, which came out at midnight, and the *Press*, the afternoon giant against which we were trying to compete.

The *News* was like the lowly St. Louis Browns, short of funds and short of staff. As I recall we had only four in our sports department, while the *Press* had at least triple that number and was the city's circulation leader.

This, though, was a break for all of us on the *News* sports staff. We had to do it all, not only work on the desk, rewrite, but we also did sidebars and clubhouse stories on the team.

And all the time we were trying to beat the giant *Press*, seeking to scoop them with a front-page story that would sell a few extra papers. Never was there a more glorious year to be part of the newspaper scene as a sportswriter. The competition for stories was nearly as intense for us as the pennant race was for members of the Indians.

It put a heavy burden on Ed McAuley, who not only covered the Indians on the field, he also wrote a daily column. Small wonder that he was totally exhausted at the end of the season.

McAuley, an exceptional writer and a warm, compassionate man, had become very close to Boudreau. The manager, I thought, almost looked at Ed as a father figure. When everyone was wondering who would pitch the playoff game against the Red Sox—most guessers figured it would be Bob Lemon or Bob Feller—McAuley already knew. Boudreau had told him the night before, after the clubhouse meeting in which the manager put the issue before the team, that it would be Gene Bearden, a rookie who had pitched just a few days earlier.

We ran the story in our early City edition, but at Ed's request asked the Associated Press to put an embargo on it so it wouldn't be on the wires until Bearden actually went on to the mound at game time. This was the kind of scoop that sold papers by the bundles in that sizzling baseball season.

The Veeck-Boudreau clash was another. In Cleveland, Boudreau was unquestionably the most popular athlete of that era. From the day he became the regular shortstop to his advance to boy-manager to his continued leadership and performance, he was everybody's hero. Except Veeck's. The boss thought he was a poor manager and, as Schneider so thoroughly recounts, was trying to trade him.

We capitalized on the story by publishing the "Boudreau Ballot." Should Boudreau by traded?

Fans bought extra papers by the thousands to vote a resounding "No." The post office had to put on extra trucks to deliver the ballots.

Veeck used us. When he was unable to make the deal because the other party, the St. Louis Browns, backed off, he told the fans, "You win. I'm calling off the deal."

How Boudreau responded is a center point in Schneider's insightful account, rich with quotes and details, that brings the manager's exploits back to life.

Another personal gem from Russ's treasure chest provided the flashback to my most challenging assignment. McAuley's heavy burden that season allowed me to get an up-close-and-personal look at the most interesting and most unusual baseball character I've ever met—Satchel Paige.

Veeck had signed Paige, the legendary pitcher from the Negro Leagues, in June and he soon captivated fans with his ability—at an unknown age—to fool hitters with his unusual deliveries and remarkable control.

Nat Howard, editor of the *News*, became so fascinated by Satch, as were the fans, he wanted to know much more about him. Satch's story would sell papers, he thought. He commissioned McAuley to make a deal with Satch: The *News* would give Paige $500 if he would tell his story to McAuley.

Satch agreed and soon there were billboards all around town: "Read Satchel Paige's Life Story in the *News*, starting next week."

I was sitting at the copy desk when Nat approached. "Grab a plane to Washington (where the Indians were playing)," he said. "McAuley has too much to do. He asked for somebody else to handle the Paige story. It's your assignment."

On the way to the airport I saw the billboards and I had yet to meet my subject. Talk about being frightened. I was almost as scared when I knocked on Satch's room at the Shoreham Hotel. His roomie, Larry Doby answered. I told him my mission.

Satch, as usual, was elsewhere, but Larry warned me, "Be careful. He carries a gun." Paige did, one that had been with him since his barnstorming years in Latin America, where he felt protection was essential.

The most difficult problem throughout the series was to find Satch. He never would keep appointments, so I'd have to talk with him when he was on the trainer's table in the clubhouse or I'd wait for his arrival at the Majestic Hotel, on East 55th and Scovill, where he lived. In those days it would have been difficult for a black man to get a room in one of the better downtown hotels.

Often he wouldn't arrive until 2 in the morning. But the wait always was worthwhile, for Satch provided some highly readable stories.

After the series had run the planned two weeks, Howard ordered, "Keep 'em coming. Our circulation is zooming."

One piece was about his indeterminate age. Veeck had suggested Satch was at least 50, maybe 60. Although it added to the legend and ticket sales, this bothered Satch. "The ladies don't want to truck with an old man," he said. He insisted he began to pitch professionally in 1927, when he was 17, and offered $500 to anyone who could prove otherwise. A reader located a box score showing Satch was off one year. He had started in 1926, which meant in 1948 he was not quite 40. "That's better," said Satch, although he never paid off the $500. Our paper did.

I finally managed to stretch out the stories for three weeks. Satch's boost to our circulation had been phenomenal. The day the stories ended sales fell back to normal.

When the baseball season ended, the *News* capitalized again, sending me to Gene Bearden's home to do the life story of the pitching hero of '48. The Hollywood-handsome Bearden had been photographed coming out of the clubhouse with a puppy under his arm. So many readers asked for the photo the *News* printed up several thousand. With the photo and stories, again we experienced a hefty circulation boost, once more revealing the impact that team and its players had on the city.

The following year was a disappointment and as Veeck later said, "You can't recapture the rapture."

Schneider actually has, however, by revisiting Bearden and all the other members of that remarkable team who are still alive, and by rekindling the memories of that wonderful year. And for those who were yet unborn he'll capture for them, what they missed.

Read and remember. Read and enjoy.

— *Hal Lebovitz, who was the sports editor of* The Plain Dealer *in Cleveland from 1964-84, is a syndicated sportswriter whose columns appear in four Ohio daily newspapers, and nationally in New Haven, Connecticut and West Chester, Pennsylvania.*

PROLOGUE

Nineteen forty eight.

It was a year unlike any—before or since—in Cleveland sports history.

It was the year Cleveland proclaimed itself the "City of Champions," which nobody could deny.

Not only did the Indians prevail in the American League and World Series, the Cleveland Browns went 15-0 to capture their third consecutive All-America Football Conference championship, and the Cleveland Barons won the American Hockey League's Calder Cup.

The Indians—the Boys of the Summer of '48—kept the fans in a state of near frenzy most of the season, partly because it had been 28 years since they'd previously won a pennant.

Excitement also was generated by their style, the *way* they often won, and the adversity they overcame in one of the tightest and most hotly contested races ever in the major leagues.

They were involved in a fight to the finish with Boston and New York, wound up in a regular season tie with the Red Sox forcing an unprecedented one-game playoff for the pennant and had to recover from an opening-game loss marred by an umpire's incorrect ruling in the World Series to beat the National League champion Boston Braves.

The promotional genius of Bill Veeck, the intrepid owner of the Indians, also was instrumental in locking in the attention of the fans through that hectic, roller coaster season of 1948.

While winning was the most important thing for Veeck, it wasn't the only thing, to twist a phrase made famous by Vince Lombardi.

Called the "Barnum of Baseball," Veeck, then 34, arrived in Cleveland like a whirlwind on June 22, 1946, when he bought the Indians for $2 million, and never stopped whirling during a brief stay that ended 3 1/2 years later. He made the games fun.

In his first season and a half at the helm of the then-floundering franchise, Veeck relied on gifts and gags to attract fans to the Cleveland Municipal Stadium, all the while wheeling and dealing to improve the Indians on the field, which he did with surprising swiftness.

As player-manager Lou Boudreau said of Veeck's promotional efforts, "We weren't very good when Bill bought the club, so he used diversionary tactics to get fans to come to the games until he was able to put together a good team."

And of Veeck's efforts to improve the Indians, Boudreau quipped, "It seemed we always had three teams ... one on the field, one coming and one going."

Among Veeck's major acquisitions were second baseman Joe Gordon, pitcher Gene Bearden and outfielder Allie Clark from the New York Yankees; outfielder Walt Judnich, pitchers Bob Muncrief and Sam Zoldak, and infielder Johnny Berardino from the St. Louis Browns; outfielders Thurman Tucker and Bob Kennedy from the Chicago White Sox and pitchers Don Black and Russ Christopher from the Philadelphia Athletics.

However, it also was a trade he didn't make—Boudreau to the Browns for shortstop Vernon Stephens—that was also important in shaping the success of the Indians.

Without Boudreau, it's doubtful the Indians would have prevailed.

In that season-long, four-team race, the Indians were in first place for 114 games, though seldom by more than two lengths, second for 18 games, and third for 24. Most of the latter was during a three-week period from August 28-September 18 when even many of their most zealous fans had given up hope.

It got so intense for the Indians in mid-September that Boudreau asked the media to stay out of the clubhouse after games. "I don't want anything said in anger or distress by a player or a writer that will create a situation ... I'm asking you to help us all in this," Boudreau was quoted by Franklin Lewis in his 1949 book, *The Cleveland Indians*.

Equally surprising, the media agreed to honor Boudreau's request.

Bill Veeck was an ex-Marine who suffered a crushed right foot during the firing of an artillery weapon in the South Pacific during World War II, an ex-owner of the minor league Milwaukee Brewers of the American Association, an ex-treasurer of the Chicago Cubs of the National League, and ex-

Cleveland Indians owner Bill Veeck and player-manager Lou Boudreau in the club house.

peanut vendor at Wrigley Field when his father was president of the Cubs.

He kept the promotional pot boiling in Cleveland even after the team became respectable on the field, giving away nylon stockings, orchids, perfume, bats, balls and a variety of other gifts; he shot off fireworks after home runs by the Indians; had a special night for an "average fan" named Joe Earley; presented trainer Lefty Weisman $6,000 in silver dollars in a wheelbarrow that was too heavy for him to push off the field; and staged other stunts that amused and attracted fans.

Obviously, Veeck never met a promotion he didn't like and the Indians set a major league attendance record of 2,620,627 in 1948 that stood until the Los Angeles Dodgers attracted 2,755,184 fans in 1962.

Neither was there any doubt about his popularity among the players, according to Marsh Samuel, who grew up with Veeck in Hinsdale, Illinois, a suburb of Chicago, and was the Indians' public relations director in 1948.

Samuel told how Veeck negotiated a contract with Ken Keltner during the winter of 1947-48, calling it "typical" of the way Veeck dealt with his players.

"Keltner was to get a bonus if he hit for a certain average," said Samuel. "In the first or second game of the season, he hit a couple of line drives right on the nose, but right at somebody. Veeck called me into his office and told me that, from then on, I should put a little red dot next to each at-bat which Keltner hit the ball hard.

"I did and, come the end of the year, I gave Veeck the total, though he already knew that Keltner had hit a lot of 'at-em' balls, you know, right at somebody. He counted them as hit which raised Keltner's batting average high enough for him to get the bonus."

Samuel also recounted the celebration the Indians had after winning the World Series in Boston. "It has to be one of the more memorable train rides of all time," he said.

"We were in the club car and it was wild. A lot of guys were drinking burgundy wine, you know, the red stuff, and sloshing it all over everything. I remember, somebody soaked Elaine Robinson, Eddie's wife then. She was wearing a new dress that got soaked and made a big fuss about it. Bill (Veeck) told her to buy another and send him the bill.

"He also went to the head trainman, the conductor or somebody, because the car was in terrible shape from the guys spraying wine and champagne over everything, and jumping on the seats. Bill asked the trainman how much damage he thought the players had caused, and sat down and wrote out a check, right there, for $25,000."

Rudie Schaffer, then the Indians' business manager and also Veeck's close friend, talked about the hectic last two weeks of the season.

"We had accepted orders for World Series tickets and were inundated with the response, even though we weren't sure we were going to win (the pennant)," said Schaffer.

"I'll never forget how low we felt the last day of the season when we were in the (Stadium) offices filling orders and listening to the game on the radio, with the Tigers beating us (7-1 and dropping the Indians into a tie with the Red Sox).

"What made it especially tough was that Bill (Veeck) wanted to spread out the tickets … to try and satisfy as many people as possible by not letting anybody get tickets for all three games we'd have in Cleveland.

"It was a terrible feeling when we lost to the Tigers, but we had to keep filling the orders even though it might be necessary to return the money. I'll tell you that nobody—and I mean

Hank Greenberg (left), Bill Veeck's "right-hand man," with the Indians owner.

Lou Boudreau with the 1948 Indians coaching staff (left to right): Bill McKechnie, Muddy Ruel and Mel Harder.

Lou Boudreau

nobody, except maybe Bill—was happier when we beat the Red Sox for the pennant than I was."

Though he'd lost part of his right leg to amputation, later developed emphysema, and was partially deaf in one ear, Veeck seemed to have the energy of three men, all younger.

He'd promote the Indians at a breakfast meeting, drop in on a civic luncheon where he'd talk some more about the team, then go to the ball park for the game. Afterwards, Veeck would sit in the press room, drink beer with the media and tell stories, often until dawn—or until nobody remained to listen.

Sometimes after a game he would leave the Stadium, fly to New York, go to the Copacabana in time for the late show, drink more beer and swap more baseball stories, and fly back to Cleveland in the early morning.

Fortunately for Cleveland (if not necessarily for the rest of the American League in 1948), Veeck was rebuffed in his attempt five years earlier to buy the inept Philadelphia Phillies, whose record in 1943 was 64-90.

It was Veeck's intention to stock the Phillies with players from the Negro League which, of

Lou Boudreau with Babe Ruth (center) and Red Sox Manager Joe Cronin on "Babe Ruth Day" in 1947, a year prior to Ruth's death.

Lou Boudreau (second from left) with spring training instructors Tris Speaker (left) and Hank Greenberg (third from left) and Bob Hope, minority investor.

course, was four years before Jackie Robinson broke the color barrier in the National League, and Larry Doby did so in the American League.

As Veeck wrote in his autobiography, *Veeck As In Wreck*, "With Satchel Paige, Roy Campanella, Luke Easter, Monte Irvin and countless others, I had not the slightest doubt

Indians broadcasters Jimmy Dudley and Jack Graney.

Author Russell Schneider (center) is signed to a minor league contract as a catcher in December 1948. Muddy Ruel (left) was a coach and Hank Greenberg (right) was a V.P.

that … the Phils would have leaped from seventh place to the pennant."

However, before closing the deal to buy the Phillies, Veeck revealed his plans to then-Commissioner Kenesaw Mountain Landis. A day later Veeck was informed that the Phillies were no longer for sale (though, shortly thereafter, they were sold to somebody else).

When he purchased the Indians, one of Veeck's "partners," though only to a very limited financial extent, was movie star-comedian Bob Hope, who was raised in Cleveland and, he said, had spent may afternoons as a youth watching the Indians play at old League Park.

And, during the winter of 1947-48, Veeck brought in former Detroit Tigers slugger Hank Greenberg, then 37, who had been released by the Pittsburgh Pirates after playing for them in 1947.

Veeck initially wanted Greenberg to continue his playing career in Cleveland, but the future Hall of Famer—and future front office chief of the Indians—declined, saying he wanted to get involved in the administrative side of baseball.

Though he wore a uniform and helped coach Indians hitters (and even played a couple of games) in spring training in 1948, Greenberg served primarily as Veeck's right hand man and confidante. The following season Greenberg was appointed farm director of the Indians, and became general manager when Veeck sold the club for $2.2 million on November 21, 1949.

After leaving the Indians, Veeck purchased the St. Louis Browns in 1951, gaining fame for sending Eddie Gaedel, a 3-foot, 7-inch midget, to the plate in a game against Bob Cain and the Detroit Tigers. He sold the Browns in 1953, when the American League rejected his attempt to move the team to Baltimore (which new owners were permitted to do in 1954).

About that failed endeavor, Veeck said, "I am the victim of duplicity by a lot of lying so-and-sos. Every reason they give for voting me down is either silly or malicious, and I prefer to think they were malicious."

Veeck made an aborted attempt to return to Cleveland by purchasing the Indians in 1958 when the news surfaced that then-owner William R. Daley (with Greenberg as general manager) was considering moving the franchise to Minneapolis-St. Paul. Newspaper accounts said he was ready to pay $4 million for the Indians, but shortly thereafter Veeck backed off, giving as his reason, "It would be impossible to recapture the rapture."

Thereafter, Veeck was involved in several ventures outside of baseball, including an attempt to buy Ringling Brothers Circus, and he also reportedly tried unsuccessfully to obtain an NBA franchise for Cleveland.

Veeck returned to his first love, baseball, when he bought the Chicago White Sox in 1959, sold the team two years later, then returned as their owner again from 1975-80. He died of lung cancer on January 2, 1986.

Greenberg, upon leaving the Indians in 1957, rejoined Veeck as a part owner and vice president of the White Sox from 1959 until he retired in 1963. Greenberg, who was an unsuccessful nominee (by Veeck) to be elected commissioner of baseball in 1962, died on September 4, 1986.

As for the "rapture" of 1948, that Veeck said would be impossible—even for him—to recapture, there's no doubt it was the highlight of the greatest year in the sports history of Cleveland, then the "City of Champions."

Veeck and Boudreau were civic heroes, and household names were Ken Keltner, Joe Gordon, Bob Lemon, Bob Feller, Jim Hegan, Dale Mitchell and Eddie Robinson, and any of the other players who wore Indians uniforms that season.

Children who were too young to stay up late got up early just to find out who won.

Housewives ironed and washed dishes and scrubbed floors to the accompaniment of Indians games as they were broadcast by Jack Graney and Jimmy Dudley over radio station WJW.

Bill Veeck, the "Barnum of Baseball."

Husbands read the sports pages while dinner got cold, if they didn't stay downtown late to go to a ball game.

And grandmothers, who didn't know a strike from a double play, rejoiced when the Indians won and were remorseful with the rest of the family when they lost.

It was indeed one helluva year in Cleveland.

THE 1948 WORLD CHAMPION CLEVELAND INDIANS

CHAPTER ONE

When They Were The Boys

of the Summer of '48

It all began for the Boys of the Summer of '48 the previous winter, on November 24, 1947, to be exact, as Cleveland Indians owner Bill Veeck unabashedly acknowledged in the euphoria of what was then the franchise's greatest moment.

"We didn't win the pennant in 1948," Veeck said a half-century ago, in the wake of the Indians' 8-3 victory over the Boston Red Sox in the American League's first one-game playoff for the championship, vaulting them into the World Series.

"We won it the day I rehired Lou Boudreau," Veeck spoke of the player-manager he'd been determined to trade to the St. Louis Browns, but didn't—or couldn't—depending upon whose explanation is believed.

Veeck claimed he called off the deal to placate the Cleveland fans who idolized Boudreau and were outraged when news of the impending trade was reported in the city's three daily newspapers, the *Plain Dealer, Press* and *News*.

The Browns were to get Boudreau—enabling Veeck to hire a new manager which, in reality, was his purpose for making the trade— and the Indians would receive shortstop Vernon Stephens and three other players.

However, in the midst of the tumult that ensued on November 17, the Browns sent Stephens and pitcher Jack Kramer to the Boston Red Sox for six players and $310,000. It lent credence to speculation that St. Louis general manager Bill DeWitt called off the deal, not Veeck. Seven days later, Veeck re-signed Boudreau.

Whether Veeck did so to appease the fans, as he said, or whether the Browns decided it was to their advantage to deal with the Red Sox instead, was never clarified by either party.

Whatever the truth, Boudreau, who was called, sometimes with derision, the "Boy Manager" when he was hired at the age of 24 to lead the Indians in 1942, kept his job, despite Veeck's lack of confidence in him.

That lack of confidence became evident shortly after Veeck purchased the Indians in June 1946.

In one of his early meetings with the local media, Veeck admitted his interest in hiring the veteran Jimmy Dykes who, a short time earlier, had been fired during his 13th season as manager of the Chicago White Sox. Later, in his book, *Veeck As In Wreck*, he said that Casey Stengel was "waiting in the wings" to become manager of the Indians.

Veeck couldn't make a change, however, unless Boudreau would be willing to step down and serve only as the Indians' shortstop, which he steadfastly refused to do.

It left Veeck with only one alternative, short of firing Boudreau— which also would have cost the Indians the best shortstop in the game.

It was to trade him, and then hire Dykes or Stengel, though the Browns, by turning their back on a deal for Boudreau (or if, indeed, it was Veeck, bowing to the wishes of the fans) nullified that possibility.

Another managerial candidate during the winter of 1947-48 was Leo Durocher, whose feisty style Veeck also

The unorthodox, but highly successful batting stance of Indians player-manager Lou Boudreau.

admired. Durocher had managed the then-Brooklyn Dodgers from 1939-46, and was coming off a one-year suspension imposed by Commissioner Happy Chandler for "acts detrimental to baseball," none of which bothered Veeck one whit.

Also considered by Veeck at that time was Al Lopez, who'd been the Indians' back-up catcher to Jim Hegan in 1947 before he retired, ending a 19-year major league playing career.

But Boudreau prevailed, despite Veeck's obvious low regard for his ability as a strategist and leader, if only because he stubbornly refused to acquiesce to the owner's "request" to step aside for a new manager.

Veeck's low opinion of Boudreau also was manifested by the hiring of veteran coaches Bill McKechnie and Muddy Ruel to the staff. They replaced two of Boudreau's closest friends and trusted lieutenants, Oscar Melillo and George Susce.

The owner also insisted that Boudreau accept Tris Speaker, the Hall of Fame outfielder who managed the Indians from 1919-26, and Hank Greenberg as spring training instructors in 1948.

Hank Greenberg in spring training in 1948.

Spring training instructor, Hall of Famer, Tris Speaker.

Speaker's job was to coach Larry Doby on the finer points of playing the outfield, while Greenberg, resisting Veeck's urging to play one more season, reluctantly donned a uniform to work with some of the Indians hitters.

Greenberg's primary project was Pat Seerey, an outfielder nicknamed "Fat Pat" for obvious reasons who, despite (or perhaps *because* of) his avoirdupois, could hit baseballs great distances, if he was lucky enough to make contact. Unfortunately, he did not do so with much regularity.

McKechnie, who'd managed in the National League from 1922-46, was hired in 1947, and Ruel, the 1947 manager of the St. Louis Browns, was added to the staff in 1948, along with Mel Harder, who had pitched for the Indians from 1928-47.

Thus, the stage was set for Boudreau and the Boys of the Summer of '48 to forge what would become the Indians' greatest—*most thrilling, exciting, wondrous, glorious,* take your choice—season in the history of the franchise, which previously had won only one American League pennant, in 1920.

Three Hall of Famers, Al Lopez (center), Tris Speaker (left) and Lou Boudreau at an Old Timers game at Cleveland's Municipal Stadium in 1954.

When Boudreau and his players arrived in Tucson, Arizona for spring training in 1948 they were greeted at the train station by Mayor E. T. Houston, wearing a full Indian headdress, accompanied by what the local media said was "nearly half the town's population," then about 60,000.

Tucson's best hotel, the newly refurbished Santa Rita, where rooms rented for "two dollars a night and up," was the Indians' headquarters. The then-New York Giants, whose camp was in Phoenix, was the only other major league team that trained in Arizona.

At the time, Harry S. Truman was president of the United States and would upset Thomas E. Dewey in the election in November, and Thomas A. Burke was the mayor of Cleveland; the Soviet Union was blockading Berlin, escalating the impending "Cold War" between the two World War II allies; the most popular film was the "Al Jolson Story;" Ingrid Bergman and Bing Crosby were the favorite movie stars; and "Fibber McGee and Molly" was the No. 1 radio program; a new Plymouth was selling for $2,095; and a sale at Taylor's in downtown Cleveland advertised women's satin dresses for $16.95; Citation won thoroughbred racing's Triple Crown, Joe Louis knocked

Hank Greenberg (left) with Bill Veeck.

Lou Boudreau (left) with second baseman Joe Gordon.

out Jersey Joe Walcott and then retired after winning 25 consecutive heavyweight title bouts in 12 years; and the hated—especially in Cleveland—New York Yankees were baseball's reigning World Champions after capturing their 15th American League pennant and beating the Dodgers in the 1947 World Series.

It was a difficult spring for Boudreau, for many reasons, not the least of which was the knowledge that the one-time "Boy Manager," then 30, knew better than anyone the pressure he was under to win. It would not be good enough to merely improve upon the Indians' record of finishing fourth, third, fifth twice, sixth and fourth again in the six years Boudreau had been manager.

As he said, "I felt we *could* win, Veeck thought we *should* win." That, along with his supreme pride, undoubt-

edly provided Boudreau with more than enough motivation to prove that his critics, especially Veeck, were wrong.

But it wasn't easy, especially in the beginning.

Boudreau and his decisions were routinely scrutinized, evaluated and, as he said, "second guessed" by not only Veeck, but also Greenberg, the former slugger who had joined the Indians in a strangely undefined role the previous winter.

Greenberg had retired as a player after hitting .249 with 25 homers for Pittsburgh in 1947, then accepted Veeck's offer of a job in Cleveland.

He was listed as a vice president and, according to subsequent published comments by Veeck, Greenberg also made a financial investment (later reported as "very minor") in the Indians, making him a part owner.

To Boudreau, Greenberg's presence often was a distraction. In fact, when this book was being researched, Boudreau said in an interview that he believed Greenberg had managerial aspirations himself.

Veeck's explanation was that he had "chased" Greenberg all winter, when asked, as he often was, about the addition of Greenberg to the Indians' hierarchy.

"We talked some about buying a minor league club as partners (because) Hank wanted to get into the administrative end of baseball. When that deal fell through, I tried to think of something else. I wanted him with me. I didn't care whether he came along as a coach, a player, or a stockholder, just so he came."

Later, Greenberg became the Indians' farm director and, after Veeck sold the club (in November 1949), served as general manager under three ownership syndicates from 1949-57. He remained a stockholder and director of the franchise until 1959.

But, that first year with the Indians, Greenberg was mainly Veeck's confidante. He also was Boudreau's severest critic, according to the manager, all of which increased the pressure to win, not merely improve upon the Indians' 80-74 record that landed them in fourth place, 17 games behind the Yankees, in 1947.

There were several personnel problems to re-solve and questions to answer in the desert proving grounds that spring of 1948. One, in particular, involved Doby, who'd been the American League's first black player and second to Jackie Robinson in the major leagues the previous summer.

Because of the color of their skin, Doby and his wife Helyn were not allowed to stay with his team-mates in the Santa Rita Hotel, which remained ra-cially segregated well into the 1950s, as did other Southern cities in which the Indians played.

A second baseman for the Newark Eagles in the Negro American League prior to his purchase by Veeck in July 1947, Doby had an undistinguished first season with the Indians when he batted only .156 in 29 games.

Initially doubtful, too, was Doby's ability to switch to the outfield, which Boudreau planned. There obviously was no place for Doby to play in the infield as Joe Gordon was still in his prime as the Indians' second baseman, Eddie Robinson was an up-and-coming, power-hitting first baseman, Ken Keltner was firmly entrenched at third base, and the manager him-self was the American League's all-star shortstop from 1940-45, and 1947.

Even more important than the uncertainty about Doby was the need to round out a starting pitching staff.

At the onset of spring training and through the first three weeks of the season, only two pitchers could be con-sidered regular starters, Bob Feller and Bob Lemon—and, at least until early May, there was more hope than certainty that Lemon would live up to the promise he showed in 1947.

Lemon was a third baseman in his first five minor league seasons (1938-42) before spending three years in the Navy during World War II, and was switched to the out-field as an Indians rookie in 1946. Then, because of his strong throwing arm (and low batting average) he was given a trial on the mound later that season.

Used mainly in relief (in 27 of 32 games), Lemon went 4-5 with a commendable 2.49 earned run average. He be-came a pitcher full-time in 1947, when his record was 11-5 in 37 appearances, 15 as a starter.

Bob Lemon (left) with Ken Keltner.

But it wasn't until May 7, 1948, when Lemon blanked Washington, 8-0, on a four-hitter for his third victory in four decisions, that the Indians were assured that he had turned the corner as an effective starting pitcher.

The uncertainty about the starting pitching rotation, beyond Feller and Lemon, was even more pronounced.

When spring training began, and throughout the weeks that followed leading up to the April 20 opener, Boudreau kept saying that the Indians' "second-line pitchers" had to come through. Otherwise, he grudgingly admitted, there was little chance the Indians could finish higher than third, which was the position most of the "experts" predicted they'd be in on October 3.

As the Yankees were everybody's odds-on favorite to win their 16th pennant, Gordon Cobbledick in the *Plain Dealer*, Frank Gibbons in the *Press*, and Ed McAuley in the *News* picked the Indians to finish behind New York and Boston, while Franklin Lewis in the *Press* tabbed them for fourth, behind Detroit as well as the Yankees and Red Sox.

Boudreau himself picked the Indians for second place, behind the Yankees, though he did so for a book that was being published by the team.

At the head of those potential "second-line" pitchers— 13 in all— who went under Boudreau's microscope in spring training, were newcomer Bob Muncrief, 8-14, for the Browns the preceding season; three who'd pitched for the Indians in 1947: Don Black, 10-12; Al Gettel, 11-10; and Steve Gromek, 3-5; and several previously unheralded rookies named Gene Bearden, Calvin Dorsett, Mike Garcia (though he was identified as "Ed" Garcia in the media guide), Ernie Groth, Bill Kennedy, Bob Kuzava, Lyman Linde, Dick Rozek, and even Les Webber, whose 1947 club was listed as "semi-pro," which offered further testimony as to the desperation the Indians apparently felt when spring training began.

Before it ended, Veeck purchased the contract of Russ Christopher, a lanky right hander who had a history of heart trouble, from the Philadelphia Athletics. His role was to anchor the relief corps which, in those days, was composed primarily of pitchers who weren't good enough to be starters.

Included in that latter category were Ed Klieman and Charley Wensloff—though early on Bearden was penciled in as a probable reliever because he wasn't a hard thrower and had a less than average curve ball. Bearden's best pitch was a knuckle ball, the control of which had to be near-perfect for him to be effective.

Otherwise, the Indians were set behind the plate, with Hegan recognized as the best defensive catcher in the American League, and certainly in the infield, with veterans Keltner, Boudreau, Gordon and Robinson.

In the outfield, Dale Mitchell, a singles hitter who batted .316 as a rookie in 1947, was firmly entrenched in left field, and the early projection had Thurman Tucker, another singles hitter acquired during the winter from the Chicago White Sox in center field, with Walter Judnich, who played for the Browns in 1947, and Indians veteran Hank Edwards in right field, though that was the position Veeck and Boudreau expected Doby to play when, or *if,* he proved capable of hitting major league pitching.

Veeck, in fact, on the very first day of practice made very clear to the media his expectation that Doby would erase any doubts about his ability.

"Doby will be in our starting lineup," Veeck predicted, without specifying a position, though Boudreau offered no such assurance, and most of the reporters remained skeptical.

In reserve, the Indians had Seerey who, in 1947, struck out an average of once every 3.2 times at bat; former Yankee outfielder Allie Clark, who could hit but couldn't throw; and Hal Peck, another good hitter, but who also had trouble in the outfield because he, too, had a weak arm in addition to missing two toes on his foot after shooting them off in a hunting accident.

Among the rookie candidates were Joe Tipton and Ray Murray, who competed for the back-up catcher's job, along with another player up from the minor leagues, Ray Boone,

Gene Bearden

who was listed as a catcher, but would become a short-stop before the season was over (and later an out-standing third baseman); Al Rosen, getting his first chance in the major leagues after a monster season— .349 average, 25 homers, 141 RBIs —as Oklahoma City's third baseman in the (Class AA) Texas League, but whose progress with the Indians obviously was blocked by Keltner.

Available, too, was veteran infielder Johnny Berardino, a jack-of-all-trades but master of none who was another player picked up from the Browns (and who would later change the spelling of his name to "Beradino" and become a television star on the soap opera "General Hospital").

The pre-season roster was rounded out by Hank Ruszkowski, who grew up on the Cleveland sandlots and had been the Indians' opening-day catcher in 1945 but, after spending part of that season and all of 1946 in the Army, fell out of Boudreau's favor because of his unorthodox theory about hitting; and veteran first baseman Elbie Fletcher, who had played 11 sea-sons in the National League and, at age 32, was mak-ing one last attempt to stay in the major leagues after being released by Pittsburgh.

Bill Veeck (right) giving tryout to Satchel Paige.

That's the way the Indians shaped up at the be-ginning of the Cactus League, which then comprised the Gi-ants and three teams from the (Class AAA) Pacific Coast League (Los Angeles Angels, Oakland Oaks and San Fran-cisco Seals), though exhibition games also were played against the University of Southern California, as well as the Browns, White Sox, Pirates and Chicago Cubs as major league teams barnstormed en route to their Opening Day cities.

Realistically, the Indians had so many holes to fill they were not held in high esteem outside of Cleveland where the media, as well as the fans, were more hopeful than practi-cal, eager as they were to accept Veeck's optimism.

They *wanted* to believe ... after all, it had been 27 years since the Indians had won the franchise's only pen-nant, and only three times since then were they able to finish as high as second.

A record Opening-Day crowd of 73,163 fans in Cleveland's Municipal Stadium welcomed the Indians home on April 20. They were rewarded with 4-0 victory over the Browns, as Feller pitched a two-hitter.

Hegan, who homered while going 3-for-3, drove in three runs and Boudreau one. The Indians cracked 11 hits, at least one by everyone in the lineup but Feller and Doby who, true to Veeck's prediction of seven weeks earlier, opened the season in the starting lineup. He played right field, but later would be switched to center.

The Indians went on to win six straight and, by the end of May when their record was 23-11, a very definite case of pennant fever was becoming evident among the fans in Cleve-land.

By then Lemon, with seven victories in nine decisions, had provided every indication that he would be as good as Boudreau and the coaches had expected.

By then, too, Bearden had shown signs of being more than the mop-up reliever that some thought would be his role.

It was virtually out of necessity that Bearden got his first chance to start on May 8, when the Indians were in second place with a 7-4 record.

He responded with a gem, beating the Washington Senators, 6-1. Bearden allowed only three hits, not one of which was a "loud" blow, according to sportswriter Harry Jones in the *Plain Dealer,* until he needed relief help from Christopher with one out in the ninth.

That game also was noteworthy for another reason.

Doby cracked his first major league home run, a shot that, Jones reported, "made history at Griffith Stadium," and that, he said, "11,902 spectators saw with wide-open eyes but still didn't believe."

In his account of the game, Jones wrote: "Not since 1922, when Babe Ruth hit a home run in this spacious park has any athlete hit one further.

"The powerful young Negro drove the ball into dead center field. It struck the top of a 35-foot wall, the base of which is marked 408 feet from the plate, and it hit a loud speaker set and bounced back into the playing field. Had the ball continued on its course, it undoubtedly would have traveled 500 feet.

"Neither Doby nor those who saw the historic blow will ever forget it, nor the eight innings of near-perfect baseball that the rookie Bearden pitched until he tired in the ninth inning."

On May 23, 78,431 fans, comprising the second largest crowd in the history of baseball until then—and the largest ever in Cleveland— jammed their way into the Stadium to see the Indians split a double header with New York. It kept the Indians in first place by a half game over Philadelphia, and two ahead of the Yankees.

That same day, Boston, which had been a pre-season favorite to contend for the pennant, was lodged in seventh place with a 12-17 record. However, from the All-Star Game (July 13) through the end of the season, the Red Sox would go 57-24 for a .704 winning percentage in the second half.

Bearden went on to win three of his next four decisions, through May 31, solidifying his grip on the No. 3 spot in the starting rotation.

Realizing by then that the Indians had a chance to go all the way —in 34 games through the end of May, the Boys of the Summer of '48 held first place for 18 days, and never were out of the lead by more than two lengths—Veeck swung back into action.

Needing to strengthen their defense, partly because the depth of the pitching staff was still questionable, Veeck acquired from the Chicago White Sox strong-armed outfielder Bob Kennedy on June 2.

Thirteen days later, Veeck followed with another trade that would prove to be even more significant, getting left-handed pitcher Sam Zoldak from the Browns.

Both deals could be attributed to, first, Veeck's and Boudreau's satisfaction with Doby, and, second, their dissatisfaction with the efforts of Black, Gettel and Muncrief to take over the No. 4 spot in the starting rotation.

To get Kennedy from the White Sox, Veeck traded Seerey and Gettel. Though Seerey was hitting .261 in 10 games, only one of his hits was a home run, and he'd struck out eight times in 23 at-bats. Gettel was 0-1 in five games, two as a starter.

To get Zoldak, a 9-10 pitcher for the 1947 Browns—whose manager that season was Ruel, an Indians coach in 1948—Veeck sent Bill Kennedy, who was 1-0 in six appearances, three as a starter, and $100,000. It was considered at that time to be a very steep price to pay for any player, especially one whose record was only 2-4, which Zoldak's was with the Browns in the first two months of the season.

Veeck took another big swing three weeks later, on July 7, purchasing from the Kansas City Monarchs the contract of Satchel Paige, the legendary Negro League pitcher. Paige claimed that he was "about 40 years old, pretty soon," though some believed he was closer to 50.

While many were pleased that Paige had finally reached the major leagues, becoming the sixth black player to do so, others—J. G. Taylor Spink, editor and publisher of *The Sporting News*—was outraged at what Spink considered an audacious publicity stunt by Veeck.

In a scathing denouncement, Spink, in a *Sporting News* editorial, accused Veeck of "exploiting" Paige.

"To sign a hurler of Paige's age is to demean the standards of baseball in the big circuits," Spink wrote. "In criticizing the acquisition of Paige, *The Sporting News* believes that Veeck has gone too far in his quest for publicity, and that he has done his league's position absolutely no good in so far as public relations is concerned."

Veeck initially ignored the criticism, although, after Paige proved he could still pitch effectively, the Indians owner in turn "exploited" Spink himself.

Veeck's obvious willingness to go all-out to win the pennant, combined with some off-the-wall promotions—as well as the outstanding play of the team through the first half of the season—had Indians fans in a state of near frenzy.

More than 1.2 million of them, an average of 36,706, spun the turnstiles in 33 games through the first half. It was more than Indians teams had drawn in all but one of the 47 entire seasons previously, and only about 300,000 fewer than the 1,521,978 fans who attended all the games in 1947.

Veeck gave away nylon stockings, which were then hard to get, to attract women to one game, and another time flew in orchids from Hawaii as gifts to the ladies. He staged a "Good Old Joe Earley Night," in which he paid tribute to, and showered gifts upon "Mr. Average Fan," and held a special night for Black, after the pitcher suffered a cerebral hemorrhage, raising $40,000 for the ailing pitcher.

Even more significant than Veeck's promotions was the play of the Indians.

On June 12, Gordon smashed three homers against his former teammates as the Indians swept a double header from the Yankees;

On June 20, another record crowd, 82,781, filled every seat and overflowed onto the field behind the outfield fence to see the Indians win a double header from the surprising Philadelphia Athletics, who had become the fourth team, joining Cleveland, New York and Boston in the most torrid pennant race in the American League's 48-year history.

On June 22, Zoldak paid his first dividend with a 5-2 victory over the Yankees. On June 30, Lemon hurled a no-hitter against Detroit raising his record to 11-6, after he'd earlier pitched 28 consecutive scoreless innings. It gave rise to speculation that Lemon had a shot at becoming the first 30-game winner in the major leagues since Dizzy Dean in 1934.

And, on July 13, with the Indians, whose record was 45-28, a half game ahead of the Athletics (48-32), five Cleveland players were members of the American League all-star team: Boudreau, Gordon, Keltner, Lemon and Feller.

Feller subsequently declined the honor, however, which underscored the only negative aspect of the season to date.

Without a doubt the best pitcher in the American League the two previous seasons, Feller, in 1946, was 26-15 with a 2.18 earned run average in 371 innings while pitch-

Bill Veeck signing Satchel Paige to an Indians contract.

ing 36 complete games and setting a major league strikeout record with 348. In 1947, Feller was 20-11 with a 2.68 ERA in 299 innings, while pitching 20 complete games.

But in 1948, with an uncharacteristic 9-10 record at the All-Star break, Feller was in the throes of a slump that would trouble him and the Indians until the final month of the season.

It was a slump for which Feller's first wife, Virginia, tried to take the blame and deflect criticism of her husband. She said that Feller's problems were caused by the worry and distraction she had caused him because of complications that developed during the birth of their second child.

Veeck, too, got involved, urging Feller to fake an injury in order to avoid the All-Star Game played that season at Sportsman's Park in St. Louis.

Bob Feller (right) with arch rival Hal Newbouser.

When the Indians resumed the season after the All-Star Game, they took another double header from the Athletics. Gromek, a spot starter-reliever, pitched a four-hitter for his third victory in the opener, and then Paige won his first major league game in relief of Lemon (who was slightly injured when hit in the head by a thrown ball).

That day, July 15, when the Indians played their 74th and 75th games of the season, also was noteworthy for another reason.

Doby, the quiet, introverted and sensitive former infielder who'd played all season in right field and was hitting a solid .286, became the Indians' center fielder. It was a position Doby would continue to play well for 11 more seasons, including seven as an American League all-star.

By then, pennant fever was raging in Cleveland and, on July 22, after splitting a double header with the Yankees to maintain their half- game lead over Philadelphia, Boudreau went on record for the first time with a dauntless prediction.

"We're as good as anybody," he said. "We've stayed up there without Feller at his best, and I still think he will come around."

But Feller, to his credit, would have none of it. He simply said no to the honor, that he didn't deserve it, that he had been picked "for old times' sake."

Through those first three months of the season, Boudreau, a self-described "hunch" manager, played like a man possessed, determined as he was to prove that Veeck was wrong in attempting to get rid of him the previous winter.

At the All-Star break, Boudreau was hitting .355 with eight homers and 54 RBIs, and was well on his way to winning the American League Most Valuable Player award.

He did everything—including going behind the plate to catch two innings of the second game of a double header against the White Sox, won by the Indians, 13-8, on May 30. It became necessary after Hegan had been replaced by a pinch hitter, and Tipton was injured.

Murray, who made the team as the Indians' third catcher in spring training, had been returned to the minor leagues, but was immediately recalled by Veeck, who warned Boudreau, "If you ever do that again, I'll have a heart attack—and you'll be gone."

Eddie Robinson

Then, "I think we will win. The Athletics have good pitching and just fair hitting. The Yankees can't win without the big guy (injured Joe DiMaggio) in good shape and at his best. The Red Sox are the main danger, but they will be on the road most of September. Besides, I think we can beat them in their park with our right-handed power."

But then, almost as though they'd been jinxed by Boudreau's prediction, the Indians proceeded to lose four straight and six of seven. They fell out of first place to third, three games behind Boston, their largest deficit of the season to date.

Significantly, the last of those six losses, to the Red Sox, 8-7, on July 30, was administered by Denny Galehouse. His performance in relief that day—he gave up one run on two hits in 8 2/3 innings—earned Galehouse the starting assignment in Boston's most important game of the season two months later.

That last loss to the Red Sox also apparently served as a wake up call for the Indians, then with a 52-38 record, as they reignited their pennant aspirations and went on to win 45 of their last 65 games.

Two of the biggest victories—in fact, *the* two biggest victories— that generally are credited with having spurred the Indians in the stretch run, were delivered on August 8.

They were literally delivered by Boudreau himself, in another double header against the Yankees witnessed by another massive crowd of 73,484 fans in the Stadium.

With the Indians clinging to a percentage points lead over Philadelphia, they were in jeopardy of losing the opener as they trailed, 6-1, in the seventh inning.

Boudreau, who'd come through in the clutch time after time, was on the bench and unable to play, nursing ankle, knee and shoulder injuries incurred three days earlier in a collision at second base with Washington outfielder Gil Coan.

The fans, hushed with apprehension and fearing the worst, roared to life when the Indians scored twice, cutting their deficit to 6-4, and loaded the bases on singles by Hegan and Mitchell, and a walk by Clark with two outs.

Yankees ace southpaw reliever Joe Page was summoned from the bullpen to pitch to Tucker, a left-handed batter, to end the rally— except that Boudreau, despite his injuries, refused to let it happen.

Replacing his left shoe, which he'd removed to soak his ankle in a bucket of ice, Boudreau hobbled to the bat rack, selected his favorite Louisville Slugger, and limped to the plate, accompanied by an ovation that, he said later, sent chills up his spine.

It also thrilled Veeck, who was in the press box with Greenberg, and remarked, "Even if Boudreau doesn't get a hit, this is the most courageous thing I've seen in baseball."

Boudreau stepped in against Page and, four pitches later—after a ball, a foul and a called strike—the inspirational player-manager whom Veeck had wanted to trade, lined a hit to center field. It scored two runs, deadlocking the game at 6-6.

As Boudreau joked later, "I doubled and stopped at first," because that's all the farther he could run.

And, as he left the field for a pinch runner, Boudreau received another ovation, this one greater than the first. Even Greenberg, alongside Veeck in the press box, stood and applauded.

The Indians didn't score again that inning, but broke the tie with two runs in the eighth when Robinson hit his second homer of the game for an 8-6 victory. It was credited to Paige, the third of four pitchers used by the Indians, with Christopher getting the final out.

Then, in the nightcap, Robinson homered again, in the fifth inning, breaking a scoreless tie, accounting for what amounted to the winning in a 2-1 victory for Gromek, with relief help by Klieman, for a clean sweep of the twin bill.

And the next day the headline on Page One of the *Press* announced: "Now It Looks Like the Pennant."

Indeed it did, though 56 games remained on the schedule—plus one that would have to be added.

However, once again the exultation proved to be premature. The Indians lost three of their next five games before rebounding again—and again spurred on by their manager, who was obsessed in his determination to show up Veeck.

Eight consecutive victories followed, the last of which, on August 20, was a 3-0, three-hitter pitched by Paige against the White Sox in front of 78,382 fans in the Stadium.

It brought to 201,829 fans who paid their way in to see the three games Paige started, and triggered a facetious, caustic barb by Veeck in a telegram to *The Sporting News*.

It was addressed to Spink and read: "Paige pitching—no runs, three hits. He definitely is in line for *Sporting News*' rookie of year award. Regards. Bill Veeck."

In blanking Chicago, Paige extended to 39 a consecutive scoreless-inning streak by Indians pitchers. It was two shy of the American League record, which Lemon broke the next day, August 21, when he shut out the White Sox through the eighth, running the streak to 47.

However, with the major league record of 56 in sight, Lemon relinquished a two-run homer to Aaron Robinson, and a solo homer by Dave Philley in the ninth, and the Indians suffered a 3-2 setback, launching another emotional roller coaster ride.

They lost four straight, the last of which on August 24 was administered, 9-8, by the Red Sox, boosting Boston back into first place.

The Indians' skid continued as they went 8-10 through September 4 and, after splitting a Labor Day double header in Chicago, found themselves in third place again, this time by 4 1/2 games, with a 78-53 record.

The Red Sox, continuing their torrid pace by winning 22 of 26 games, were in first place, and the Indians also trailed New York by three.

Even the indomitable Veeck, by then, was ready to give up.

"There's not much chance left now . . . it will take a miracle for us to win," Veeck was quoted in the *Press.*

Which is when Feller came to the rescue.

"Rapid Robert," as he was called—and who was instrumental in stealing the signs of opposing catchers through a telescope commandeered from Feller's World War II ship, the *U.S.S. Alabama* —suddenly regained the form that had made him the American League's premier pitcher.

With a rare losing record of 9-12 as late as July 23, and then 12-14 on August 22, Feller proceeded to win seven straight. He beat New York, 8-1, on August 27; Philadelphia, 8-1, September 1; Chicago, 1-0, September 6; Washington, 4-1, September 17; Boston, 5-2, September 22; Detroit, 4-1, September 26; and Chicago, 5-2, September 29, bringing his record to a commendable 19-14.

Bearden also was outstanding, even prior to the stretch run, going from a 6-3 record on June 27, to win 13 games while losing only four, including six straight from July 8-August 17, and five more in a row from September 10 through the second last game of the regular season.

With Feller and Bearden leading the way, the Indians went on to win seven straight, and 14 of 16, climbing into second place on September 19.

Three days later they tied Boston atop the American League as Feller won his fifth game in a row, against the Red Sox. It came on "Don Black Night," when 76,772 fans filled the Stadium to pay their respects to the pitcher who had been stricken with a cerebral hemorrhage on September 13. It provided him with a $40,000 get well purse.

From Labor Day through the end of the regular season, the Indians won 11 of 16 games and, after tying the Red Sox for first place with 11 days left, clung tenaciously to the lead, winning six of their last nine games. They were deadlocked with the Red Sox and Yankees from September 22-25, but were all alone at the top from September 26-October 1, when only two games remained.

Then Bearden hurled his sixth shutout to beat Detroit, 8-0, on October 2, maintaining the Indians' one-game lead over Boston and two ahead of New York, clinching at least a tie for the pennant.

And with Feller slated to face the Tigers in the finale, seeking an eighth straight victory, it seemed the Indians were home free.

However, Feller lost to his arch rival, Hal Newhouser, 7-1, on October 3, while Boston was beating New York, 10-5, and the Indians'— and their fans'—worst fears were realized.

A playoff schedule had been set up in the event that two, or even all three of the teams were still deadlocked at the end of the season, and it seemed that fate was working against the Indians.

In a coin-tossing ceremony by American League President William Harridge in Chicago on September 24, when the Indians, Red Sox and Yankees were tied with 91-56 records, it was determined that:

If the Indians and Red Sox tied, the playoff game would be played in Boston (where the Red Sox's season record would be 55-22); if the Indians and Yankees tied, the game would be played in New York; if the Red Sox and Yankees tied, the game would be played in New York; and if all three teams tied, the Indians and Red Sox would play one game in Boston, and the winner would play the Yankees on the home field of the Cleveland-Boston winner.

By the fourth inning of the Indians' loss to the Tigers in that final game in Cleveland where 74,181 fans were in the Stadium were hoping —*expecting*, really—to celebrate the pennant clincher, gloom and doom replaced optimism and enthusiasm.

*Bill Veeck signing
Lou Boudreau to
a new contract.*

The Tigers erupted for four runs in the third, knocking out Feller, and added two more in the fourth, while Newhouser was pitching one of his best-ever games.

And, as the scoreboard informed the fans—and the Indians—the Red Sox were romping over the Yankees through six innings in Boston, where the game had started an hour earlier.

By then the outcome of the tightest race in the history of the American League was becoming crystal clear—the Indians and Red Sox would be tied with 96-58 records, two games better than the Yankees, at 94-60, while Philadelphia, which fell out of the race earlier, finished fourth with an 84-70 record.

Even before Newhouser retired Keltner on a fly ball to left for the final out in the loss to the Tigers, Boudreau called Gordon aside in the seventh inning. He said, "It looks like we'll have to go to Boston tomorrow ... what's your idea about our pitcher" to face the Red Sox?

Gordon asked, "Who's your man?" and Boudreau said, "I was thinking about Bearden."

Then, "You just took the words out of my mouth. So was I," said Gordon.

With that, Boudreau sent word to the bullpen for Bearden to stop warming up; he'd been throwing easily, keeping loose in case the Indians got back in the game.

"Come into the dugout and sit down," Boudreau told the rookie pitcher who, less than 24 hours earlier, had pitched nine strong innings.

When the game finally ended and the disappointed Indians trudged into the clubhouse, Boudreau closed the doors, met with his coaches, then said to the players, "What the hell, we were planning to go to Boston (to play the Braves in the World Series) anyway.

"All this means is that now we have to go to Fenway Park first, a day early. It's that simple."

Then he said it was his opinion that Bearden should pitch the all-or-nothing game, but told the Indians as they sat silently in front of their lockers, "We're all in this thing together ... it's your money as well as mine, and if you have any ideas of your own, speak up."

Berardino was the only one who did, questioning the wisdom of starting a left hander in Fenway Park where the left field wall is a friendly target for right-handed hitters.

Boudreau obtained the records of the Indians' starting pitchers against the Red Sox that season. They showed Bearden was 3-1, Lemon 3-2, Feller 2-2, Zoldak 1-1, and Gromek 1-2, and the matter was discussed some more until, finally, Gordon spoke up.

He said, "Lou, we went along with your choice for 154 games and finished in a tie. There's not a man in this room who, two weeks ago, wouldn't have settled for a tie. I'm sure we can go along with you for another game."

And with that, Berardino said, "I'll go along with that, too," and the issue was settled.

It would be the rookie Bearden who'd hold the fate of the Boys of the Summer of '48 in his left hand the next day in Boston.

CHAPTER TWO

A One-Game Season

Just about everyone *except* Gene Bearden was speculated as the Indians' pitcher in the playoff game against Boston, but nobody knew for sure except Lou Boudreau, his coaches and players, as the manager was determined to keep it a secret until game time.

Boudreau's reasoning: "I didn't want the media bothering (Bearden) . . . let's keep everybody guessing." Which he did.

Boudreau made clear, however, that Bob Lemon, along with every other able-bodied pitcher on the staff, including Bob Feller, who'd pitched $2\frac{1}{3}$ innings the day before, would be in the bullpen keeping ready from the start of the game in case Bearden faltered. It was a suggestion that Bearden said was "insulting."

"What the hell do you mean?" he demanded. "There isn't going to be any change of pitchers," and there wasn't.

When Boudreau talked about keeping "everybody guessing," it included, of course, the Red Sox, though they, too, kept the identity of their starting pitcher a secret until it was time for Denny Galehouse to warm up for the biggest game of the season for both teams.

Galehouse got the assignment because he'd pitched so well against the Indians in relief of Mel Parnell three months earlier, in an 8-7 victory on July 30. But still, Boston manager Joe McCarthy also was second guessed for his choice of the 37-year old veteran who'd worn a Cleveland uniform from 1934-38.

Some wondered if McCarthy bypassed Jack Kramer (18-5) and Parnell (15-8), two of Boston's most effective pitchers, because he'd either lost confidence in them—or they'd lost confidence in themselves and begged off.

Also bypassed in favor of Galehouse, whose record going into the playoff game was 8-7 in 26 appearances, 14 as a starter, were Joe Dobson (16-10), who'd pitched the day before in the 10-5 victory over New York, and Ellis Kinder (10-7), who started 22 games and relieved in six in 1948.

The game turned out to be no contest, to the dismay of a capacity crowd of 33,957 at Fenway Park, at least after the fourth inning when the Indians erupted for four runs. Three came on a homer by Ken Keltner that sent Galehouse to the showers, replaced by Kinder, who pitched the rest of the way for Boston.

Boudreau, who again put himself on the spot even before the first pitch—resulting in more second guessing of his managerial acumen by Bill Veeck and Hank Greenberg—also was remarkable again on the field.

Boudreau solo homered in the first inning, singled to trigger the fourth-inning uprising, hit a second homer in the fifth, drew an intentional walk in the seventh, and singled for a perfect 4-for-4 performance in the ninth, when the Indians put the finishing touches on the 8-3 victory that won the pennant.

Amazingly, in that final plate appearance, Boudreau received a standing ovation by the Red Sox fans, despite their disappointment in the way the game had progressed.

Playing his hunches to the hilt, Boudreau, in addition to rejecting the long-held theory that left-handed pitchers were at a disadvantage in Fenway Park, started Allie Clark, a

Gene Bearden reports to Fenway Park for the playoff game.

right-handed batter, at first base in place of left-handed hitting Eddie Robinson.

Boudreau also installed Bob Kennedy, another right-handed batter, in right field, the position Walt Judnich had played most of the second half after Larry Doby was switched to center field.

Not only had Robinson been the regular at the position all season, Clark had never—that's *never ever, anywhere*—played first base previously. He'd always been an outfielder and was as surprised to see his name in the lineup with "1b" after it, as were Veeck and Greenberg, both of whom hotly debated with Boudreau the wisdom of the move.

But, when the game ended and the pennant finally was won, and as Bearden was carried off the field on the shoulders of his exuberant teammates into the clubhouse, Veeck was among the first to congratulate the new American League champions.

"I have only one word to say," he told the Indians. It was, "Thanks."

Galehouse, who would spend most of the next two seasons pitching and coaching for Seattle in the (Class AAA) Pacific Coast League, then go into scouting, a job he still

holds, said he wasn't comfortable explaining why McCarthy chose him to start the playoff game against the Indians.

"It's something I don't feel right talking about," said Galehouse. But then he did, though not in great detail.

"(The day before the game) Birdie Tebbetts was sent around by McCarthy to ask some of us (pitchers) a few questions about pitching the game. I was one of them and when Birdie asked me how I felt about starting the next day, I told him, 'If (McCarthy) wants me to pitch, OK, that's what I'm here for.' That's all I know about that part.

"Then, about 25 years later, Birdie told me that, after he talked to us, though he never said what anybody else told him, he went into McCarthy's office to tell him what everybody had said, to give his opinion as to who should start the game.

"But before Birdie could say anything, he told me, McCarthy turned over a piece of paper that was on his desk and it had my name on it. Obviously, I was his choice to pitch, even before he sent Tebbetts around to talk to us.

"When Birdie came out of McCarthy's office, he said to me, 'I think it will be you,' which was fine with me. I was as ready as I could be.

Lou Boudreau crosses the plate after his first inning home run in the playoff game, and is greeted by teammate (No. 4) Joe Gordon. The Boston catcher is Birdie Tebbetts.

Hank Greenberg (left) with Bill Veeck.

"But I don't want to say anything more about it," said Galehouse. "It was a long time ago and wouldn't help anybody to talk about it now."

Galehouse said the Red Sox also tried to keep secret the fact that he would pitch, just as the Indians didn't let anybody know that Bearden would be their starter.

"McCarthy told me to go to the outfield and just stand around while we (the Red Sox) were taking batting practice, which I did."

It wasn't until Galehouse started to warm up that anybody knew that he had been given the assignment to pitch the most important game of the season for both the Red Sox and Indians.

"Sure, I was pleased," Galehouse answered the obvious question. "That's what you work for, to pitch the big games. I figured it was a chance to do something for the club, although it didn't turn out too well.

"The play that killed us, even though it meant only one run, was the homer that Boudreau hit in the first inning.

"The wind was blowing out to left field at a pretty good clip, and when Boudreau hit the ball—a curve with the count 3-and-2—(Ted) Williams, who was playing left field, came in like he was going to catch it behind the shortstop.

"Then Williams backed up and kept backing up like he was going to catch it against the wall. Then he turned around and backed up toward the infield like he was going

Former Indians pitcher Denny Galehouse, who started for the Red Sox in the playoff game.

Boston catcher Birdie Tebbetts, who would manage the Indians from 1963-66.

remembered that the last time Galehouse pitched against Cleveland, he slammed the door on them. I think that was the basis of his decision to pitch Galehouse.

"What the hell, if it had been the other way around, if Galehouse had beaten Bearden, Boudreau would have gone down in Cleveland history. Everybody would have said, 'That dumb sonofabitch, why'd he pitch a rookie in a big game like that?'

"Instead, Boudreau comes across as real smart and everybody wants to make McCarthy out to be the dumb sonofabitch for pitching Galehouse. But I don't buy it, and I never did.

"We thought we were going to win . . . we *knew* we'd win because we'd played so well the last six weeks of the season, and we were playing at home," continued Tebbetts.

He was Boston's 35-year-old catcher in 1948 and, in fact, made the last out in the playoff game, on a grounder to Keltner. Tebbetts later played for the Indians in 1951-52, and was their manager from 1963-66.

to play the ball off the wall. But it hit right at the top of the wall and bounced into the netting (atop the wall).

"If the wind hadn't been blowing out, it would have been only a fly ball," added Galehouse, as disconsolately as though Boudreau had hit the home run the day before our interview, instead of nearly a half century earlier.

Of Keltner's three-run homer in the fourth inning, Galehouse said, "He decoyed me. The count was 2-and-2 and he was leaning out over the plate. I thought he was looking for an outside pitch, so I threw a fast ball inside, about neck high. It would have been ball three if he let it go. But he didn't. He tomahawked it (over the left-field wall)."

Tebbetts said he didn't know why McCarthy picked Galehouse over the others to start for the Red Sox, but didn't question the choice.

Neither would he confirm that he'd met with Galehouse and other Boston pitchers, at the behest of McCarthy, the day before the game, as Galehouse said.

"Hey, McCarthy was the manager and, in my opinion, to be a good manager you have to have a long memory, which he did," said Tebbetts. "McCarthy

Ken Keltner, who starred for the Indians for 11 seasons, smashed a single, double, and three-run homer in the historic playoff game against the Red Sox.

"The Indians had a couple of Hall of Famers (Feller and Lemon) on their staff, and they're going to pitch a guy (Bearden) that nobody knew? We were happy about that. We thought facing anybody was better for us than Feller or Lemon, and we were satisfied with Galehouse.

"But all of a sudden, bam, bam, bam, home run, home run, home run, and before we knew it, we're beat."

When asked what the Red Sox clubhouse was like after the game, Tebbetts said, "If you want to know if there was any finger pointing, there wasn't. We just got beat, and then we showered, dressed and went home. The season was over."

Don Fitzpatrick, an 18-year-old batboy for the visiting teams at Fenway Park in 1948, and later a Red Sox clubhouse attendant until he retired in 1991, also said he didn't know why McCarthy picked Galehouse.

But he stoutly denied that it had anything to do with speculation that Parnell and Kramer didn't want to pitch.

"I've heard that story, but it's bullshit, believe me. And anybody who knew those guys knows it's bullshit," he said.

Gene Bearden after winning the playoff game.

As for the atmosphere in the Indians dugout during the game, Fitzpatrick said, "What I remember best is that (Allie) Clark was so stressed out, so worried that he'd make an error, he couldn't even sit down between innings."

And Boudreau? "He was a pro. All business. He knew what the stakes were and went right at the Red Sox."

What about Bearden? "I don't know how he was mentally, I just think, at first he was awed by it all, by the whole situation," said Fitzpatrick. "The trainer (Lefty Weisman) was always with him between innings, patting him on the back and rubbing his arm, and giving him a couple of shots to keep him calm."

A couple of shots? "Yes." Of what? "I heard it was brandy, or something, some kind of liquor, I guess," said the old batboy.

"Then, when the Indians got that big (5-1, fourth inning) lead, Bearden just kept getting the outs . . . bang, bang, bang, and the next thing we knew, it was over."

And when it was over, Fitzpatrick said, "Veeck, gimping around on that wooden leg, jumped over the short wall be-tween the dugout and the box seats, happy as hell, as thrilled and excited as anyone could be. He hugged Boudreau and then everybody went into the clubhouse."

Another who was among the first to congratulate Boudreau and the Indians, Fitzpatrick said, was Red Sox owner Tom Yawkey. "I felt bad, because I wanted the Red Sox to win. Mr. Yawkey patted me on the shoulder as he left the clubhouse and said, 'Hang in there, Donald. We'll get there.' He was really a nice man."

"Boudreau had everybody in the Red Sox clubhouse screwed up that day," said Vince Orlando, then the 32-year-old attendant in the Indians' locker room, who was often accused of "spying" on visiting teams— the validity of which he didn't deny.

"Sure I did," Orlando said of the speculation that he passed information to the Red Sox. "What the hell, I worked for the Red Sox, didn't I? Why wouldn't I help them, if I could?" He worked for the Red Sox from 1934 until 1990, when he retired at age 74.

Gene Bearden (left) with Lou Boudreau and Coach Mel Harder celebrating the playoff victory.

The Red Sox were "screwed up" that day, Orlando said, because they couldn't believe that Bearden, and not Lemon or Feller or even Steve Gromek, would pitch the playoff game for the Indians.

As was the custom, the manager would put a new baseball under the cap in the locker of the pitcher who would start the game that day.

But because Boudreau suspected Orlando would try to find out who would pitch for the Indians and inform the Red Sox, he placed baseballs under the caps of Feller, Lemon and Bearden.

"I looked (in the lockers) and realized what Boudreau was doing," said Orlando, "but it didn't matter because I found out it would be Bearden and told my brother (Johnny Orlando, who was the Red Sox clubhouse attendant). But by then I think everybody knew, anyway.

"I was more surprised that Galehouse was going to start for the Sox. Even my brother was surprised. We thought it would be Kramer or Parnell. Everybody did, although everybody liked Galehouse.

"But you had to know McCarthy. He had a funny way about him. I used to say that he talked to gremlins, you know, because he was always thinking, thinking, thinking, how to win, how to beat you. I never saw a guy who thought so much. He was a real intellectual.

"When we'd be in spring training and I'd come in late at night, the light would still be on in his room. Even at one or two o'clock in the morning he'd still be up.

"McCarthy didn't need a hitting coach or a pitching coach because he did it all himself, and he knew everything, which is why I think he picked Galehouse. He must have talked it over in his head all night the night before."

And what about the report that Tebbetts met with the Red Sox pitchers on behalf of McCarthy to help him select the starter? "That makes sense to me," said Orlando. "Birdie was a smart guy, too. He was a brilliant manager when he managed the Indians, though sometimes too brilliant. But I liked him. He was a nice guy. He was great."

Orlando said he also was surprised by the atmosphere in the Indians clubhouse prior to the game because "there was so much clowning around," he said. "You never would have known it was such an important game. Those guys were loose as a goose."

He also confirmed what Fitzpatrick said about Weisman keeping Bearden calm. "I heard that story, too," said Orlando, "that the trainer was feeding Bearden brandy between innings. Can you beat that! I really think Bearden was drunk by the time the game was over. That's the way it seemed to me.

"Oh, Jesus! They were really a loose team. And, my God! What a celebration they had after they won, though most of it was later at the Kenmore Hotel (where the Indians were housed in Boston)."

Though he worked for the Red Sox, Orlando said, "I loved those guys, the Indians, especially (Johnny) Berardino and Boudreau. We were good friends even before he came over to the Red Sox (as a player in 1951, and manager from 1952-54)."

Another of Orlando's favorites was Lemon. "One time he came in with the Indians and gave me money to bet a horse with a bookie friend of mine. The horse won and the bookie had to pay Lemon $2,000. I thought the bookie would be mad, but instead, he gave me a $100 tip.

"I asked him, 'What's that for?' and he said, 'When you told me one of the ball players was betting the horse, I bet it, too, with another bookmaker and I won big.'

"I took Lemon's money to him in a brown paper bag and he got a big kick out of it when I told him about the bookie.

"I loved those guys. Those were really good times."

"We didn't lose the pennant in the playoff game, we lost it early in the season," said Bobby Doerr, the Red Sox 30-year-old second baseman in 1948 who would be elected to the Hall of Fame in 1986.

"We had a good team that year, but started poorly because we couldn't hold a lead. We'd be ahead, like 5-3, 4-2 or 6-5, going into the eighth or ninth inning, and then our relief pitching would blow it.

"It wasn't until about the middle of the season that it got better because our pitching started to come around. Parnell was pitching pretty consistently by then, and so were Kramer and Kinder, though they made a reliever out of Kinder in 1949.

"But if we hadn't lost so many games in the first half, we would have built up a big lead the way we played in the second half. Even at the end we thought we had a good go at it, and when they (American League President William Harridge) flipped a coin that decided the playoff game would be in Boston, we considered it was a big advantage for us.

"I really believe, if we'd had a big relief pitcher we would have won the pennant, not only that (1948) year, but also in 1949 and 1950."

As late as the end of May the Red Sox were mired in seventh place, didn't make it out of sixth place until mid-June, and were fourth with a 39-35 record at the All-Star break.

Doerr admitted he was puzzled by McCarthy's choice of Galehouse. "We all thought Parnell would pitch that day," he said. "(Parnell) had a good sinker and was more successful than most left-handed pitchers in Fenway Park.

"It's a funny story why Parnell's ball broke the way it did. Some time in his career he broke the ring finger on his left hand. When it healed, the finger was stiff and some way or another it caused him to give the ball a funny twist when he released it, which made it break away from right-handed batters.

"It might have been enough to make some guys break their finger on purpose, to give them the kind of sinker that Parnell had.

"I think the reason McCarthy picked Galehouse was because he thought we had the home advantage and the type of club that probably could beat anybody. We had a lot of hitters in the lineup . . . (Ted) Williams, (Vernon) Stephens, (Johnny) Pesky, (Dominic) DiMaggio, and (Billy) Goodman."

Williams, another Hall of Famer on that team, won the batting championship with a .369 average, 25 homers and 127 RBIs that season, and Doerr himself hit .285 with 27 homers and 111 RBIs.

"What McCarthy should have done was ask the eight guys in the starting lineup who they thought should pitch," Doerr said. "I think every man on the team had his own individual feelings, but McCarthy was a very dominating person and I'm sure he thought he was making the right decision.

"No disrespect against Galehouse, but he hadn't started a game for two or three weeks. I just think McCarthy felt Parnell wasn't quite rested enough (though Parnell would have been working with three days' rest, having pitched 6 2/3 innings on September 30 in a 7-3 victory over Washington, and prior to that, three innings on September 26).

Red Sox Manager Joe McCarthy

"Parnell probably was our best pitcher that year and anytime I ever talked to him about it, he always said he was ready (to pitch) and that he was surprised that he didn't start."

On the other hand, Doerr also indicated that the Red Sox were glad to see Bearden, instead of Lemon or Feller, on the mound against them that day.

"We thought it was to our advantage because we didn't consider Bearden to be one of their real strong pitchers, though he sure pitched a helluva game that day," said Doerr.

"(Bearden) had that little knuckler and we didn't have enough sense to move up on him and hit the ball before it broke. In other words, when you are anticipating swinging at that pitch, it was a strike. Just like split-finger fast balls now. But when we swung, we were way out in front of the ball.

"We didn't get smart until the next year. We moved up on him about a foot or two (at the plate) and hit the pitch before it had a chance to break.

"I guess after you get kicked in the fanny so many times, you wake up, which we finally did," added Doerr.

"Which might have been what happened to Bearden in 1949. He didn't have a very good season, did he?" asked Doerr.

Later, when he and Boudreau became teammates in Boston in 1951, Doerr said, "I remember that we talked about that (playoff) game one time when we were having dinner. I asked him, 'Lou, what did you think when you heard that Galehouse would start for us?'

"He said he didn't believe it, and that he sent, I think, Berardino all around Fenway Park, under the stands, everywhere, to see if McCarthy had somebody else warming up."

Parnell, one of the American League's best young pitchers in 1948 when he was 26 years old, said it was a "nightmare," what happened to the Red Sox in the playoff game.

"We thought we were in the driver's seat, the way we'd been playing, the Indians losing their last game against Detroit—and with the game in Fenway Park."

And he also adamantly denied allegations that surfaced periodically that he, as well as Kramer and Kinder, but not Galehouse or Dobson, didn't want to face the Indians in that one-game playoff for the pennant.

"I've heard that for years, over and over and over, and it's absolutely not true," said Parnell. "There was a writer up there (in Boston), Dave Egan—Col. Egan, they called him—who started it, and it was a total lie.

"Hell, any one of us would have welcomed the opportunity to pitch that game, it meant so much to all of us."

The fact is, Parnell said, "The night before the game I was in bed at nine o'clock because I thought I'd be the pitcher the next day. My mother and dad were in town and everybody in my family kept telling me, 'Get some sleep . . . you've got the biggest game of the year tomorrow.'

"It wasn't that McCarthy told me I would pitch. With him there never was much conversation. I think that he, like the rest of us, just took too much for granted, that we were going to (beat the Indians). We'd pretty much counted them out after Labor Day, when they were 4 1/2 games behind. I guess we got too excited too soon.

"When I went to the ball park on the morning of the playoff, I thought it was my game to pitch. I took my time in the clubhouse, like pitchers do when you're going to start. You don't go out and shag flies in batting practice or anything, you just take it easy until it's time to warm up.

"I was standing in front of my locker when McCarthy came alongside me and said, 'Kid, I'm going with the right hander (Galehouse). The elements are against a left hander today. The wind is blowing out.'

"But, hell, that shouldn't have made any difference. I pitched a lot of games with the wind blowing out at Fenway.

"Then (McCarthy) called the clubhouse boy (Fitzpatrick) over and said, 'Fitzie, go out and get Galehouse off the field and bring him into my office.' The kid did and, when McCarthy told Galehouse he was pitching, (Galehouse) got white as a ghost, it was such a shock to him. He didn't expect it.

"With that, I put on my uniform and went out to the field for the rest of batting practice. When the guys saw me, they said, 'What are you doing out here?' I told them, 'I'm not pitching,' and they couldn't believe it.

"I was very disappointed, very upset . . . I sure was," said Parnell. "I was stewing inside, but I didn't argue. I didn't say anything to McCarthy. It was his choice. I liked him as a manager, but I was upset about not pitching," Parnell said again.

"And when we found out Bearden was pitching for the Indians, I thought to myself, 'Hell, if they can pitch a left hander in this park, why can't we?'

"I kind of think that Boudreau felt that way, too. That McCarthy probably was going to start Galehouse, then bring me into the game, which might have been the reason Boudreau loaded up his lineup with right-handed hitters, Clark and (Bob) Kennedy.

"I also understand that Boudreau sent Clark around underneath the stands to see if I was somewhere warming up," said Parnell (though Doerr said he heard it was Berardino who went looking, and Boudreau, in his book, *Covering All The Bases*, said he sent Indians traveling secretary Spud Goldstein on that mission).

When told that Galehouse said he knew the day before that he would pitch, and that Tebbetts had met with members of the Boston pitching staff at McCarthy's request, Parnell said, "I kind of doubt that story. I don't know of anybody (Tebbetts) talked to. I know damned well he didn't talk to me."

Parnell said he remained in the Red Sox dugout the entire game, not even going to the bullpen in case he was needed in relief. When it was over, "We were really down, disappointed after having played so well and coming so close. It really hit us all pretty hard. We expected to win.

"McCarthy didn't say anything, that I recall. At least, I didn't hear anything. We just showered, got dressed and got the hell out of there. The season was over."

After Boudreau joined the Red Sox, Parnell said they never talked much about the playoff, but did discuss at length another game between the two teams at Fenway Park earlier that season.

It was a 2-0 Indians victory on June 8 that came on a two-run homer by Boudreau off Parnell. Losing that game was particularly distressing because, the pitcher said, it was the result of an incorrect call by first base umpire Charlie Berry.

"Boudreau hit the ball down the right-field line that didn't even reach the foul pole before it sliced into the stands," said Parnell. "It started fair and then Berry lost sight of the ball and called it a home run. But a guy sitting five or six rows in foul territory told me later that he caught the ball at least five yards in front of the pole.

"It was a foul ball all the way, but Berry wouldn't ask the plate umpire, Ed Hurley, for help. Hurley told me, 'Mel, I can't make a call on it . . . Berry has got to ask me, and he didn't.'

"Boudreau said he knew it was a foul ball, too, but of course he didn't say anything at the time, and Bill McKechnie (who was coaching first base for the Indians that day) also admitted the ball had gone foul. But nothing could be done about it and we lost.

"Think of it, if we had won that game, there might not have been a tie at the end of the season and we, not the Indians, would have won the pennant."

Johnny Pesky recalled the Red Sox's final game, against New York, which they had to win to retain any hope of finishing in a tie with the Indians.

"We were watching the scoreboard all the time we were playing, and when the Indians lost—I guess we were in the middle innings of our game against the Yankees—we had all the momentum we needed. I thought we were going to do it, win the pennant handily," recalled Pesky.

He was Boston's 29-year-old third baseman in 1948 and, after retiring as a player in 1954, managed in the minor leagues from 1956-62, and was manager of the Red Sox in 1963 and 1964. Pesky returned as a coach for the Red Sox (1975-84), and still serves the team in an advisory capacity.

"I thought McCarthy was a helluva manager, after all, he'd won all those pennants with the Cubs and Yankees (nine, from 1926 until he joined the Red Sox in 1948), so how could you not have confidence in him?" Pesky wanted to know. "You don't second guess a guy who has a record like that.

"Because I did (have confidence in McCarthy) I didn't think twice about his decision to start Galehouse, although, I admit, most of us expected it would be Parnell. I guess McCarthy figured Galehouse had the most rest and was the proper guy to pitch.

"What really surprised me wasn't that Galehouse was pitching for us, but that Boudreau picked Bearden to start for the Indians. But I guess Old Louie knew what he was doing, too.

"The thing that killed us, no matter if Walter Johnson could have come out of the grave and pitched against Cleveland that day, was Boudreau.

"Nobody, and I mean *nobody,* could have stopped him. He was terrific. He was terrific all year. He was a helluva player.

"So, put everything else to rest. There was no other reason we lost and Cleveland won, than Boudreau. He was the one. He was it. Nobody else," said Pesky.

It would be difficult to refute Pesky's contention.

But then, what Boudreau did in the playoff game simply mirrored what he'd done the entire season. He was, again, irrefutably, the Indians' inspirational and physical leader, this time to the great delight of Veeck who was no longer looking for a new manager.

With his perfect game at bat, as well as his flawless play in the field in the victory over the Red Sox, Boudreau more than secured his already established status as the Most Valuable Player in the American League, virtually by acclamation.

The intensely competitive shortstop-manager wound up with a .355 batting average, second only to Williams' .369, delivered 18 homers and 106 RBIs, both of which were career highs. Amazingly, he struck out nine times in 560 at-bats.

In the euphoria that followed the Indians' cherished triumph, Ed McAuley, in the *Cleveland News*, wrote the fol-

lowing tribute to Boudreau: "They laid the big dough on the line and the greatest money player of them all just stepped up and collected."

And later in his column, McAuley said "there wasn't a dry eye in the room" when Gordon toasted his teammate and manager during the postgame celebration, saying, "Let's all drink to the greatest major leaguer in the business, Lou Boudreau."

Left fielder Dale Mitchell, playing only his second full season in the major leagues, was third in the race for the batting championship with a .336 average, and Doby, about whom there'd been so many doubts six months earlier, went 2-for-5 against the Red Sox to surge to .301.

Keltner just missed the .300 mark, finishing with .297 and 31 homers, one fewer than Gordon, who batted a solid .280. Clark and Kennedy, in limited opportunities, also hit well, .310 and .301, respectively, and while Robinson's average was .254, he was part of the infield that drove in a major league record 432 runs. In addition to Gordon's team high 124, and Boudreau's 106, Keltner had 119 and Robinson 83.

Hegan batted only .248, but caught 142 games and was recognized as the best at his position in the American League.

Bearden, 20-7, after beating the Red Sox in the finale, and Lemon, 20-14, were the Indians' most successful pitchers, though Feller finished strong, going 10-2 from July 27 to the end of the season, and 6-1 in the last five weeks, for a final 19-14 record.

Satchel Paige, 6-1 as a spot starter-reliever, also was a major contributor to the Indians' success, as were Gromek, 9-3, and Sam Zoldak, 9-6, both of whom won several key games, and Russ Christopher, the submarine-style right-handed reliever who appeared in 45 games with a 3-2 record and 2.90 earned run average.

Had there been Cy Young and Rookie of the Year awards presented in 1948, Bearden most certainly would have been the leading candidate for both. Lemon and Hal Newhouser (21-12) were the only other American League 20-game winners that season and, arguably, only Alvin Dark, then with the Boston Braves, would have been in competition with Bearden for rookie honors.

And in the wake of, not only the pennant, but also, the 2,620,627 fans who jammed the Stadium during the regular season, comprising what was then a major league attendance record, Veeck, the master promoter, was named "Executive of the Year" by *The Sporting News*, which was vicariously satisfying to the Indians owner.

It had been *The Sporting News* whose editor and publisher, J. G. Taylor Spink, was so harshly critical of Veeck three months earlier when he signed Paige.

So ended the Indians' most exciting regular season—which had to be one of the greatest in the 48-year modern era of major league baseball—and which also had to be, by Boudreau, one of the greatest (if not *the* greatest) individual accomplishments by any player.

With even more to come.

Satchel Paige

CHAPTER THREE

End of the Rainbow

The World Series that followed the Indians' often frenzied roller coaster ride to the pennant might have been anticlimactic, if Lou Boudreau had allowed it.

But he wouldn't, and the Indians, after appropriately celebrating the most satisfying victory in the 48-year history of Cleveland's baseball franchise, regrouped to face the other Boston team, the Braves, who'd clinched the National League pennant on September 26, one week earlier.

When the Indians showed up for a workout on October 5, the day after they'd beaten the Red Sox and the day before they'd face Johnny Sain in the opener of the World Series at Braves Field, Boudreau looked at them and exclaimed, "What a sorry-looking bunch of hung-over guys!"

But with understanding.

"They'd earned the right to enjoy what they'd accomplished," said the player-manager, who also—perhaps even more so—was entitled to relish the spotlight directed his way.

For the opener, Boudreau nominated Bob Feller to face Sain, then a 31-year-old right-handed curveball virtuoso who'd been the biggest winner in the major leagues that season, with a 24-15 record.

But first, even before the World Series schedule had been established, Bill Veeck pulled off a stroke of genius, something of which Sain said "hardly anybody realized the importance of at the time."

But Sain did, only too well.

"Veeck talked the Braves into doing away with a travel day, to play all seven games on consecutive days (October 6-

12)," said Sain. "I don't know why (Boston owner Lou Perini) agreed, unless it was to save money.

"It bothered me, but there was nothing we (the players) could do about it."

By playing without a day off in Cleveland between the second and third games the Braves hotel expenses were minimized, as were the Indians' expenses in Boston between the fifth and sixth games.

More importantly, had the Series been stretched out over nine days instead of seven, and if it went seven games, as Sain pointed out, "I could have started four of them because I'd worked with two days' rest many times that year."

It also was the season that Sain completed 28 of his 39 starts, as well as pitching in relief three times.

The Braves' other big winner in 1948 was Warren Spahn, who started 35 games, going all the way in 16, giving rise to their facetious—but accurate—pennant-winning formula, "Spahn and Sain and pray for two days of rain."

Instead, because of the elimination of the two so-called "travel days," Sain would have been able to start only three games, the first, fourth and seventh. "I don't know if that was Veeck's intention (when he talked the Braves into eliminating the travel days), but it worked in the Indians' favor," said Sain.

But not at first glance . . . not the way Game One turned out—a 1-0 victory achieved by the Braves with the help of a hotly disputed decision at second base by National League umpire Bill Stewart in the eighth inning.

Lou Boudreau poses with manager Billy Southworth (left), manager of the Boston Braves, prior to the opener of the 1948 World Series.

*Bill Veeck (left)
and Lou
Boudreau prior to
Game 1 of the
World Series.*

Until then, Feller was working on a one-hitter, allowing only a fifth-inning single by Marv Rickert, while the Indians had four hits. "I had a very good curveball that day," said Sain, who went on to become one of the best pitching coaches in baseball for six teams over 17 years, between 1959 and 1986.

In that World Series opener, with the teams locked in a scoreless tie in front of 40,135 screaming fans at Braves Field, Feller committed what he called a "fatal mistake." It was, in his opinion, even worse than what Stewart would be guilty of perpetrating.

Feller walked Bill Salkeld, the Braves catcher, on a 3-and-2 count, leading off the eighth. Phil Masi ran for Salkeld and was bunted to second, and Eddie Stanky was intentionally walked, setting the stage for the controversy that followed.

Feller and Boudreau collaborated on their patented, precisely timed pickoff play that had worked so often that season—and which worked again, though Stewart disagreed.

With Sain the next batter, Boudreau sneaked behind Masi, and Feller, after counting to himself, "one thousand one, one thousand two," then wheeled and threw the ball to second base.

Boudreau, who'd also been counting to himself after giving the pickoff signal to Feller, was at the base, caught the throw and, as virtually everyone in the park believed, tagged Masi as he tried to slide back to the bag.

To the dismay of the Indians, however, Stewart saw it differently. He ruled that Boudreau had tagged Masi high, after the runner's feet already had reached the base, though films of the play proved the call was wrong and Masi should have been declared out.

The ensuing argument didn't change it, of course—though Stewart, many years later, admitted he "blew" the play—and, after Sain lined out to right, Tommy Holmes, a .325 hitter, singled to score Masi with what would be the only run of the game.

Feller was charitable, saying that Stewart's ruling on Masi didn't cost him the game. "It beat me out of a tie," he said. I lost because I walked the leadoff batter."

Sain said he was "relieved" that the umpire made the call he did. "I was at the plate when it happened, and from where I saw it, I was afraid Masi was out. When Stewart called him safe, I was relieved. We (the Braves) all were," said Sain.

"And we all felt even better when Holmes hit that little quail (bloop single) over third base that brought Masi home."

All that remained was for Sain to retire the Indians in the ninth, which he did, though not without one last threat by the Indians.

"I got the first two (Boudreau on a fly to center and Gordon on a foul to shortstop Alvin Dark). But then (Ken) Keltner hit a bounder to (third baseman) Bob Elliott who came up with the ball but threw it ten feet over the first baseman's head," said Sain.

"Now I was in the same position Feller had been the inning before, a runner on second and two men out, but I was lucky enough to strike out (Walter) Judnich on three pitches to end the game.

"The last pitch, which in my mind was the most important pitch I ever got to throw, was a side arm curveball that Judnich took for strike three.

"I got kidded a lot for making that pitch; you just don't throw side arm curveballs to left-handed batters, but I did because I didn't think he'd be expecting it.

"The first two pitches also were curves, my 'hammer,' as I called it, and then I dropped down and threw another big breaking ball that started way outside. Judnich sort of dropped his bat and took the pitch, and the umpire (George Barr of the National League) called it strike three.

"It wouldn't have been a good pitch to make if Judnich had been looking for it. But that's what I was counting on. That he'd be surprised."

Boudreau, as he'd done all season, took matters into his own hands in Game Two, when Bob Lemon and Spahn were the pitching opponents, and again an umpire's decision figured in the result, this time a 4-1 victory by the Indians.

It happened in the very first inning with Lemon struggling. The Braves had taken a 1-0 lead on an error by Gordon and singles by Earl Torgeson and Elliott, leaving runners at first and second with one out.

With Marv Rickert at the plate and Torgeson carelessly leading too far off second, Boudreau gave Lemon the same signal he'd given Feller 24 hours earlier. Lemon counted, "one thousand one, one thousand two," then wheeled and fired to second base, again as Feller had done the day before.

And, as Feller's also had been, Lemon's throw was on the mark and in plenty of time for Boudreau to tag Torgeson diving back to the base.

This time Bill Grieve, an American League umpire, called the runner out, and Lemon proceeded to strike out Rickert and end the inning. He went on to scatter six hits, never more than one an inning.

"I know it hurt Feller," Lemon said about the unsuccessful pickoff play in the first game, "but it might have turned out good for me." The controversy it caused, Lemon said, "might have made the umpires more alert, more aware that we might try it again."

The Indians disposed of Spahn in a hurry, scoring twice in the fourth inning on Boudreau's double and singles by Gordon and Larry Doby. They added another run in the fifth when Boudreau came through with another key hit. Dale Mitchell led off with a single, was bunted to second and scored on Boudreau's single that knocked Spahn out of the game.

A final run scored in the ninth when Jim Hegan reached on an error by Dark, took second on Lemon's infield out, third on another grounder by Mitchell, and went home on Bob Kennedy's single.

Larry Doby

Then, back in Cleveland with the Series tied, 1-1, Boudreau gave the ball in Game Three to Bearden again to break a deadlock, as the rookie southpaw had done four days earlier against the Red Sox.

And again Bearden came through, winning, 2-0, this time in front of 70,306 fans witnessing their first World Series game in 48 years. The Stadium was not sold out, Indians officials said, because of a "ticket snafu," but those who were there saw another superlative performance by Bearden.

As Harry Jones reported in *The Plain Dealer*, "Bearden's relatively easy triumph (gave) him something of a 'grand slam.'

"Within the space of a week, he clinched a first-place tie in the American League for the Indians, hurled them to a pennant by defeating the Red Sox in the playoff, and put them one game ahead in the World Series.

"With marvelous control of his celebrated knuckleball, Bearden did not issue a single pass, fanned four and kept most of the enemy batters hitting into the dirt. He saw only one Boston runner reach third base and only two advance as far as second. At no time was an opposing runner in scoring position—at either second or third—with less than two out."

Bearden yielded only five hits, two of which were erased in double plays, and also got two himself, the first a double in the third inning, after which he scored on an error.

The Indians added another run in the fourth on a walk and one- out singles by Eddie Robinson and Jim Hegan, sending Braves starter and loser Vern Bickford to the showers.

Thereafter, Bearden retired 14 of the next 16 batters with only Dark, who doubled in the sixth, getting as far as second.

When it was over, Boudreau said, "Well, men, tomorrow's the big one," which was the same thing he'd been saying all season.

Steve Gromek was the surprise starter for the "big" Game Four, opposed by Sain, working with two days' rest.

This time there was no ticket snafu, and 81,897 fans spun the turnstiles to see Gromek and Doby beat Sain and the Braves, 2-1, in the near-record time of one hour and thirty one minutes.

The game also had its share of controversy, though it didn't surface until much later when Sain and Gromek were interviewed for this chronicle of the Indians' greatest sea-son, and by then, neither expressed any rancor in recalling the episode.

The run that made the difference for the Indians came on the wings of a third-inning homer by Doby, who drilled a change up by Sain over the right-field fence, becoming the first black player to hit a home run in a World Series.

Sain well remembers. He claimed that Doby knew a change up was coming, and was ready for it because the Indians had a "spy" in the scoreboard stealing opposing catchers' signals.

"I knew it the way Doby stood up there and hit the pitch. He wasn't a good change up hitter, but he hit the hell out of that pitch. He had to be looking for it," said Sain.

"Doby may deny it," which Doby did, "but when Jim Hegan and I were together on the coaching staff of the Yankees (1961-63), I used to bug him about it. Finally, one day, he said, 'Hell, John, yeah, we did (have a spy in the scoreboard).'"

Doby insisted that, not only was he not tipped off about what pitches to expect, he said, "I didn't even know anything like that (a spy in the scoreboard) was going on during the season. The other guys might have known, but I didn't."

Gromek, who'd pitched effectively as a spot starter-reliever all season, indicated, also without rancor, that he still remembered how he'd resented a statement by Boudreau prior to that fourth game.

According to Gromek, the manager originally planned to start Feller, but changed his mind and said he would "sac-rifice" the game by pitching Gromek, then use Feller the next day.

But Gromek's subsequent, complete Game Seven hit-ter, in which his only mistake was a too-fat pitch that Rickert hammered into the right- field stands leading off the seventh inning, wiped away any lingering resentment he might have harbored.

So did another key hit by Boudreau, whose double scored Mitchell in the first inning, and preceded Doby's homer two innings later.

Afterwards, in the flush of victory, Gromek was photo-graphed as he hugged Doby. It was a picture that was pub-lished in virtually every major newspaper in the country the next day, the memory of which, Doby said, he would cherish forever.

Feller, who had achieved virtually every honor avail-able to a major league pitcher except one—winning a World

Series game—failed again with a chance to secure the world championship for the Indians and, this time, he had nobody to blame but himself.

Unlike the opener, when he allowed but two hits, Feller was manhandled by the desperate Braves in Game Five, to the dismay of a then-record crowd of 86,288 fans in the Stadium.

The Braves prevailed, 11-5, clubbing three homers off Feller and driving him from the mound in the seventh inning, sending the Series back to Boston for the sixth game and, as the Braves hoped, also a seventh.

Feller offered no excuses. "All I can say is that I just didn't have it."

His trouble began almost immediately as the first two Braves singled in the first inning and, one batter later, Elliott homered.

Mitchell retaliated with a leadoff homer off Nelson Potter in the Indians' half of the first, but Elliott homered again, this one a solo shot in the third, for a 4-1 Boston lead.

The Indians went ahead, 5-4, with a four-run rally in the fourth on two singles, a walk and Hegan's homer, but Feller couldn't hold it. He yielded a game-tying homer to

Salkeld in the sixth, and was banished in the seventh when Holmes and Torgeson singled around a sacrifice bunt by Dark.

But reliever Ed Klieman, who had pitched well most of the season, making 44 appearances with a 2.60 ERA, also failed this time. He gave up one hit and two walks without retiring a batter as the Braves took an 8-5 lead.

Boudreau summoned Russ Christopher, who also had been an effective reliever with a league-leading 17 saves in 45 games (though the save rule was different in those days), but also couldn't stop the suddenly ferocious Braves. The next two batters singled for two more runs, and Satchel Paige shuffled to the mound.

Paige retired the next two batters, one on a sacrifice fly that produced Boston's 11th run, and Bob Muncrief blanked the Braves in the eighth and ninth, but to no avail.

Spahn, who replaced Potter when the Indians took the lead in the fourth, allowed only one hit in 5 2/3 innings. He retired ten straight batters from the fourth until Boudreau doubled leading off the eighth, and 15 of the last 16, striking out seven for the victory that extended the season at least one more game.

Gene Bearden (center) celebrating with Bob Lemon (left) and catcher Jim Hegan after Bearden saved Lemon's victory in Game 6 to win the World Series.

Thousands of fans celebrate at Cleveland's Public Square after the Indians beat the Boston Braves in the World Series.

The next morning Boudreau was soundly criticized by Gordon Cobbledick, sports editor of *The Plain Dealer*, for not replacing Feller earlier, after the Indians had taken a 5-4 lead and the victory would have been credited to the long-time ace of the pitching staff.

"Bob Feller waited 12 years for the chance all pitchers dream of —the chance to pitch in a World Series. When it came, he could make nothing of it, save the dubious distinction of losing the only games in which his team has been beaten.

"And yet there should be no defeat charged against Feller in the 1948 World Series. He didn't deserve to lose the first game because he was so good. He didn't deserve to lose (Game Five) because he was so bad that he should have been out of the game long before the Braves broke a tie with a six-run explosion in the seventh inning.

"Feller is a great pitcher when his fastball is hopping. When he has to rely on his curve and change of pace, he is not a good pitcher.

"It became apparent in the first inning that the fastball that has broken all strikeout records in baseball history wasn't there. They don't hit home runs off Bob Feller when he is

fast. The fact that the Braves hit three home runs in six innings was proof that he didn't have it.

"And yet, he was still in the box when the seventh inning rolled around. He was still in there when Tommy Holmes led off for the Braves with a single, still in there when Alvin Dark moved the tie-breaking run to second with a sacrifice, still in there when Earl Torgeson came to bat and drilled a single to center field that knocked in the winning run.

"Only then was Lou Boudreau convinced. And then it was too late."

Boudreau's only explanation: "I wanted to see (Feller) go all the way, but in retrospect, I realize I went too far with him. The Braves just out-slugged us, and they got the relief pitching, which we didn't."

Then, striving for something positive, Boudreau said, "The only good thing that happened was that Satchel Paige, who never got a chance to show what he could do in the major leagues before this season, was finally able to make an appearance in a World Series game."

Three hours after the loss to the Braves, as the Indians were bused to the Terminal Tower where they would board a train to Boston, they were pleasantly surprised by a crowd estimated at 15,000 fans there to wish them luck in Game Six the next day.

As reported on page one of the October 11 edition of *The Plain Dealer:*

"A phalanx of humanity lined each side of the concourse from the far end clear down to Gate 22. Police kept open a narrow lane for the heroes.

"It was for all the world like a gigantic fraternity initiation, except that those running the quarter-mile-long gauntlet were greeted with cheers instead of chastisement.

"Some fans had cowbells. Others had vestiges of once-powerful lungs. Bobby soxers whistled, and it was easy to tell when a particular favorite approached because swells of applause would roll down the concourse and echo off the ceiling."

All of which might have helped as the Indians put the finishing touches on their greatest season with a 4-3 victory over the Braves the next day. It won the franchise's second world championship—which still, a half century since, hasn't been repeated.

It was appropriate that Bearden was on the mound, making the final pitch that landed in the glove of Bob Kennedy in left field, to finalize the cherished victory.

Until then, the Indians had constructed a 4-1 lead against Braves starter and loser Bill Voiselle.

Mitchell and Boudreau doubled for a run in the third, but the Braves tied it in the fourth on Elliott's infield single, a walk and Mike McCormick's single. Gordon's homer leading the sixth, followed by a walk, Eddie Robinson's single and an infield out, put the Indians back on top, 3-1, and in the eighth, Keltner, Thurman Tucker and Robinson singled for what proved to be the deciding run.

Though Bearden wasn't credited with the victory, he saved it after taking over for Lemon when the Braves loaded the bases with one out in the bottom of the eighth.

And, while Bearden claimed he'd been more lucky than skillful in maintaining the lead, the pressure was squarely on him again, as it had been so often in the final weeks of the season—although Boudreau also put himself on the spot by bringing Bearden into the game.

Bob Lemon with his wife, Jane, in the World Series celebration parade.

As the manager said later, "I had to ask myself whether I should relieve with Bearden and possibly lose him for the seventh game if the Braves won? Or do I save Bearden, give him as much rest as possible in case we need him (in Game Seven), and go with somebody else, and hope for the best?"

Boudreau, as he'd done all season, went with his gut instinct, and again it paid off, although, as Bearden confessed, "I never was hit so hard in all my pitching career."

Holmes, who'd led off with a single, was on third, Torgeson was on second after he'd doubled with one out, and Elliot, who'd walked, was on first.

Clint Conatser, the first batter to face Bearden, flied out to Tucker with Holmes scoring after the catch, and Torgeson, representing the tying run, taking third.

But Conatser's fly was not routine. It traveled more than 400 feet and, as Bearden said, "was almost gone (for a home run)."

Then, as Bearden continued, "Masi blasted the left-field wall with a long double," and the Indians' lead was

Allie Clark, wife Francis and Jim Hegan in the parade celebrating the 1948 World Series.

down to one with the tying run at third and the go-ahead run at second, Boudreau was forced to sweat another decision.

Should he stick with the left-handed Bearden to face McCormick, a right-handed batter who'd hit .303 and driven in the Braves' first run of the game with a single in the fourth inning? Or make another pitching change?

He decided to stick with Bearden. "How could I not go along with him, after all he'd done?" Boudreau said.

Indeed, all Bearden had done in the previous 16 days was to start —and win—five games, including the one that clinched a tie for the pennant, then the one that won the pennant, and finally Game Three of the World Series.

And so, "lucky" or skillful, he induced McCormick to slap the ball back to the mound and was thrown out at first base, though Bearden said he had "no choice" but to "stop (the ball) or get killed." He added, "If it had hit me, or gone past me, the runners on second and third would have scored."

Whatever, the play ended the inning and, as it turned out, the Braves' last real chance to stay alive in the World Series.

Though Bearden walked Stanky to start the ninth, pinch hitter Sibby Sisti, attempting to lay down a sacrifice bunt,

popped up. Hegan caught the ball and turned it into a double play as Connie Ryan, running for Stanky, had broken for second and couldn't get back to first.

Then Holmes lofted a fly to Kennedy and the Indians' dream season was over. They'd reached the pot of gold— in this case, $6,772 per player—at the end of the rainbow. Each of the Braves got $4,570.

"No doubt about it, it was Bearden's series, all his, all the way," chortled Boudreau.

It also could have been said without fear of contradiction that it was Boudreau's *season*, that it belonged to the once unwanted manager, that it was all his, all the way.

And in the midst of their celebration en route to Cleveland, where an estimated 500,000 revelers lined Euclid Avenue for a parade honoring the Indians the next day, Gordon again toasted Boudreau.

"To the greatest leatherman I ever saw, to the damnedest clutch hitter that ever lived, to a doggone good manager," Gordon said of, and to Boudreau.

And so ended the Indians' greatest—*most thrilling, exciting, wondrous, glorious,* take your choice—season in the history of the franchise.

It was a long time coming, and would be even longer before another would come again.

Lou Boudreau with wife Della and Indians owner Bill Veeck in the parade celebrating the Indians winning the World Series.

Lou Boudreau being congratulated by Cleveland Mayor Thomas A. Burke after the Indians win the World Series.

CHAPTER FOUR
· · · · · · · · · ·

From the U.S.S. Alabama

To a Spy at the Stadium

Though nobody involved could pinpoint the date with any certainty, it happened "sometime" at mid-season, about the time the Indians themselves were convinced—and had made believers of everybody else—that, indeed, they could win the pennant in 1948.

"I think it was during a game against the Red Sox, and it was either Joe Gordon or Ken Keltner, though it might've been Jim Hegan . . . I'm not sure," said Bob Feller.

And in his book, *Veeck As In Wreck,* Indians owner Bill Veeck wrote that it happened against the Yankees, with ace reliever Joe Page on the mound, and that it was done by Gordon.

Whenever, whoever, or against which team, there was no disagreement as to what took place.

Somebody—Gordon or Keltner or Hegan or even another player —swung mightily at a 3-and-0 pitch and drove the ball into the upper deck of the left-field stands.

Even before the ball landed in the seats, in fact, almost the moment the batter made contact with the pitch, a half-dozen players from the opposing team leaped out of their third-base dugout, screaming and pointing at the scoreboard in center field.

"They knew what happened," said Feller, chuckling as he recalled the incident. "They knew, but there wasn't anything they could do about it, although, after that we had to be a little more careful."

What happened in that game was something that happened a lot with the Indians in 1948—and which they claimed other teams also were doing—stealing opposing catchers' signs and relaying the information to the batter so he'd know what kind of pitch to expect.

"Hey, all's fair in love and war, and when you're trying to win a pennant," quipped Feller who, along with Bob Lemon and groundskeepers Marshall and Harold Bossard, and their father Emil, were the primary perpetrators of the thievery.

"I think it was No. 5 (Manager Lou Boudreau) who got it started, though I'm not real sure about that," said Marshall Bossard, who was one of the spies in the scoreboard.

Boudreau acknowledged his awareness of the sign-stealing, but denied speculation that he was responsible for getting it started.

"A few of the guys wanted to try it, so I said OK, let's do it, but it wasn't my idea," said Boudreau. "I was willing to go along with it because I felt, as a lot of us did, that other teams were doing it. Does that make it right? I don't know. Were we wrong? I don't know that either.

"I guess it isn't legal, but if you suspect somebody is stealing your signs, either from the scoreboard or by a runner on second base or even by the third-base coach, it's up to you to do something about it. You use different sets of signs, or do something to camouflage them. That's what we did when we thought somebody was picking off our signs."

Feller explained how the Indians did it—and didn't shirk responsibility for his part in the subterfuge.

"I don't know who came up with the idea, and I don't give a damn, never did, though I guess I probably was one of the leaders," said Feller.

Bob Lemon (left) with catcher Jim Hegan.

Lou Boudreau (left) with Bob Feller prior to a 1945 game played in Cleveland for the benefit of United States servicemen. Feller was then in the Navy.

"Once I had it focused on the pitcher and, when he suddenly whirled around, I instinctively ducked, that's how close he seemed to be. The 'scope was that strong."

Bossard, 34 at the time, said it all began "about six weeks into the season" when he was approached by Boudreau. "He told me, 'Everybody else in the league is stealing signs, so we're going to try it, too.' He said he knew that Detroit and Boston were getting (the catchers' signs) from guys in the bullpen, and I told him we could do it from the scoreboard (in center field)."

The telescope was mounted on a tripod and was aimed out of the scoreboard through one of the small openings that otherwise was used to post numbers.

"My brother (Harold) or I would be behind another (opening)," said Bossard, "and if one of the guys on the telescope (Feller or Lemon) called 'curveball,' I'd maybe stick my face in the window so the batter could see me, and if it was a fastball, maybe I'd stick my arm out. If we didn't know for sure what the pitch would be, I'd duck down so nothing showed, although we changed it around a lot.

"Sometimes I'd stick my face in the (opening) if it was a fastball, and hang my arm out if it was a curveball. We'd never do the same thing all the time. Sometimes, sticking my arm out or showing my face meant we weren't sure what was coming. And we always had to be careful.

"The important thing was that the batter had to be quick, he'd have to keep his eyes glued on the scoreboard until the pitcher was ready to throw the ball. But that was easy because the scoreboard was right out there, above and behind the center field fence."

Bossard said the sign-stealing wasn't done all the time, "just against certain clubs . . . you know, the tough clubs, the teams (the Indians) had to beat."

Were they ever caught?

"No, but a few times we stopped because we thought (the visiting team) suspected something," he said. "A couple times guys came out looking to see if anything was going on, but we always kept the door (to the scoreboard) locked, just in case."

"The way I felt about it, it was like in the war, you had to decipher a code, break it down, which we did against the Germans and the Japanese, and we won (World War II), right?"

It was Feller, in fact, who provided the telescope that was used in the scoreboard. "It was the 'scope I'd used on the (U.S.S.) Alabama, during the war," said Feller, then a gunnery officer in the Navy. "I used it to pick up enemy aircraft coming in at us. It's only about three feet long, maybe a little less, about 2 1/2 feet. I've still got it at my home."

How powerful was it?

The question was answered by Bob Lemon, who took turns with Feller "working" the telescope. When Feller pitched, Lemon would be in the scoreboard. When Lemon pitched, Feller would be there. They also took turns when anybody else on the staff was on the mound.

"It was so powerful," Lemon said of Feller's telescope, "when you looked through the damned thing, you could actually see the dirt under the fingernails of the catcher.

And once the Indians won the pennant, they didn't continue the thievery during the World Series, or after the 1948 season.

"Don't ask me why," said Bossard. "Maybe Boudreau thought they didn't need it . . .I don't know why."

But Johnny Sain, who gave up what amounted to the game-winning homer to Larry Doby in the Indians' 2-1 victory in Game Four of the World Series, doesn't believe it. He is still convinced that Doby knew a change up was coming, and was ready for it when he smashed his home run over the right-field fence.

However, Doby said, "I've heard that story, but it's not true. I didn't even know (during the season) we were getting the catchers' signs. Nobody ever told me."

Several other Indians didn't want to know what pitch to expect because they were fearful the information might not be correct, said Bossard. "We were right most of the time, but some of the guys never were convinced and didn't want to take any chances."

While some of the players interviewed for this book weren't sure it was the appropriate thing to do—Al Rosen, Bob Kennedy, and Eddie Robinson were among them— former pitchers Gene Bearden and Mel Harder were ambivalent.

"If I was on the other team and pitching against the Indians, yeah, sure, I'd resent them stealing our catcher's signs," said Bearden. "But like everybody said, other teams were doing it, so we might as well, too.

"The thing that always puzzled me was that nobody ever caught us. I mean, take a guy like Birdie Tebbetts, as smart a man as he is. I think he knew something was going on, but he couldn't pinpoint it.

"Shoot, that year, as soon as a pitcher would cock his arm, one of our guys was ready to hit a frozen rope, which should have made people sit up and wonder. I know I would. 'Sonofabitch,' I'd say to myself, 'they're hitting my best pitches like they know what's coming.'

"But nobody ever did, so that's their fault."

Groundskeepers Marshall Bossard (left) and Harold Bossard.

As for Harder, who was a coach for the Indians in 1948, he said, "I personally don't see anything wrong with it. It's the same as somebody sitting in the dugout, or on the coaching line, or at second base and picking up the catcher's signal and giving it to the batter.

"There's nothing wrong with that," he said again, "although, if I were pitching and they were calling my pitches, I wouldn't like that at all —and I'd do something about it to stop them."

Kennedy disapproved, though not strongly, and so did Robinson, who was reluctant to even discuss the subject.

"It was done," Robinson admitted when asked about the Indians having a spy in the scoreboard. "But I really don't want to talk about it . . . I'm not going to divulge any of those secrets."

Rosen, while conceding that at least on one occasion in 1948 he benefited by knowing what pitch to expect, strongly disapproved of the sign thievery.

"One time I got a hit off Bob Porterfield (who then pitched for the Yankees) because I saw this hand hanging out of a window in the scoreboard and knew to look for a curveball. But it was only that once," he said.

"That stuff (sign stealing) has been going on since the game began and, while I can accept a coach or a base runner doing it, I can't condone it being done with a telescope or television camera or anything of that nature.

"To me, that's as unsportsmanlike as anything I can think of," added Rosen, a former major league executive for the New York Yankees, Houston and San Francisco, after ending his playing career in 1956.

"I was with the Indians only that last month (of 1948), so I just went along with what they were doing. But (sign stealing from the scoreboard) is not something I would participate in, or approve of, and it's something we didn't do after that season."

When asked what his reaction would be if his manager—when he was with the Yankees, Astros and Giants—used a spy to steal opposing catchers' signals with a telescope, Rosen replied, "First of all, I can't answer that question because it never happened.

"But second, I don't think any manager I ever had would have such a lack of respect for me that he wouldn't tell me if he was going to do something like that.

"And if he did, I would have told him, no, we are got going to do that . . . I absolutely would not approve."

Bob Lemon

Jim Hegan

CHAPTER FIVE

Lou Boudreau

"Tell all the guys I wish we could do it all over again."

There was no mistaking the glint of a tear in the eyes of Lou Boudreau as he fondly recalled the greatest season of his 20-year major league playing and managerial career.

Without a doubt, 1948 also was the greatest season in the 98-year history of Cleveland's American League baseball franchise.

Hobbled with arthritis in his back, knees and ankles, Boudreau hardly resembles the handsome, dashing, inspirational shortstop-manager who, in 1948, led the Indians to their first pennant and world championship in 28 years, and second since becoming a charter member of Ban Johnson's new league in 1901.

Then 31 years old but still regarded as major league baseball's "Boy Manager," Boudreau batted a career-high .355 and won, practically by acclamation, the A.L.'s Most Valuable Player award in the wake of what would have been then-owner Bill Veeck's biggest mistake.

Now, halting in his steps and walking with the aid of a cane, Boudreau and Della, his wife of 60 years, live in a comfortable but modest home in Frankfort, Illinois, about 30 miles southwest of Chicago. They were married June 5, 1938, a few days before Boudreau began his professional baseball career at Cedar Rapids, Iowa

Boudreau was alternately cheerful and somber—often almost sad—as he remembered the "good times," and frowned, sometimes even scowling, when the not-so-good times, of which there also were many, came to mind.

"Mostly, the memories are pleasant because, all things considered, we did pretty well," he said. "Oh, sure, we could have done better, anyone who ever played the game would tell you they could have done better. I wish we'd won (the pennant) more than once, but that one time was wonderful, and a lot of guys didn't win even once."

And the not-so-good times?

Boudreau used the same choice of words to respond. "Anyone who ever played the game had bad times, same as we did," he said after pondering the question. "I have no great regrets. If I had it all to do over again, I wouldn't do anything different, at least nothing I can think of now."

Certainly, however, there's one thing Boudreau obviously wished someone else would have done differently—namely Chicago radio station WGN, as well as one of its counterparts in Cleveland, and he made it clear several times during our interview.

After retiring as a manager in 1957, Boudreau embarked upon a 30-year broadcasting career with WGN that ended in 1988. He was replaced by Dave Nelson, another former player who, after two seasons on the air, subsequently joined the Indians as a coach in 1992.

Though Boudreau carefully avoided criticism of WGN, there was no mistaking his disappointment in not being retained as one of the voices of the Chicago Cubs.

It also was obvious that he would have appreciated an invitation to join the broadcasting team in Cleveland covering Indians games after his contract with WGN was not re-

Lou Boudreau looks at his trophy emblazoned with the words, "The Greatest Shortstop Ever Left Off an All-Star Team, Boston, July 9th, 1948." The trophy was presented to Boudreau by the Cleveland Indians Baseball Club on behalf of Cleveland fans.

newed. Boudreau made clear his availability, but an offer was never forthcoming.

"That (returning to Cleveland) would have been great . . . but I guess it was time for me to quit," he said. "The time to go comes to everybody."

It was during the winter of 1947-48 that Veeck first thought it was time for Boudreau to go. He tried to trade Boudreau the shortstop—because he did not want Boudreau the manager—to the St. Louis Browns for Vernon Stephens in a deal that would have included eight players, four from each team.

Boudreau, the American League shortstop in the 1947 All-Star Game, was coming off a .307 season that included four homers and 67 runs batted in, while Stephens, 27 at the time, had hit .279 with 15 homers and 83 RBI.

"I didn't want to go, but I had told Veeck that if he didn't want me as a manager, he couldn't have me as a shortstop, that I wouldn't step down and play for somebody else," said Boudreau.

The majority of baseball fans in Cleveland didn't want Boudreau to go, either. He had come to the Indians as a rookie shortstop in 1939, quickly established himself as a coming star, and was hired as player-manager by then-owner Alva Bradley in November 1941. Boudreau was only 24 at the time, making him the youngest manager in major league history to start a season.

Devoted as they were to Boudreau, who'd been a basketball star at the University of Illinois, the fans were outraged by Veeck's audacity.

"No way!" they howled in protest, vocally and through the media, at the proposed trade. Veeck, no dummy in the fine art of public relations, quickly realized the error of his ways—or what *would have been* the error of his ways.

As one Cleveland sportswriter reported the controversy, "It smashed and splintered and shook the community by its civic heels until all hell popped loose."

Another wrote, "It is evident that Veeck didn't know Boudreau was immortal in Cleveland. (Previous Indians owner) Alva Bradley used to say that he hired the managers and the public fired them.

"Boudreau is the one Bradley hired, but apparently only an act of God can fire him."

Veeck finally—publicly—broke off negotiations with the Browns, calling it "the will of the fans."

Lou Boudreau with wife Della.

There is ample evidence, however, to indicate that St. Louis owner William O. DeWitt already had decided to trade Stephens to the Boston Red Sox instead of the Indians, because he considered their offer better than what Veeck had proposed.

In addition to Stephens, the Browns sent pitcher Jack Kramer to Boston for six players and $310,000, which in those days was a huge amount of money.

Not only did it mean that Boudreau would remain in Cleveland— Veeck gave him a new, two-year contract—the failed transaction, for whatever reason, also served as motivation for the dark-haired, boyishly handsome shortstop-manager.

Boudreau was driven, almost maniacally, to prove that Veeck and, subsequently, Veeck's right-hand man, vice president Hank Greenberg, were wrong in their low opinions of his managerial ability.

"It could not have been more perfect, the way it turned out," Boudreau said of the 1948 season in Cleveland as we sat under the watchful gaze of a portrait of himself wearing his Indians uniform. It was painted at the height of Boudreau's playing career, when he was the best shortstop in baseball.

It wasn't simply a matter of ego that motivated Boudreau to excel, to produce one of the all-time, all-around greatest performances a player could hope to achieve, he insisted. "I was challenged. I was determined to prove that Veeck was wrong.

"It also was important to me to win for the fans who had been so great in their support of me. I'll never forget them, and I'll always be grateful for what they did.

"Imagine how different things might have been if Veeck had gone ahead and made that trade."

If the deal had been consummated, Stephens would have gone to Cleveland, probably along with outfielder Paul Lehner, and pitchers Bob Muncrief and Kramer, for Boudreau, pitchers Red Embree and Bryan Stephens, and outfielder George Metkovich and $100,000.

To complete the scenario, either Al Lopez or Jimmy Dykes, both of whom Veeck greatly admired, probably would have taken over as manager of the Indians.

As it turned out, both Lopez and Dykes eventually did manage the Indians; Lopez from 1951-56, and Dykes in 1960 and 1961.

And if Boudreau had gone to St. Louis? "Who knows what would have happened?" Boudreau answered the question with one of his own.

Indeed. The Browns were a rag-tag franchise that was deeply in debt and a perennial also-ran in the American League since winning their only pennant in 1944. They never finished higher than sixth (in the eight-team A.L.) from 1948 through 1953, after which they moved to Baltimore.

Which is not to say that Boudreau, had he been traded to the Browns, would not have made it to the Hall of Fame.

He was, truly, "remarkable," as then-Commissioner Bowie Kuhn intoned during the induction ceremonies for Boudreau at Cooperstown, New York, July 27, 1970.

"The most remarkable thing about this remarkable man was the way he stretched the wonderful skills he had into superlative skills.

"As a shortstop, he was a human computer; he knew all the hitters' habits, he knew all the moves of the base runners, he knew what the pitcher was going to pitch, he had an instinct for where the ball would be hit, and from all of this he fashioned the wonderful ball player that we knew as Lou Boudreau.

"There are hitters in the Hall of Fame with higher lifetime batting averages, but I do not believe there is in the Hall of Fame a baseball man who brought more use of intellect and advocation of mind to the game than Lou Boudreau."

It also was in 1970 that Boudreau's uniform No. 5 was retired by the Indians.

One "advocation of mind" for which Boudreau always will be remembered—especially by Ted Williams, perhaps the greatest hitter of all-time—was his invention of the "Williams Shift," though Boudreau prefers to call it the "Boudreau Shift."

Boudreau conceived the unorthodox defensive alignment between games of a double header in 1946 after Williams had blasted three home runs in the opener, all of them to right field.

"The charts we kept showed that 95 percent of Williams' hits against us—and he got many—were to right field, which gave me the idea for the shift," said Boudreau, while acknowledging that the strategy also was partially motivated by sheer frustration.

In the first game of that double header, Boudreau himself delivered five extra base hits, a homer and four doubles,

Lou Boudreau (left) with Indians Vice President Hank Greenberg.

establishing an American League record that still stands, but Williams' three homers gave the Red Sox an 11-10 victory.

"I knew Ted Williams, and I knew he wanted to be recognized as being the greatest hitter in the game of baseball," said Boudreau. "I also knew his disposition. I knew what it meant to him to beat a challenge."

Thus was born the shift, in which Boudreau deployed the Indians' first baseman and right fielder on the foul line with the second baseman closer to first than to second, the shortstop on the right side of second base, and the third baseman behind second. The center fielder moved to the right fielder's normal position, and the left fielder moved in about 10 yards.

But the shift wasn't designed by Boudreau simply to protect the right side of the field against Williams' hits. "Actually, I wanted him to try to slap the ball to left field, or to bunt so we could hold him to a single, though I knew he wouldn't," added Boudreau.

The first time Williams saw the defensive deployment, he laughed. But not for long.

And Boudreau proved to be correct. The shift did present a challenge that Williams constantly tried to beat, but often didn't.

"After we used the shift regularly, our records showed we were 37 percent better against Williams than we were prior to the shift," said Boudreau, "so we used it all the time I managed the Indians."

Other teams quickly followed suit, either duplicating Boudreau's deployment of defensive players, or employing a version of it.

As he reminisced, Boudreau was ambivalent when he was asked if his enshrinement in the Hall of Fame represented the greatest day of his baseball career.

"Yes and no," he replied. "I'll just say it was tied with a few others, especially a couple in 1948."

One of them was October 4, 1948, when Boudreau went 4-for-4 with two home runs and two singles in leading the Indians to an 8-3 victory over the Boston Red Sox in a then-unprecedented one-game playoff for the American League pennant.

It was during the ensuing celebration that Veeck unabashedly conceded he'd been wrong in his judgment of Boudreau the manager.

"We didn't win the pennant today," he said. "We won it on November 25, 1947, the day I rehired Lou Boudreau."

That simple, though eloquent admission by Veeck, also served to somewhat—though not entirely—lessen Boudreau's animosity toward Greenberg, who joined the Indians during the winter of 1947-48 as a minor stockholder and vice president.

"Greenberg did not like my management of the team," said Boudreau. "He ridiculed me all the time . . . criticizing, second guessing me. I figured he wanted my job."

To emphasize his point, Boudreau said, "After almost every game I'd have to meet with Veeck and Greenberg. If we were at home, we'd meet in Veeck's office at the Stadium. If we were on the road, it'd be on the telephone.

"They'd have their scorebooks in front of them and would ask me, 'Why'd you do this?,' and, 'Why'd you do that?'. Especially Greenberg. He wanted a reason for everything I did. I resented it, though I kept it to myself most of the time.

As for his relationship with Veeck, who purchased the Indians in June 1946 and sold them in November 1949, Boudreau said, "Actually, it was pretty good when we were one-on-one. He seemed to go along with me 90 percent of the time, although that might have been because we were doing OK.

"Had we not been successful in 1948, if we'd been having a bad year, it might have been different. I don't know what might have happened . . . I probably would have been gone, fired."

Greenberg, who died in 1986, did fire Boudreau in November 1950, a year after Veeck sold the Indians. Greenberg had taken over as vice president and general manager of the team under the new ownership of a group headed by Ellis Ryan.

Though the animosity that Boudreau harbored toward Greenberg —and that which Boudreau perceived Greenberg harbored toward him —never totally became public, the two men did engage openly in a heated discussion prior to the playoff game for the pennant.

According to Boudreau, though other surviving members of the 1948 team said they were unaware of the argument that transpired between the then-manager and then-vice president, with Veeck also in attendance, "Greenberg thought I was wrong to start Allie Clark at first base instead of Eddie Robinson. He also second guessed me for pitching Gene Bearden."

Neither Veeck nor Greenberg had been informed in advance of Boudreau's plans. When the lineups were posted, both hurried down through the stands at Fenway Park to the edge of the visiting team's dugout where they questioned Boudreau. "It got pretty hot between Greenberg and me," recalled Boudreau.

"I knew Clark had never played first base, but I wanted to get as many right-handed bats in the lineup as possible because of that short left-field wall at Fenway Park. I figured we'd need a lot of runs."

Lou Boudreau embraces Indians players Bob Feller (left) and Ken Keltner.

As for his decision to pitch Bearden, Boudreau said, "It was my feeling that he was our best bet because of his knuckleball. It's much tougher to hit a long ball off a knuckleball, if (Bearden) had his control.

"And if he didn't (have control of his knuckleball), I planned to have everybody else in the bullpen ready.

"I would not have stayed very long with Bearden . . . if we'd have been two runs behind, he would have been gone," said Boudreau.

But Boudreau himself made sure it never reached that point.

Obviously relishing the memory of that game, Boudreau recalled, "I was determined to prove that my 'hunch'—as Greenberg referred to my choice of Bearden to pitch and Clark to play first base—was right, a good one."

And prove it, he did.

With two out in the first inning, Boudreau hit a 2-and-1 pitch from Denny Galehouse into the screen atop the left-field wall, staking Bearden to a 1-0 lead, to the dismay of the capacity crowd of 33,957 hostile Boston fans.

Lou Boudreau stands next to a painting of himself hung over the fireplace in his suburban Chicago home.

The Red Sox retaliated with a run in their half of the first inning on a double by Johnny Pesky and a two-out single by Vernon Stephens—yes, *that* Vernon Stephens, who had been the object of Veeck's affection and almost was traded to the Indians instead of to Boston.

Bearden promptly slammed the door, blanking the Red Sox in the second and third innings, which set the stage for the game's turning point, which Boudreau triggered with a fourth-inning leadoff single.

His dark eyes flashing behind the bifocal glasses he now wears, Boudreau smiled as he talked about another "hunch" of his that paid another large dividend.

After second baseman Joe Gordon followed with another single, putting Indians on first and second with nobody out and the score tied, those who managed by the "book" would have ordered the next batter to advance the runners with a sacrifice bunt.

But not Boudreau.

"Even before Greenberg joined the club, I was accused of being a hunch manager, though it didn't bother me because it was true," he said. "I wanted to do things different. I wasn't going to read a book and do things (manage) by that book."

Whatever his logic, Boudreau, standing on second, signaled the next batter, third baseman Ken Keltner—whom he affectionately called "Benny Beltner"—a .296 hitter, to swing away.

And swing away Keltner did. On a 2-and-2 count, Keltner also drove Galehouse's next pitch into the screen above the wall known as the "Green Monster."

"It probably was the best hunch move I ever made. That and picking Bearden to pitch the playoff game," said Boudreau.

The homer by Keltner—or "Benny Beltner," if you will—sent Galehouse to the showers, replaced by Ellis Kinder, who was no improvement for the Red Sox. Larry Doby greeted Kinder with a shot off the wall in left center for a double, was sacrificed to third, and scored on catcher Jim Hegan's infield grounder.

The four-run outburst gave Bearden and the Indians a 5-1 lead, after which Robinson, the regular first baseman, replaced Clark, who was flawless in the field, despite Veeck's and Greenberg's trepidation, though he grounded out in his only two trips to the plate.

An inning later, with one out in the fifth, Boudreau added an exclamation point with his second homer of the game and 18th of the season. It put the Indians ahead, 6-1, and all but won the game and the pennant.

The Red Sox scored twice in the sixth when Williams reached on an error by Gordon and Bobby Doerr homered, but Bearden yielded only one hit the final four innings to more than justify Boudreau's faith.

The Indians increased their lead to 7-3 in the eighth, and in the ninth, after Robinson led off with an infield single, the partisan fans in Fenway Park gave Boudreau a standing ovation when he approached the plate as the next batter.

"It was another memory I'll cherish forever," said Boudreau, who responded to the cheers with his fourth hit of the game, a single, and Keltner's double-play grounder scored the final run for the 8-3 victory.

It gave Boudreau "the greatest sense of excitement, of achievement, of pride, I'd ever felt," he said.

As Bearden was being carried off the field on the shoulders of his teammates, Veeck hobbled into the Indians clubhouse, threw his arms around Boudreau and, with tears in his eyes, said to the manager he'd tried to replace, "Thanks. Just thanks."

And Greenberg?

Boudreau said, "He congratulated me, shook my hand and said, 'Nice going.'"

The World Series that opened two days later against the Braves, also in Boston, could have been anti-climactic for the Indians, considering how the regular season ended and the pennant had been won.

But Boudreau wouldn't let his players—or himself—be satisfied.

"We had a celebration to end all celebrations, but the next day, the day before the Series began, I reminded everybody that we hadn't reached our final objective," said Boudreau.

The Braves and Johnny Sain beat the Indians and Bob Feller, 1-0, in the opener of the World Series on a disputed

Boudreau filling in as a catcher in a game in 1948, the only time in his baseball career he went behind the plate.

pickoff play at second base. Phil Masi, who scored the only run, later admitted he was out, picked off on a throw from Feller to Boudreau, but that umpire Bill Stewart blew the call.

"It was a terrible disappointment, especially for Feller, who pitched a great game and deserved to win," said Boudreau. "But we bounced back to beat the Braves the next three games and were on a roll."

Doby and Boudreau each got two hits as the Indians won Game 2, 4-1, with Bob Lemon out-pitching Warren Spahn; Bearden hurled a five-hitter and blanked the Braves and Vern Bickford, 2-0, in Game 3 in Cleveland; and Doby's third-inning homer proved to be the decisive blow, giving Steve Gromek and the Indians a 2-1 victory over Sain and the Braves in Game 4.

But Feller, in front of the largest crowd ever to see a baseball game—86,288 fans at the Stadium—couldn't wrap up the Indians' "final objective" in Game 5. Feller was knocked out in the seventh inning and the Braves prevailed, 11-5, to keep their hopes alive, though only for one more day.

With Lemon pitching seven strong innings before running out of gas and needing help from Bearden, the Indians won Game 6, 4-3, in Boston. Robinson drove in Keltner with what proved to be the winning run in the top of the eighth inning.

Only then did Boudreau admit that the World Series was, indeed, "somewhat" anticlimactic.

"Winning the pennant was the big thing," he said, "and I would have been disappointed if we had lost the World Series. But that would have been nothing compared to the disappointment I would have felt if we had lost the playoff game."

When the Indians partied again, this time aboard their train to Cleveland where a civic celebration awaited them, Gordon called for silence and saluted the shortstop-manager who, twelve months earlier, almost was replaced, traded to St. Louis.

Gordon raised his glass and toasted Boudreau: "To the greatest leatherman I ever saw, to the damnedest clutch hitter that ever lived, to a doggone good manager."

As Gordon's words were recalled, there was no mistaking Boudreau's pride in the tribute offered by his close friend and confidante, who died in 1978. Gordon had been acquired from the New York Yankees in a 1946 trade for pitcher Allie Reynolds and, after retiring as a player in 1951, managed the Indians from 1958-60, as well as Detroit in 1960, the Kansas City Athletics in 1961, and Kansas City Royals in 1969.

When Boudreau said at the onset that his induction into the Hall of Fame was "tied with a few others" as the greatest day of his life, it also was a reference to August 8, 1948, when it became evident that the Indians were for real in the American League pennant race.

It was the day Boudreau limped out of the dugout as a pinch hitter and delivered a two-run single that led to a double-header victory, 8-6 and 2-1, over the New York Yankees in front of 73,484 initially worried, then deliriously happy fans in the Stadium.

At the time, Boudreau was nursing an assortment of injuries— bruises of his right shoulder, right knee and right thumb, and a sprained left ankle—that had prevented him from playing the previous day, and was expected to keep him out of a couple more games.

The Indians, with a 58-39 record, had won six straight and were ahead of the Yankees and Philadelphia Athletics by a mere two percentage points, with the Red Sox in fourth place by one and a half games.

"I wasn't even wearing a shoe on my left foot, which I was soaking in a bucket of ice during the game, my back and thumb were taped up, and I had a brace on my knee (and) Johnny Berardino played shortstop in my absence," Boudreau recalled in his book, *Covering All The Bases.*

"Sam Zoldak, the left-handed pitcher we acquired from St. Louis in the middle of June, started but was knocked out. We were losing the opener, 6-1, in the seventh inning, and were in deep trouble, the way Spec Shea was pitching for the Yankees.

"But Ken Keltner walked and, after Shea got the second out, Berardino homered into the left-field stands. Eddie Robinson followed with another homer and we were only two runs behind. Jim Hegan kept the rally alive with a single, Allie Clark walked, and Dale Mitchell also singled to load the bases.

"(New York manager) Bucky Harris came out of the Yankees' dugout to talk to Shea. With Thurman Tucker, a left-handed hitter due next, Harris brought in Joe Page, their ace left-handed reliever. I'm sure Bucky figured I couldn't hit because I was hurt, and knew the only other right-handed batters we had on the bench were Joe Tipton and Bob Kennedy.

"I looked at Lefty Weisman, our trainer, and asked him what he thought. Should I bat for Tucker? Lefty said no, that if I reinjured myself, I'd miss a lot more time.

"But I felt this might be our last shot, and also—however, immodest it sounds—I knew I was the best we had available.

"While Page warmed up, I put on my sock and shoe and went to the bat rack. Nobody said anything, though I remember seeing (coach) Bill McKechnie nod his head and smile.

"When I stepped out of the dugout with a bat in my hand and field announcer Jack Cresson intoned, 'Attention please. Batting for Tucker, No. 5, Lou Boudreau,' the fans went crazy. Their cheers were deafening and sent a chill up my spine. I forgot about how badly my ankle hurt, or that my back was stiff, or that my thumb was so sore.

"Page's first pitch was a ball. I fouled off his second. His third pitch was inside for ball two, and then umpire Art Passarella called Page's fourth pitch a strike. I didn't like it and told Passarella.

"Now, with the count 2-and-2, the crowd was hushed, expectant, probably fearing the worst.

"I figured Page would come in with another fastball. He did and I was ready for it. I hit a line drive to the right of second base into right-center field. It might have been a double, but I barely made it to first base, my ankle and back hurt so much."

Boudreau's clutch hit scored two runs, tying the game, and the ovation the player-manager received as he limped off the field was deafening, even greater than the one he got when he was announced as a pinch hitter.

"It was second only to winning the playoff game—and we never would have gotten to the play-offs if we hadn't beaten the Yankees that day," he said.

An inning later Robinson hammered another homer to break the tie and win the game for reliever Satchel Paige. The Indians went on to capture the nightcap as Gromek pitched seven strong innings and Robinson bashed his third homer of the day.

As *Cleveland Press* sports editor Franklin (Whitey) Lewis wrote, "If Boudreau could do it, so could his men, it seemed."

And Gordon Cobbledick reported in the *Cleveland Plain Dealer* that Veeck had said in the press box as Boudreau limped to the plate, "Even if he doesn't get a hit, this is the most courageous thing I've ever seen in baseball."

Remembering Veeck's compliment pleased Boudreau, of course.

But the smile it brought to his face soon faded, as did the euphoria of that glorious season of 1948, when the Boy Manager and his Indians were at the height of their popularity.

The decline began with their inability to repeat as the American League champion, followed by Veeck's sale of the franchise that, essentially, left Greenberg in charge. It was culminated with Boudreau's departure a year later after the Indians failed again to win another pennant.

Boudreau with wife Della in their Frankfort home.

They finished third, behind New York and Boston, in 1949, and when they dropped to fourth place in 1950, Boudreau was fired, replaced by Lopez.

It was the low point of Boudreau's career, coming as it did two years after reaching the pinnacle.

Boudreau was informed of his ouster in a succinct and seemingly insensitive telephone call from Ryan. Only two weeks earlier Greenberg had led Boudreau to believe he'd be rehired.

In that call to Boudreau, Ryan said, "Lou, we've decided to make a change. We've hired Al Lopez to manage the club."

Basically, that was it. Ryan offered no elaboration. Boudreau admitted that he was too stunned to react other than to ask about his status as a player, to which Ryan replied, "Let me talk it over with Hank. I'll call you back."

Before Ryan did, Boudreau called him, saying, in effect, "Forget it . . . give me my unconditional release."

Greenberg immediately complied.

It ended Boudreau's playing career with the Indians, which began in 1938 when he batted .290 in 60 games with their Cedar Rapids farm club in the Class B Three-I League. In 1939, his second season as a professional, at Buffalo of the Class AA International League, Boudreau hit .331 in 115 games, earning a promotion to Cleveland for the final six weeks of the season.

Boudreau's firing also concluded his Indians managerial career with a nine-year won-lost record of 728-649, the most victories in franchise history, though it didn't finish him in baseball.

Declining offers to play for the New York Yankees, Pittsburgh and Washington Senators, Boudreau signed with the Red Sox as a utilityman under his old friend and mentor, Steve O'Neill, then the Boston manager.

As manager of the Buffalo Bisons in 1939, O'Neill helped develop Boudreau into a major league shortstop, then served as a Tribe coach under Boudreau in 1949.

Boudreau played all shortstop, third base and first base in 82 games for the Red Sox in 1951, hitting .267 with five homers and 47 RBIs, before suffering a broken thumb when hit by a pitch from Virgil Trucks late in the season. It all but ended his playing career.

When the Red Sox wound up third in 1951, after having been favored to win, O'Neill was fired and replaced by Boudreau, who managed the team the next three seasons, though without great success.

The record shows that he played in four games in 1952, batting only twice without a hit as the Red Sox were sixth in 1952, and fourth in 1953 and 1954.

Boudreau managed the Kansas City Athletics, newly relocated from Philadelphia, the next three seasons with even less success, finishing sixth and eighth twice, before he was fired August 5, 1957.

But instead of ending Boudreau's career in baseball, his dismissal by the Athletics opened another door, this one in broadcasting.

Except for a brief interruption in 1960, Boudreau sat behind a WGN microphone in Chicago the next 30 years. He was primarily an analyst and color commentator for the Chicago Cubs, and also did interviews before and after Chicago Bulls and University of Illinois basketball games, and Chicago Blackhawks hockey games.

"One thing I *never* did," Boudreau was quick to interject, "was second guess the manager or coach."

Jack Brickhouse, who got Boudreau started in radio and was his longtime partner on Cubs broadcasts, said of the former shortstop-manager, "Listening to Lou on the radio was like sitting next to an old friend at the ball park and having him explain what's going on before you even asked."

That brief interruption in Boudreau's broadcasting career occurred in 1960 when Philip K. Wrigley, then owner of the Cubs, asked him on May 5 to leave the radio booth and replace Charlie Grimm as manager of the team.

Lou Boudreau in a full Indian headdress presented to him by the Tucson, Arizona Chamber of Commerce during spring training in 1948.

At the time, the Cubs were floundering in last place in the National League with a horrendous, 6-11 record.

Boudreau could not resist the opportunity to return to the field and accepted Wrigley's offer. "I had mixed emotions because I was comfortable in my broadcasting job, but the fact is, I was only 43 years old and, I guess, I was still a manager at heart."

It did not prove to be a good move, for either the new manager or the team.

Under Boudreau the Cubs went 54-83. Except for a brief period shortly after Boudreau's arrival when they temporarily climbed into sixth place, the Cubs spent most of the season trying to stay out of the basement. They finally did, finishing seventh, one game ahead of Philadelphia and 35 behind Pittsburgh, which won the pennant.

The following season, 1961, Wrigley initiated the unique—and short-lived—"College of Coaches," in which 10 coaches were employed, four of whom took turns rotating as "head coach."

Boudreau was not one of them, by his own volition, ending his managerial career. It showed a 16-year won-lost record of 1,162-1,224 for a .487 winning percentage, one pennant and world championship. His teams finished third twice, fourth five times, fifth twice, sixth three times, seventh once, and eighth twice.

Boudreau returned to WGN where he remained behind a microphone until 1988, when the station declined to renew his contract.

"There's no doubt this is a very sad time for me," Boudreau said when he was replaced by Nelson. "I feel capable of continuing, but (WGN) has made up their mind. I felt it coming."

And so, Boudreau's career was ended, retired as a broadcaster, major league baseball player, and manager—sadly, but also happily for the man who did, indeed, cover all the bases, as expressed in his 1993 book.

It was a joyride that began in 1935, when Boudreau was awarded a basketball scholarship by the University of Illinois, and took flight when he had the unmitigated audacity, at age 24, to apply for the job of managing the Indians.

Despite his resistance to Veeck's attempt to trade him to St. Louis in November 1947, Boudreau had, and still has great respect for the former Indians owner who died in 1986 at the age of 71 after undergoing two operations for lung cancer.

"Bill was a great showman, a great entertainer, and while we didn't always see eye-to-eye, he was a darned good baseball man," Boudreau said of Veeck. "He was a man who put himself in the fans' shoes, as well as the executives' and ballplayers' shoes. He knew baseball, he made the trades. And he was the type of individual who took care of his players.

"We had a good relationship, though he was closer to Greenberg after Hank joined the organization. A lot of that had to do with the fact that Bill liked to go out after games, have a few drinks and talk about what happened. He liked wine and, for awhile, I'd have a few (glasses) with him.

"But then it started to get to me and I realized I couldn't hit and field, play my best if I were going to drink with Bill and stay up late every night, so I told him I couldn't keep it up. He understood and that's about the time Hank (Greenberg) sort of took my place spending a lot of time with Bill."

Boudreau admitted that Veeck "occasionally tried to influence" his decisions on the field—though not as strongly as Greenberg did— but denied that the owner "interfered."

"Oh, I'm not saying he never tried (to force his opinion), but I never let him and he knew I wouldn't go for it."

Especially not after Boudreau had gained the upper hand in their relationship and was signed on November 24, 1947 to a new two-year contract at a salary of $49,000 each season, $25,000 as a manager, and $24,000 as a player.

Now Boudreau spends much of his time watching baseball and other sports on television, and visiting Balmoral race track in suburban Chicago.

Especially Balmoral race track.

Though it's difficult for Boudreau to walk because of the arthritis in his back, knees and ankles, he is able to drive. Three or four times a week he goes to Balmoral where he is met at the entrance by an attendant with a wheelchair and rides to the clubhouse while his car is being parked.

In December 1994, while climbing the steps to the clubhouse at Balmoral, Boudreau tripped and fell, breaking a bone in his left shoulder. Ever since then he gets V.I.P. treatment at the track.

"They take great care of me . . . probably because they think I'm a lousy handicapper and want me to keep coming back and betting their horses," he quipped.

Lou and Della Boudreau raised four children—daughters Barbara and Sharyn, and sons Lou and Jim —who have given them 17 grandchildren and two great grandchildren.

Barbara, the oldest, is married to a former University of Illinois football player, Paul Golaszewski, and lives a few blocks from Lou and Della in Frankfort. "The big reason we moved here (from Dolton, Illinois, another suburb of Chicago) was to be close to Barbara and Paul," said Boudreau.

Sharyn is married to former Detroit Tigers pitcher Denny McLain who, a year ago, was convicted of stealing from the pension plan of a company he owned and was sentenced to eight years in prison. It was the second time McLain was convicted of a felony and imprisoned.

A two-time American League Cy Young Memorial Award winner (1968 and 1969), and the last pitcher to win 30 games in one season (1968), McLain previously served 29 months of a 23-year sentence imposed in 1985, before an appeals court overturned his convictions of racketeering, drug dealing and extortion.

McLain later pleaded guilty to federal racketeering and drug charges to avoid a retrial and was sentenced to time served and five years probation.

Then, nine years later, after embarking upon a promising radio career as a general talk show host in Detroit, McLain was back in trouble and incarcerated again.

It is, of course, a source of great consternation to Boudreau, who acknowledges McLain's troubles are embarrassing, but is reluctant to discuss the situation in much detail.

"We've always gotten along, but we never had what I'd call a good father-in-law, son-in-law relationship," said Boudreau.

"I let Denny know that I was available, that if he wanted me for anything, advice or help of any kind, he could come to me. But I could never really reach him. He is a flighty individual and always seemed to have something on his mind. I have to give Sharyn a lot of credit. She has stuck by Denny through thick and thin."

Their lives, and the lives of Lou and Della Boudreau, also were scarred by tragedy on March 20, 1992, when Sharyn and Denny's 26-year-old, newly wedded daughter, Kristin, was killed in a truck accident near Detroit.

"You never get over something like that; you only survive it," said Boudreau.

Boudreau's oldest son, Lou (who is not a junior because his middle name is Harry, after Della's father), served with the Marines in Vietnam where he was wounded three times during his six-month tour of duty. Boudreau's pride in

his son is unmistakable. As he stated in *Covering All The Bases:*

"We in sports often talk about the courage it takes to stand 60 feet from a pitcher throwing a baseball 90 or 95 miles an hour, sometimes even faster, or to go over the middle to catch a football, or to take a chance of being undercut while leaping to shoot a basketball through a hoop, or to get checked into the boards by a hockey player skating 35 miles an hour, or to block a puck traveling 80 miles an hour.

"But it takes real courage to put your life on the line as did Lou."

Boudreau's fourth child, Jim, was a left-handed pitcher who was drafted by the Cubs in 1982. He played in the minor leagues four years, two with the Cubs and two with Baltimore, but never made it above the Class AA level.

While Boudreau always was careful as a broadcaster to avoid second guessing managers and coaches, he was candid and outspoken in expressing his opinion of baseball today.

As we concluded our interview in his car—speeding back to Frankfort from Balmoral, where he'd picked a few winners and, consequently, was smiling broadly—Boudreau said, "I don't envy managers and the way they have to operate now, primarily because of the way the people in charge are running the game, the owners and leaders in the Players Association.

"For one thing, I'm amazed at the money the players are being paid. Now, it's more business than baseball. The players get multi-year contracts and high salaries. They have security, which has to change their perspective. In my day, a two-year contract was a rarity."

Boudreau's peak salary was $62,000, which he received in the form of a new contract after the Indians won the pennant and World Championship in 1948. It represented a raise of $13,000 over the two-year contract he'd been given by Veeck in November 1947.

"I'm not saying players shouldn't get as much as the owners are willing to pay. But I think that, with salaries as high as they are, it changes the attitude of the ball players.

"In 1948 we—and I mean *everybody*—had a great attitude, which was a big reason we were successful. We were like a bunch of college athletes, all together on the same page, and everybody knew what had to be done when he was called upon.

Lou Boudreau enjoys Bill Veeck burning his contract and signing him to a new one after the 1948 season.

"To me, there's also a question of loyalty, the way things are today with agents being so prominent, and so important. Instead of a player owing his total allegiance to his team, his manager and his teammates, it seems that too many are loyal primarily to their agent, the guy who got them their big contract, and will be negotiating their next contract.

"I don't know what to do about it, but I do know that, what baseball needs today, more than anything, is a strong commissioner, another Judge (Kenesaw Mountain) Landis. If he were still around, you can bet your bottom dollar a lot of the things that are happening wouldn't be happening, and the game would be a lot better off."

By then we were back in Frankfort and Boudreau eased his Buick into the garage of his home on Cedar Lane.

"What more can I tell you?" he asked.

"Nothing more that I can think of," I told him.

"OK," he said, grunting as he got out of the car and slammed the door.

Then, shifting his cane to his left hand and shaking my hand with his right, Boudreau, the former, but not forgotten, "Boy Manager" said, "Tell all the guys I said hello, and that I wish we could do it all over again."

I said I would . . . and I wish they could, too.

CHAPTER SIX

Bob Feller

"I must have been the cleanest guy in baseball because the writers kept saying I was all washed up."

Without a doubt the greatest pitcher the Indians ever had—and one of the greatest in the history of baseball—Bob Feller laughed often as he reminisced about the 1948 season, even though it was not one of the best in his Hall of Fame career.

"I must've been the cleanest guy in the game . . . because the writers kept saying I was all washed up that season," quipped Feller, major league baseball's "Strikeout King" before Sandy Koufax, Nolan Ryan and Roger Clemens came along.

Feller threw three no-hitters, twelve one-hitters, and held the single-game and season strikeout records (18 and 348, respectively).

Those marks were bettered by Koufax, who pitched four no-hitters, and then Ryan, who pitched seven; Steve Carlton, who struck out 19 batters in a game in 1969, Tom Seaver, who also fanned 19 in 1970, Ryan, 19 in 1974, David Cone in 1991, before Clemens struck out 20 in games twice, in 1986 and 1996; and Koufax fanned 382 in the 1965 season, and Ryan 383 in 1973.

But, back there a half-century ago when Feller was 29 and should have been in his prime, speculation was rife, as he facetiously acknowledged, that he'd lost, not only his fastball but also the winning touch.

Feller won five of his first seven decisions in 1948, but went on to lose five straight and six of his next seven for an uncharacteristic—for him—6-8 record in late June.

Then, after July 7 when Feller beat Chicago, 10-2, for his ninth victory to go with nine defeats, it got worse. He lost three more in a row.

Just about everybody had a theory as to what was wrong, even his first wife, Virginia, who was quoted by Bob Considine in a nationally syndicated wire service story that she was to blame for Feller's problems.

"I'm the trouble with Bob," she told Considine. "I didn't recuperate too well after our last baby and it worried him. Lordy, I had to go back into the hospital not long ago and on three separate times they called Bob away from the team to see me. No wonder he's been upset. It's really my fault.

"Well, maybe nearly all my fault. Some fellow in Iowa sued Bob over one of the barnstorming games, and though Bob won, he had to go to court and it was all pretty distracting.

"But he'll come around. Don't you worry about that. I'm well now, the (law) suit's out of the way and Bob's unloading a lot of the outside work he was doing."

Another who was confident that Feller would "come around" was Gordon Cobbledick, veteran sports editor of the *Cleveland Plain Dealer*, who wrote:

Bob Feller

Bob Feller, circa 1937.

"A poll of the people of Cleveland and northern Ohio shows a sharp division of opinion about the one truly vital issue of the day, to wit: Robert William Andrew Feller.

"Somewhat more than half the populace, or 58.3%, favors hanging Feller as a habitual criminal. The moderate element, representing 41.6%, is merely worried about him. A scant .1% (one-tenth of one percent), the inevitable crackpot minority, recommends that we all keep our shirts on."

Then Cobbledick, who covered the Indians as a baseball writer and columnist for more than 30 years until his retirement in 1965, wrote, "I confess to membership in that last group," and the patience that he also advocated proved to be appropriate.

From July 27 through the final ten weeks of the season Feller went 10-2. Included were seven straight victories down the stretch, though it was a 7-1 loss charged to him on Octo-

ber 3, the last day of the season, that dropped the Indians into a tie with Boston, forcing the one-game playoff for the pennant.

Feller wound up with a 19-15 won-lost record and a 3.56 earned run average, the second highest to that point of his career that began in 1936 as a 17-year-old schoolboy fresh off his family's farm in Van Meter, Iowa.

"I had a terrible first half," acknowledged Feller as we visited in the library of his home in Gates Mills, Ohio, a fashionable suburb of Cleveland. "To this day I don't know why. I just didn't have my good stuff."

Although Feller hurt his arm the previous season when he slipped on the mound while delivering a pitch against the Athletics in Philadelphia on June 13, he insisted it had nothing to do with the troubles he experienced the first half of 1948.

"It was nothing physical . . . I just wasn't doing my mechanics properly," Feller said, offering no excuse.

Neither could he explain why he improved in the second half of the season.

"I got better as the season went on, and I was selected for the All-Star Game," said Feller, though his record at the time was only 9-10. "But I knew I didn't belong (on the American League squad"; I was picked for old times' sake and I didn't go."

Feller was subjected to great criticism for "backing out," as he was accused of doing, but in his opinion, "I didn't deserve to be on the team, which was the reason I gave. It was that simple."

The fact is, Indians owner Bill Veeck urged Feller to fabricate a reason for skipping the All-Star Game, to save himself for the pennant race in the second half. At the time the Indians were locked in a four-team battle, along with New York, Boston and Philadelphia.

"Veeck told me, 'Don't go to the All-Star Game, say that you cut your finger on a razor blade,' but I told him I wouldn't lie," said Feller.

"Then Marsh Samuel (the Indians public relations director) released a statement that said I was withdrawing for 'unknown reasons,'" which obviously angered Feller.

Feller confronted Veeck and, he said, "I had a few words with him that weren't very pleasant. Though (Veeck) apologized, nobody wanted to hear my explanation.

"All the writers wanted to do was throw rocks at me because I withdrew. You know how the media was —and is even worse now. They want to throw rocks at anyone who is halfway successful."

When asked if the criticism affected him, Feller replied, again facetiously, "Oh, yeah, it must have bothered me a lot because I won nine of my last ten games."

Then, seriously, he said, "If anything, it might have motivated me in some respects, though I never needed anybody else to motivate me. I motivated myself."

Obviously, Feller's personal motivation was more than enough. Pitching his entire career with the Indians, Feller was a 20-game winner six times while compiling a 266-162 record in 18 seasons from 1936-56. He undoubtedly would have won 300 games had it not been for World War II.

Two days after Pearl Harbor was attacked by the Japanese on December 7, 1941, Feller enlisted in the Navy, serving aboard the U.S.S. Alabama as a chief gunnery mate. He was discharged 44 months later, on August 14, 1945.

Ten days after being released by Uncle Sam, Feller made a dramatic, triumphant return on August 24 to the Cleveland Stadium. There, in front of the largest crowd of the season, 46,477, he faced—and beat —longtime rival Hal Newhouser in a 4-2 victory over Detroit.

Feller allowed only four hits and struck out twelve, two of them against future Hall of Famer Hank Greenberg, who would become one of Feller's bosses with the Indians three years later.

Ironically, that loss by Newhouser to Feller cut the Tigers' first- place lead over Washington to a half game, though Detroit went on to win the pennant—just as the Indians did by defeating Boston in the playoff in 1948, after Newhouser beat Feller on the final day of the season.

"I don't know about anybody else, but I figured as early as spring training that we had a chance to win the pennant (in 1948)," Feller said. "We didn't have much of a pitching staff in 1946 when Veeck bought the team, but he hired some pretty good players and lucked out with some trades.

"He got Joe Gordon and Gene Bearden (in separate deals) from the Yankees, Walt Judnich and Bob Muncrief from the (St. Louis) Browns, and then he picked up Sam

Bob Feller (left) with Joe Gordon.

Zoldak (also from the Browns) during the (1948) season, and signed Satchel Paige.

"By then Dale Mitchell had come into his own, so did Larry Doby, (Ken) Keltner had a good year and, of course, (Lou) Boudreau had the best season of his career.

"Gordon was a great second baseman and clutch hitter, a real leader on the field, along with Boudreau, who was absolutely the best manager, the best player-manager I ever saw. No doubt about it, he was better as a player-manager than he could have been as a bench manager, maybe because he was such a great player that year.

"I don't know why I was so bad in the first half," Feller said again. "Some days I had a pretty good fastball, but I wasn't consistent with my curve and slider. I think my best game was against the Red Sox the night they had for Don Black (September 22)."

A crowd of 76,772 fans jammed the Stadium for that game as Feller pitched a three hitter to beat Boston, 5-2. All the proceeds were donated by Veeck to Black, a right-handed pitcher who had suffered a brain aneurysm nine days earlier while batting in a game against the Browns.

Feller went on to beat the Tigers and Newhouser, 4-1, with a five-hitter on September 26. It boosted the Indians into undisputed possession of first place by one game over the Red Sox and Yankees.

Three days later Feller hurled another gem, and Keltner and Gordon homered to beat the Chicago White Sox, 5-2, giving the Indians a two-game lead over Boston and New York with three left to play.

However, the best the Indians could do was split the next two games with the Tigers, while the Red Sox were winning two and the Yankees one. That left it up to Feller to wrap up the pennant with a victory over Detroit in the season finale.

But he couldn't. The Tigers, with Newhouser seeking—and getting—a measure of revenge, knocked Feller out of the box in the third inning with a four-run explosion, and went on to win, 7-1.

It was Newhouser's 21st victory, Feller's 15th loss, and with Boston clobbering New York, 10-5, the Indians and Red Sox were tied, forcing the playoff.

"Newhouser had great stuff, but when you get right down to it, he had nothing to lose and nothing to gain except his reputation," said Feller.

"As for me, I just plain and simple had a bad day, which I did a lot of times in the first half (of 1948). But the fact is, Newhouser outpitched me and we didn't score many runs."

In a 1995 interview, Newhouser said of the victory that jeopardized the entire season for the Indians, "I'd won my twentieth game four days earlier and thought my season was over. But Freddie Hutchinson, who was scheduled to start against the Indians, got sick. (Tigers manager) Steve O'Neill told me to pitch.

"'You've got to do it for baseball, for the integrity of the game,' O'Neill told me. 'If you

Bob Feller poses with his book, "Strikeout Story," in the Cleveland Indians' dressing room.

don't, the Red Sox will jump all over us for starting a second-line guy,'" Newhouser quoted the manager.

"I pitched what might have been the best game of my life. Did I feel bad about possibly knocking the Indians out of the pennant? Hell, no. My job was to pitch and win. Which I did."

When it was over the Indians regrouped in the clubhouse. "We were disappointed, of course, but we weren't demoralized, if that's what you want to know," said Feller. "Boudreau was upbeat and wanted to make sure the rest of us were, too.

"He said something like, 'Well, we were going to Boston, anyway,' though he meant to play the (National League champion) Braves, and told us right away that Bearden was his choice to pitch against the Red Sox.

"Nobody argued . . . not after Gordon said that he was willing to trust Boudreau's judgment for another game, and that's the way it was, even though Bearden had pitched the day before. My choice would have been Bearden, too.

"I know there was speculation that it would be Lemon or me, but speaking for myself, I wouldn't have wanted to pitch. At least not to start the game. I wasn't that good in Fenway Park. My record there was only like 50-50. I either pitched very good in Boston or very bad. But when the game started, Lem and I were both warming up in the bullpen, getting ready in case we were needed."

Neither was, though Bearden faltered briefly when the Red Sox tied the score, 1-1, in the first inning. It stayed that way until the fourth when the Indians added four runs, three of them on Keltner's homer that knocked Denny Galehouse out of the game. Bearden literally coasted thereafter.

"Bearden was great," said Feller. "He had good control and was able to get past their big hitters . . . (Ted) Williams, (Vernon) Stephens (1-for-4) and (Bobby) Doerr." None of them got more than one hit apiece, singles by Williams and Stephens, and a homer by Doerr.

Was Bearden nervous before he took the mound against the Red Sox?

"I'm sure he was . . . I'm sure he was as nervous as all of us would be in a game like that, with so much —*everything,* really—riding on it. But once you get past the first two or three batters, you're OK," Feller said.

The 8-3 victory over the Red Sox, of course, vaulted the Indians into the World Series.

And, even though it would have been Lemon's turn to pitch, Feller got the assignment to start Game One at Braves Field on October 6. Feller's opponent was Boston's ace, Johnny Sain, the National League's winningest pitcher with a 24-15 record.

The result undoubtedly was one of the major disappointments of Feller's career, never mind his protestations to the contrary.

Sain and the Braves prevailed, 1-0, as the only run of the game scored in the eighth inning on a single by Tommy Holmes. It happened after National League umpire Bill Stewart blew a call on Feller's attempted pickoff of pinch runner Phil Masi at second base. It was a mistake that Stewart, several years later, admitted making.

But not when it happened.

"What we should have done was tell the umpires to be alert for the (pickoff) play," said Feller. "The American League umpires knew about it because we'd used it during the season.

"The trouble was that Boudreau, in the managers' meeting with the commissioner and the umpires before the Series began, didn't go out of his way to say anything because, he said, (Braves manager) Billy Southworth was always at his elbow.

"If Lou had alerted the umpires, Southworth also would have been alerted, so everybody (except the American League umpires) were caught off guard when we (tried to pick off Masi at second base).

"At least, that's what Lou told me," said Feller.

"Some years later, it was about 1958, or thereabouts, I saw Stewart and he admitted he blew the call. He didn't apologize, he just said he blew it, which he did."

Alvin Dark, who was then the Braves shortstop and later managed the Indians (1968-71), was another who knew that Stewart was wrong.

"All of us (Braves) knew Masi was out . . . there was no question about it," Dark was quoted later.

If Feller still resented Stewart's mistake, he won't admit it.

"I didn't lose the game because Stewart blew the call," said Feller. "It didn't beat me out of a victory. It beat me out of a tie. I lost because I walked the leadoff batter (Bill Salkeld) in the inning. If you walk the leadoff man, it's nobody's fault but your own."

Masi ran for Salkeld, took second on a sacrifice bunt by Mike McCormick, Eddie Stanky was intentionally walked and replaced by pinch runner Sibby Sisti, and Sain flied out.

That's when Feller and Boudreau tried their pickoff play, which the manager said in his 1993 autobiography, *Covering All The Bases,* "saved us 18 to 20 runs" that season. "Once we showed it, many base runners were intimidated by the possibility that we'd use it."

Boudreau signaled for the pickoff by holding his glove a certain way over his left knee. When Feller saw the sign, he was to look directly at the batter and start counting, one thousand one, one thousand two, and then wheel and fire the ball to second base. Boudreau was counting, too, and raced to the bag, behind Masi.

Feller's throw was right on the mark and, when Boudreau applied the tag, Masi was a good three feet from the base.

But Stewart called him safe.

Then Holmes, a .325 hitter in 1948, looped a single to score the decisive run.

It was only the second hit allowed by Feller, though he also walked three. Sain pitched a four-hitter and didn't issue a base on balls.

By his own admission, Feller was not nearly as good when he came back to pitch the fifth game in Cleveland with a chance to win the Series for the Indians.

"I had good stuff in the opener, but not in the fifth game . . . I was struggling from the first inning," said Feller. He was hammered by the Braves, giving up seven runs on eight hits—including two homers by Bob Elliott and one by Salkeld. He also walked two batters and was replaced in the seventh.

And, neither would Feller admit to any great regret about being a two-time loser in the World Series, which the Indians won in the sixth game behind Lemon and Bearden.

"It doesn't bother me at all," he said. "We won (the World Series) and cashed the winners' checks. That's what was important."

However, Feller conceded that it was "different"—that he was "disappointed" though "not angry or upset"—in 1954 when the Indians were swept in the World Series by the then-New York Giants, and he wasn't given an opportunity to pitch by Manager Al Lopez.

Lemon started the first game and was brought back with two days' rest to pitch the fourth, while Early Wynn started the second and Mike Garcia the third.

"Lopez thought Lemon had a better chance to win (the fourth game) than I did," said Feller, whose record that season was 13-3, as his brilliant career obviously was on the wane.

"Al was desperate. We had lost three straight and we weren't hitting well, and our defense also had fallen apart.

"Everybody said when Willie Mays made that catch (of a 400-plus foot drive to center field by Vic Wertz in the eighth inning of the first game) it demoralized us, but that's not so.

"Actually, the ball could have been easily caught by any center fielder. Lemon, before he became a pitcher, could have caught it. But Willie was a good actor. He always wore a cap that was too big or too small so that it would fly off his head when he ran. And if a ball was hit right at him, he'd run around in a circle and dive for it. He was a good showman besides being a great ball player . . . one of the best ever."

When the question persisted—was he angry that Lopez did not start him in one of the four games in the 1954 World Series—Feller insisted, "I was not angry or upset . . . but I was disappointed.

"How could anybody get mad at Lopez? I felt sorry for him. I felt sorry for all of us, although I did think it was bad strategy on the part of Lopez because I don't know if Lemon ever pitched well with two days' rest.

"And those who thought Garcia should have started the fourth game were wrong, too. Mike never pitched well against the Giants in the spring.

"(Art) Houtteman is the guy Lopez should have gone with, not me—and not Lemon—though that's hindsight.

"But I do know this," continued Feller. "Leo Durocher (the Giants' manager in 1954) told his team—and Leo himself told me because we were very good friends—there was only one pitcher with the Indians they couldn't beat. It was me."

Feller chuckled and said, "Maybe that's because Leo remembered he was the first batter I ever faced (on July 6, 1936) in an exhibition game between the Indians and the old 'Gashouse Gang,' Durocher's St. Louis Cardinals. I struck him out."

*Bob Feller, then 20
years old, shows his
windup and delivery
in 1939.*

Then a precocious high school kid, Feller went on to strike out eight of the nine Cardinals he faced, after which Dizzy Dean was asked to pose with the Indians rookie and replied, "Shucks, ask that boy if he's willing to pose with me."

Shortly thereafter Feller made his first major league start on August 23 and fanned 15 batters in a complete game, 4-1, victory over St. Louis.

And three weeks later, in the first game of a double header against Philadelphia on September 13 at League Park, Feller struck out 17 members of the Athletics, tying Dean's major league record.

It was in 1938, on a cold and raw final day of the season, October 2 against the Tigers at the Stadium, that Feller struck out 18 batters to set the nine-inning, single-game record that stood for 31 years.

The game had been scheduled for League Park but was switched to the Stadium because a large crowd—27,000—was expected. The main attraction was Greenberg, who needed two homers to equal Babe Ruth's then-record of 60.

However, though the Indians lost, 4-1, to Harry Eisenstat, who pitched for the Tigers (and would be traded to Cleveland and be Feller's teammate in 1940 and 1941), Feller held Greenberg to a double in four at-bats, and struck him out twice.

The highlight of Feller's career, though he consistently declines to pinpoint any one game, probably was April 16, 1940.

It came in the wake of Feller's first 20-victory season the year before, when he —a.k.a. "Rapid Robert"—hurled major league baseball's only Opening Day (winning) no-hitter against the White Sox on another cold and overcast day in Chicago. It was witnessed by 14,000 half-frozen fans in Comiskey Park.

(One other Opening Day no-hitter was thrown, by Red Ames of the New York Giants against Brooklyn in 1909, but he yielded a hit in the tenth inning and lost, 3-0, in the thirteenth.)

Feller struck out eight and walked five, and was in trouble only once. In the second inning, with one out, Taft Wright reached as his fly ball to center was misjudged and fell for a two-base error by Roy Weatherly.

Feller got the second out, fanning Eric McNair, but walked Mike Tresh and opposing pitcher Edgar Smith, loading the bases.

Rookie third baseman Bob Kennedy, who, in 1948, also would become a teammate of Feller, then struck out. It ended the inning and the White Sox's only serious threat, though an outstanding play by Indians second baseman Ray Mack in the ninth inning was necessary to preserve the no-hitter.

With two out and Luke Appling on first via a walk, Wright slapped a sharp grounder toward right field. Mack raced to his left, knocked down the ball as he fell to his knees, and recovered in time with a throw to first baseman Hal Trosky to beat the runner by a half-step.

Right fielder Ben Chapman also stole a hit from Wright with a running catch against the wall in the fourth, and Mack also made a difficult play in the eighth, fielding a slow grounder to retire pinch hitter Larry Rosenthal.

The only run Feller needed to win that game was produced in the fourth inning after Trosky flied to Wright against the right-field fence. Jeff Heath singled to left and, after Keltner was retired, Rollie Hemsley slashed a liner to right. The ball sailed away from Wright and, by the time he retrieved it, Heath had scored and Hemsley was on third with a triple.

Feller also pitched no-hitters against New York, 1-0, on April 30, 1946—that was the season he called the best of his career—and Detroit, 2-1, in the opener of a double header on July 1, 1951.

In 1946, the first full year Feller was back from World War II, he won 26 games and lost 15 for the team that finished sixth with a 68-86 record, 36 lengths behind the pennant-winning Red Sox.

It was the fourth of six times that Feller led the American League in victories. Not only did he post his best-ever earned run average, a minuscule 2.18, he worked 371 1/3 innings, completed 36 of his 42 starts, pitched ten shutouts and broke what was then thought to be the season strikeout record of 343 set by Rube Waddell in 1904.

His no-hitter against the Yankees also came in the wake of widespread speculation in the media that Feller had lost his overpowering fast ball, and no longer was the No. 1 pitcher in baseball.

"It seemed like every time I'd lose a couple of games, the prophets of doom would come out of their closets," he said.

But, as he often did, Feller quickly quieted the critics with his performance in front of 37,144 fans in Yankee Stadium, striking out eleven and walking five.

Only Phil Rizzuto came close to getting a hit; in the eighth inning, after Keltner had dropped his pop foul for an error, Rizzuto smashed a grounder that Boudreau back-handed in the hole between shortstop and third base, and fired a strike to first baseman Les Fleming.

The only run Feller needed came on the wings of a ninth-inning homer by catcher Frankie Hayes off Yankees starter and loser, Floyd Bevens.

It also was in 1946 that Feller went into the last game with 343 strikeouts and, facing the Tigers—as well as Newhouser—he fanned five for a total of 348 in a 4-1 victory.

As fate would have it, Feller's final victim was none other than Newhouser, who was called out on a 3-and-2 pitch, although, to this day, he maintains the pitch should have been called ball four, not strike three.

Several years later a baseball historian discovered an additional six strikeouts that should have been credited to Waddell, giving him 349.

"I wanted the record, and as far as I'm concerned, (Waddell's total) was 343 . . . I have a letter from the American League office stating that it was 343," he said. "There were no official records kept by anybody back in those days (of Waddell's career).

"If I'd been told by the American League that the record was 349, I would have pitched another couple of innings and got another couple of strikeouts so I'd have gone past 349. There was nothing else for us to accomplish that year . . . the season was over for us about the middle of Mother's Day.

"A lot of people thought I hurt myself physically by going for the strikeout record, but that's not true. I started 1947 having a good year (7-5 record) and I struck out nine of the first eleven batters I faced in a game in Philadelphia (on June 13)," said Feller.

"I was throwing nothing but fastballs . . . it was the best fastball I ever had," he was quoted in an article in *The Plain Dealer* on April 5, 1981. "The ball felt small, real small and light in my hand and I thought I would go on to strike out maybe 20 batters that game. I don't ever remember feeling that good before.

"But then I threw my first curveball. It was on an 0-and-2 count to Barney McCosky. My front foot slipped in the dirt as I was striding forward in my delivery and I fell down. I tore the muscle behind my right shoulder blade, and also hurt my knee . . . and I was never the same. I never had a consistent fastball, and I had to make the transition from being just a hard thrower to a pitcher by utilizing a slider and curveball more.

"Before I hurt my shoulder I could throw ten good fastballs in ten pitches. But after that game in 1947, I could throw only, maybe, seven good fastballs in ten pitches. That was the biggest difference in me."

Despite being injured that night in Philadelphia, Feller stayed in the game through seven innings, striking out three more batters for a total of twelve, and giving up six hits and four runs. Ed Klieman relieved Feller and worked the final two innings of the Indians' 5-4 victory.

Feller's third no-hitter, enabling him to join the immortal Cy Young and another old timer, Larry Corcoran, as the only pitchers who—at that time—had accomplished the feat. It was the eleventh victory in thirteen decisions for Feller, who struck out five, mainly with curve balls and sliders, and walked three.

According to media accounts of the game, Feller was saved by the "great support" of his infielders.

Bob Feller in the press box at Jacobs Field.

Three batted balls were ticketed for hits but were turned into outs, first, by second baseman Bobby Avila on a grounder up the middle by Bob Cain in the fifth inning; then by shortstop Ray Boone on a slow bounder by Johnny Lipon in the sixth; and finally by third baseman Al Rosen who made a back-hand stab of a shot by Jerry Priddy, also in the sixth.

The last out was made by Vic Wertz, who would become a teammate of Feller in 1954. Wertz drilled a vicious liner off Feller's first pitch that sliced foul at the last moment, then, after the count went full, was called out on strikes.

The Tigers' only run scored as Lipon reached on Boone's error, stole second, went to third on an errant pickoff throw by Feller, and scored on George Kell's fly (which at that time was not ruled a sacrifice).

Singles by Dale Mitchell and Avila, and an infield out provided the Indians first run in the first inning, and they won it in the eighth on Sam Chapman's triple and Luke Easter's single.

Feller went on to post a 22-8 and 3.50 ERA in 1951, but it was his last big season for the Indians.

Never bashful about speaking his mind—or writing about it, for that matter—Feller, early in his career, expressed a perhaps too-blunt opinion of Jackie Robinson, and those words often came back to haunt him.

Because they'd barnstormed together, Feller obviously felt he knew Robinson and, at one time, indicated doubt as to Robinson's ability to play in the major leagues.

As Feller was quoted in *Legends, Conversations With Baseball Greats,* a book written by Art Rust Jr. and Mike Marley and published by McGraw-Hill:

"I think I said that because (Robinson) looked like another muscle-bound football player. It was more or less a tongue-in-cheek thing. We were playing exhibition games in California against each other and—you know, it's like Bill Veeck always said—if you've got a feud going, don't keep it a secret.

"(What was said) was more or less a little hype to help our exhibition games. Jackie was a great athlete. He never did really hit the high, tight fastball very good. I could throw a pretty good high, tight fastball in my prime, and maybe I didn't take it into consideration . . . that not too many guys were hitting it if I got it where I wanted it."

Later, in his own book, *Now Pitching, Bob Feller,* written with Bill Gilbert and published by Carol Publishing Group, Feller said of his comments about Robinson:

"I pitched against Jackie on our '46 barnstorming tour when he was playing for Satch (Satchel Paige). I got him out three times in a game at Wrigley Field, the Cubs' minor league park in Los Angeles, on a strikeout, a pop up and a ground out. When we moved down to San Diego for a game, I struck him out three times on ten pitches.

"Paul Zimmerman of the *Los Angeles Times* asked me in L.A. if I thought Jackie would be able to hit major league pitching. I said I wasn't sure, that he might be muscle-bound and unable to hit big league pitching, especially the fastballers in the American League.

"Jackie and others didn't like that, and apparently he never forgot it."

On the subject of Larry Doby, who followed Robinson by eleven weeks as the first player to break the color barrier in the American League, Feller said in our interview for this book, "Larry was a ball player, a good ball player, and what color he was didn't matter."

When reminded there were reports that some of the Indians refused to shake hands with Doby when he joined the team on July 5, 1947, Feller said, "Don't be putting words in my mouth."

And, when asked if there were players who resented Doby, Feller replied, "I don't know. I never asked them."

But then Feller elaborated. "I know there have been stories that some people wouldn't shake hands with him, and also that Eddie Robinson wouldn't let him use his ball glove because (Doby) was going to play first base.

"Well, I wouldn't let Bob Lemon use my ball glove to pitch with, because everybody has a different shape hand. It (Robinson's refusal to lend his glove to Doby) had nothing to do with race," said Feller.

As for Paige, who was signed by the Indians on July 7, 1948, Feller said that, by then, "Satch wasn't quite as fast anymore, about 90 to 95 percent of what he'd been, but he had good control and pretty good stuff, though he only had

a little wrinkle of a curveball. He also was very savvy, had great pitching instincts, could throw equally well overhand or side arm, and he never gave a hitter the same pitch twice.

"Satch also was an excellent team man, not a do-gooder, he was just happy to be doing what he was doing. He loved baseball and he loved people. Off the field he was kind of a prankster and a con man. He would tell you three different answers to the same question.

"He helped us a lot, as did Doby, to win the pennant and World Series in 1948, but the next season he lost it. Satch didn't have it anymore in 1949."

Paige was 6-1 in 1948, but only 4-7 in 1949. After the Indians let him go, Paige returned to pitch in the big leagues for the St. Louis Browns from 1951-53, and made a token appearance with the Kansas City Athletics in 1965.

"I liked Satch a lot. He was a great friend of mine," said Feller. "I played a lot of games with him, going back to our barnstorming days, and we made a lot of money together. He was, in my opinion, the best black pitcher I ever saw. As far as I'm concerned, Satch was No. 1."

And where does Feller think he should be rated as a pitcher? Feller replied, "The American public likes speed, whether it's an airplane or automobile or baseball, and I could throw hard, I had a good fastball, a live fastball. I was kind of like Sandy Koufax, or Sandy Koufax was kind of like a second Bob Feller.

"I was not a second Walter Johnson, because Walter did not have a curveball, even though, in his prime, he was faster than I was, even in my prime."

How fast was Feller?

Though he said in this interview that he wasn't sure how hard he could throw, Feller was quoted in *Bill Veeck, A Baseball Legend,* by Bill Gilbert and published in 1988 by McGraw-Hill:

"'The Army tested me in Washington, D.C. after the war. The speed (of my fast ball) at home plate was 98.6 miles and hour, and when I released the ball it was 117.2. They figured the average speed of the ball ... which of course I couldn't continue for a whole ball game—was 107.9. Maybe I could sustain 104 miles an hour.'

"'Is that comparable to anyone?'

"'The only guy who could throw as hard as I was Walter Johnson. And he didn't have a curveball.'"

Then, in this interview, Feller said, "I think Johnson was the best pitcher in history, in my opinion."

Who was second best?

"That would be very difficult," said Feller. "Those things are all very arguable. How about Christy Mathewson, or Sandy Koufax, or Lefty Grove?"

Or Bob Feller?

"I'll let my peers decide where I stand in the history of the game," said Feller, whose uniform No. 19 was the first to be retired by the Indians, in 1957.

"I don't know where my place in major league baseball will be. You never can tell because I was out four years in World War II. But I do know that I don't second guess myself for joining the Navy two days after Pearl Harbor when we were losing big in the Pacific.

"I joined the Navy on the ninth day of December, 1941. My dad was dying of brain cancer, and I didn't have to go.

"But I'm no hero. We lost 405,000 men and women who were killed in action during World War II. The heroes are the ones that didn't come back.

"That's the way I feel about it."

Reflecting on his star-studded career, Feller said, "I probably would be more careful and not walk as many hitters, which got me in trouble a lot of times. Because I had a strong arm and could pitch all day, walking a guy didn't mean that much to me then, even though a lot of them scored.

"If I had it to do all over again, I'd not be so careless. I'd probably aim the ball a little more and work at improving my control. I didn't really start pitching good ball until 1939. That's when I became a pitcher, when I was 20 years old."

That was the season, 1939, that Feller led the American League with 24 victories, while losing nine, the first of six times that he won twenty or more games.

"It's when I was 20 that I probably was as good a pitcher as anybody around, especially in the (1939) All-Star game, which is one of my high points."

He took over in the sixth inning in relief of Tommy Bridges with the bases loaded and one out, and the American League leading, 3-1. The first batter Feller faced, Arky

Bob Feller with Mel Harder (left) at a recent old timer's function.

Vaughn, grounded into a double play, and he went on to blank the National League in the seventh, eighth and ninth innings, striking out the last two batters, Johnny Mize and Stan Hack.

The American League won, 3-1, and Feller earned a save.

But trying to pin down Feller to name the highest of the high points in his career continued to be difficult.

"If I have to pick something, it probably was being with my father on our farm playing ball on our team, the Oakview team," he said. "I had very good parents, my mother as well as my father, and they gave me, not money, but time. Their time. Especially my father.

"We had our own team, and I would not have been able to do what I did, or be where I am today if it had not been for my parents."

Of today's players and the future of baseball, Feller said, "I don't know if the game is in trouble or not, the way

things are going ... the way salaries continue to climb out of sight.

"A lot depends on where you are. In certain cities it's much better than others. The new ball parks mean a lot, in terms of revenue for the owners, and for the hitters. They're built for home runs. And because of television, the games almost seem to be coincidental, it's so much show business, as well as the way products are hyped and everything is merchandised.

"The game itself is watered down because there are so many (major league) ball clubs, which means that each team has fewer pitchers with good arms, and fewer great hitters."

How much better would it be for Bob Feller if he were pitching today?

"With all the news media hype, probably a lot better," he said. "And also because you have so many hitters today who are incompetent. Now (hitters) use the thin-handled bats with no weight in the barrel to give them high swing speed because everybody wants to hit home runs. The ball parks are built for home runs, (the owners) pay off on home runs.

"You don't get paid big money for hitting singles, or hitting behind the runner, and the fundamentals (of baseball) are something (today's players) have forgotten.

"And pitchers ... they've got middle inning guys and closers, and nobody wants to go nine innings anymore. They don't know how to pace themselves because they don't want to. If you say anything, they don't even know what you're talking about.

"That's about it," said Feller.

Now Feller and his second wife, Anne, whom he married in 1974, do considerable traveling as he is in great demand to attend old timers games, memorabilia shows and other baseball promotional events around the country, and as a public relations representative of the Indians.

They also spend much time at the Bob Feller museum—officially known as the "Bob Feller Hometown Exhibit"—located in Van Meter, Iowa, where he was born and raised. It was designed by Steve Feller, Bob's eldest of

Bob Feller, in his Indians uniform, still makes promotional appearances for Major League Baseball.

three sons who was born in 1945. Feller's other two sons are Martin, born in 1947, and Bruce, born in 1950.

Feller also is immortalized by a ten-foot tall statue of himself outside Jacobs Field.

The Feller museum was opened June 11, 1995. It contains 1,750 square feet of exhibit space and was built at a cost of $250,000, financed entirely through private contributions and donated work.

Feller, who was inducted into the Baseball Hall of Fame in 1962, his first year of eligibility, said at the dedication of the Bob Feller Hometown Exhibit, "This is probably the highest honor I've ever received. This museum is not about me. It's not honoring anything except Americanism.

"I hope it motivates young people to have discipline so that they can become leaders of this great country."

All of which brought to mind a comment by Tom Keegan of the *New York Post*, who said, "When I started my job as a baseball writer, my dad told me, 'If you see Bob Feller, don't ever write anything bad about him because he is a great American.'"

Just as he also was a great pitcher.

Bob Feller shows he still has the form that made him famous.

CHAPTER SEVEN

Ray Murray

"Count them, three years, eight months, two days, six hours and fifteen minutes."

" I loved the guy, though I probably should have hated him ... he had me up and down like a damned yo-yo that year," said Ray Murray, the tough, raw-boned, plain-talking ex-catcher and old Texas deputy sheriff who still resembles the Marlboro Man.

"The guy" was Bill Veeck, the late owner of the Indians who pulled the strings and set the baseball world on its ear in 1948.

Murray's lament about being treated like a "damned yo-yo" that season was understandable.

So was the frustration that tormented Murray, a.k.a. "The Deacon," because of the time he lost serving Uncle Sam during World War II.

At the age of 30—going on 31—in 1948, Murray, then a rookie, won a job with the Indians in spring training as one of three catchers on the roster, along with Jim Hegan and Joe Tipton.

However, in mid-May, with the season less than a month old, he was demoted to Oklahoma City of the (then-Class AA) Texas League, but recalled by the Indians on May 31. Then, five weeks later, Murray was sent back to Oklahoma City where he remained until September 1, when major league rosters were expanded to 40, and he returned to Cleveland. But even that didn't end Murray's 1948 odyssey, or his frustration.

After the Indians beat Boston in the one-game playoff for the American League pennant on October 4, vaulting them into the World Series, Murray was cut off the eligibility list when rosters had to be reduced to 25.

"I stayed with the team throughout the Series, but once a game started I'd change into street clothes and sit in the stands with my dad," Murray recalled as we visited near his home in Ft. Worth, Texas.

Despite his ups and downs with the Indians that season, Murray's explanation as to why he "loved" Veeck, not "hated" him, also was easily understood.

"When I was called back to Cleveland in September, my wife Jackie and I got into town around three in the morning, went to bed and about eight o'clock the phone rang, waking us up," said Murray.

"It was Veeck. He said, 'I want you and the wife in my office in 30 minutes' because there was something he wanted to talk to me about.

"We were staying at the Hotel Cleveland (now the Renaissance Hotel on Public Square) and I told him, 'Hell, Bill, we can't walk that far, we've been traveling and we're tired. I'll come down later.' He said, 'I want to see you right away. Take a cab. I'll pay for it.'

"Well, he was the boss and what could I do? I didn't want to hurt my chances, so Jackie and I got dressed and

Ray Murray as a rookie catcher in 1948.

took a cab to the Stadium. I didn't expect to be there long, so I told the cabbie to wait.

"When we got to Veeck's office he said, 'I appreciate the way you people have cooperated with me and I want to do something for you.'

"He held up a key. 'This is for a new Pontiac car,' he said. 'If you can find it, it's yours,' though he wouldn't tell me where it was, or even where to look. He was laughing, but I knew he wasn't joking.

"I remembered, from when I was up with the club earlier in the season, that (Veeck) did business with a car dealer on the west side. I think it was called 'West Side Pontiac.' So Jackie and I jumped back in the cab and told him to take us there.

"We went in the showroom and there's a new Pontiac sitting over in the corner. I asked the salesman if I could try my key in the ignition, and when I did, VAROOM! the car started. How about that! We drove it out the door.

"It had to be worth about $4,800 at least. When the season ended, after the World Series, we drove it home and kept that Pontiac for a long time, all because I 'cooperated' with Bill. That means I didn't cuss and raise hell every time they sent me down.

"So, sure, I loved Bill Veeck," Murray said again. "Why wouldn't I?"

Murray's tangible contributions to the Indians in 1948 were hardly impressive, consisting of four appearances as a pinch hitter, in which he struck out three times, and grounded out once.

"I guess you can say I was an insurance policy," Murray said, goodnaturedly, though he thought he should have been given more of a chance to play.

"I played real good in spring training . . . hit some home runs and everybody thought I was about ready to take the danged job away from Hegan," who had been the Indians' regular catcher in 1947, primarily on the strength of his defensive ability.

"I could hit, but all the pitchers liked to pitch to Hegan. They all knew him and, what the hell, he was a damned good catcher, I'm the first to admit. So what could I do about it. If it hadn't been for Hegan, I probably would have done most of the catching.

"The other catcher was Tipton. I know I was better than him, but I guess I was the only one who thought so because he got to play more than I did."

The 1948 season was Murray's fifth in professional baseball, though his career, which began in 1940, was interrupted by World War II when he spent almost four years in the Army Air Corps (as the Air Force was called then).

"Count them, three years, eight months, two days, six hours and fifteen minutes, to be exact," said Murray.

"I guess you can also say that the Indians traded me for Satchel Paige . . . sort of," said Murray as he recounted his "yo-yo" season, and another "contribution," this one intangible, that he made to Veeck and the Indians.

To make room for Paige on the roster when the legendary Negro League pitcher was signed on July 7, Murray was demoted to Oklahoma City.

"When they sent me down, Veeck said he was sorry, but that he wanted to sign Paige. I said that was OK as long as I was going to play (at Oklahoma City) and he said I would, which was the main thing.

"I was disappointed, but I wasn't resentful because I loved to play ball. I would have rather played in the big leagues, of course. But as long as I was playing somewhere, that was important to me, and I would still be getting $5,000, which was the major league minimum then, whether I played in Cleveland or Oklahoma City," said Murray.

"And when the season was over, I received a World Series share —maybe because of Paige. Think about it. If the Indians didn't have Satch, they might not have won the pennant."

Paige, in 1948, appeared in 21 games, seven as a starter, with a 6-1 record and 2.48 earned run average.

"The old guy could still pitch, he had a sinker and great control, though he wasn't nearly as good as when I saw him in his prime, back when I was a kid in Ft. Worth," said Murray. "His velocity was down but, hell, he must've been at least 50 when we got him.

"Once, after I came back to the Indians in September, we were in the bullpen and he balled up a bunch of grass and put it on top of the plate. Then he told me, 'Big Catch,' which is what he called me, 'put your cap on top of that pile of grass and I'll show you something.'

"Satch went back to the mound and started pitching and knocked my cap off the pile of grass two out of every three pitches. Like I said, his control was amazing."

As for Larry Doby who, in 1947, preceded Paige as the first black player in the American League, Murray said, "There were some guys (among the Indians), maybe five or six rock piles and idiots, all of them Southern boys, who didn't want anything to do with him.

"But the rest of us got along with him fine."

Who were the "rock piles and idiots?"

"I'm not saying . . . it's over and done with and it's going to stay that way," said Murray who was, himself, born and raised in the South, a little town in North Carolina called Spring Hope.

"I wasn't one of them . . . the best friend I ever had was a black guy, a fellow named John Dunn, who is a heart specialist up in Boston now."

Murray said he also was a close friend of Bill White, a black man who played in the National League from 1956-69 and was the National League president from 1989-94. When Bill came down to the Texas League and we played together in Dallas in 1955, he said to me once, 'Ray, help me out,' which I did. We were good friends. Still are."

The circumstances that led to Murray being recalled by the Indians on May 31, 1948, also are interesting.

In the eighth inning of the second game of a May 30 double header in Chicago, the Indians had lost the opener, 4-2, and were getting beat in the nightcap, 6-4. Boudreau sent Allie Clark to the plate as a pinch hitter for Hegan with the bases loaded in the eighth inning.

Clark singled, driving in two runs, and the Indians went on to score nine in what turned out to be a 13-8 victory.

However, Tipton, himself a pinch hitter in that eighth inning, was hit in the wrist by a pitch and had to leave the game.

Because the Indians didn't have a third catcher on the team, as Murray had been sent to the minors a couple of weeks previously, Boudreau, who had done some catching in high school, went behind the plate for the final two innings.

The next day, in the wake of an ultimatum by Veeck to Boudreau —"If you ever do that again, I'll have a heart attack, and you'll be gone," according to reports—Murray was recalled from Oklahoma City, and stayed with the Indians until Veeck signed Paige.

"I loved that (Indians) team," Murray said. "It was a great bunch of guys, some would call them 'hard livers'— which some of them were —but they could play the game, they knew how to play the game."

Which brought to mind Bob Lemon's no-hitter against the Tigers, a 2-0 victory, on June 30 in Detroit, a game that he had not been slated to pitch.

"Lem had been out the night before and, I don't know, I guess he had a pretty good time on the town," said Murray. "When we got to the clubhouse, there he was, asleep on the floor in front of his locker.

"Boudreau got somebody to wake him up and Lem went out and pitched a no-hitter. That's the kind of team it was," said Murray, obviously relishing the memory.

And, when he's asked who was the best pitcher he ever caught, or even saw, Murray replied, without hesitation: "Lemon."

Something else Murray relished was his friendship with Joe Gordon. "Joe absolutely was one of the best guys that ever played the game of ball," said Murray. "Not only a good guy, but a good player. I've got to thank him for getting me a ring, a World Series ring.

"I wasn't going to get one because I'd been up and down with the club all season. But Joe said, 'Dammit, Deacon, you're going to get one, and I'm going to see that you do,' and he did.

"But here's how dumb I am. Awhile back, it was about 1965, I needed some money and I sold it. I got $2,500 for it . . . now it'd be worth at least $5,000, probably more.

"But I don't need a ring to remind me how great it was in 1948."

Murray spent 1949 at Oklahoma City, but was back with the Indians and played 55 games for them in 1950 when his statistics were credible, if not outstanding. Murray hit .273, on 38-for-139, and drove in 13 runs as he backed up Hegan.

It earned Murray a raise in 1951, to $12,000, the most he ever made in baseball. That was a year after Veeck had sold the Indians, leaving Hank Greenberg in charge, and Murray was traded in a six-player, three-team deal on April 30, 1951.

It proved to be one the Indians' worst-ever trades.

They gave up Murray and pitcher Sam Zoldak and outfielder Minnie Minoso, and received only relief pitcher Lou Brissie. The Philadelphia Athletics wound up with Murray and Zoldak, as well as outfielders Dave Philley and Gus Zernial from the Chicago White Sox, who also got Minoso and outfielder Paul Lehner from the Athletics.

"The perpetrator (of the deal) was Greenberg, who was not one of my favorite people even before he traded me," said Murray. "I didn't hate the man, I just didn't like his attitude, his kind of B.S.

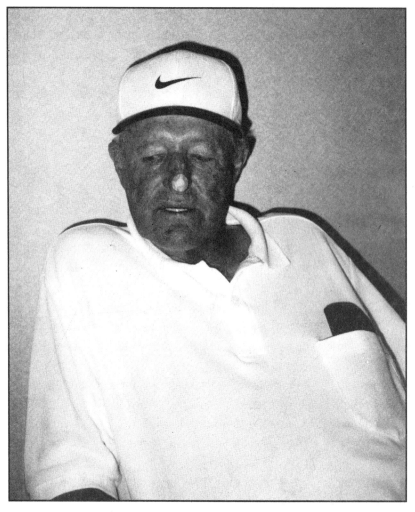

Retired rancher Ray Murray.

with 25 home runs for Dallas—and was voted the "Most Valuable Player" and "Most Popular Player" in the Texas League. That winter the (then New York) Giants bought his contract.

"But I tore up my knee in spring training and never got another chance (in the big leagues)," said Murray.

He played and managed at Springfield, Massachusetts of the (Class A) Eastern League in 1957, Corpus Christi, Texas in the Texas League in 1958 and 1959, and in 1960 and 1961 Murray managed Rio Grande, Texas, also in the Texas League.

One of Murray's pitchers in 1959 was Gaylord Perry, then climbing through the minor leagues to the San Francisco Giants (1962-71), the Indians (1972-75), and six other major league teams (through 1983), a journey that was culminated with his election to the Hall of Fame in 1991.

Murray remembered Perry well, but was initially evasive when asked if Gaylord was throwing a spitball back there in the minor leagues. "I'll let him tell you if he did or didn't," said Murray, chuckling.

When reminded that Perry admitted in his 1974 autobiography, *Me And The Spitter*, that he developed the illegal pitch in the minor leagues, Murray chuckled again and said, "Well, he learned it by practicing on the sidelines. He'd throw (the spitball) every once in awhile, when he'd get two strikes on the batter.

"Once, when he was pitching a game for me, he got two strikes on a batter and I said, 'Watch that sonofabitch's next pitch drop,' which it did, about a foot when it got to the plate. When the guy asked me what kind of a pitch it was, I said, 'Oh, he's got a good forkball,' which everybody now calls a split-finger fastball.

"Ol' Gaylord was tricky even back then . . . and a helluva pitcher," said Murray, who retired after the 1960 season.

Murray's Corpus Christi team won the Texas League playoffs in 1958, but lost the Dixie Series to Birmingham, Alabama of the Southern Association.

"I was supposed to manage El Paso (Texas) for the Giants in the Texas League in 1962," he said, "but it fell

"He always looked at me like I was some kind of trash, and we never saw eye to eye. He always wanted to be the big dog in everything. We never had much opportunity to talk, but if I had, I would have talked pretty plain to him.

"One time in 1949 (Greenberg) came in to the clubhouse and was popping off about someone. I said to him, 'If you feel that way, if you're going to talk about a guy that way, why the hell don't you get rid of him?

"Right after that I was traded," said Murray.

He had three mediocre seasons as a back-up catcher with the Athletics—hitting .213 in 1951, .206 in 1952, and .284 in 1953—and played a final year in the major leagues in 1954 as a part-timer in Baltimore, where he batted .246 in 22 games.

Thereafter, Murray played and managed in the minor leagues the next six years, including 1955, when he hit .329

through because they said they wanted a Spanish-speaking guy. Even though I rode those damn buses all over Mexico for two (winter) seasons when I was young, I couldn't speak Spanish."

Why not? "Because I never wanted to. That's when I said the hell with it and quit (baseball)."

It all began for Murray in 1940 and, even then he was his own man, who spoke his mind and never pulled his punches.

"I was playing semi-pro ball and somebody saw me and told me to go talk to a guy named Dennis Sothern, who'd played in the National League (from 1926-31). Sothern was managing Kinston, North Carolina in the (Class D) Coastal Plain League.

"He gave me a chance in spring training," said Murray, "but I never hit it off with that guy (Sothern). He never said good morning to me, go to hell, nothing.

"Early on (in spring training) I was batting with the bases loaded and went to a three-and-nothing count. I looked down at Sothern, who was coaching at third, and he nodded no. So I took the next pitch. It was right down the middle for a strike and I gritted my teeth, but didn't swing.

"Then I looked down at him again and he nodded no again. He didn't want me to swing again. But the pitch came in and it was a dinky little curve that I thought looked like a watermelon. I swung at it and popped up.

"The next day (Sothern) sent me a pink slip, a release. I went into his office and told him, 'I don't treat dogs like you treated me. When I get up in the morning I speak to my dog, feed him, take care of him. But you wouldn't do that. You don't give a damn about ball players, and I'm tired of taking crap off anybody.'

"Then I said, 'I'm going somewhere to play and I'm going to prove to you that I can get to the big leagues.'"

Which Murray did, though it took him awhile, beginning at Pocomoke City, Maryland of the (Class D) Eastern Shore League in 1940, then Tarboro, North Carolina, also of the Coastal Plain League in 1941, before Uncle Sam called Murray for service in World War II.

It couldn't have come at a worse time for Murray's career. "I was in spring training with Baltimore (which was then in the Class AA International League), when I got the finger pointed at me, you know, like they showed on those posters, Uncle Sam pointing and saying, 'I want you!'"

That was March of 1942 and, instead of wearing a baseball uniform, Murray wore Air Corps khaki for "exactly three years, eight months, two days, six hours and fifteen minutes."

Murray served most of that time as a drill instructor, teaching hand-to-hand combat at a training center in Ft. Worth, and called himself the "luckiest sonofabitch there ever was" because he didn't have to go into combat or overseas.

After those three years, eight months, two days, six hours and fifteen minutes serving Uncle Sam, he played at Baltimore and Oklahoma City in 1946, and at Oklahoma City again in 1947, after which the Indians purchased his contract.

Murray and his wife Jackie, whom he married in 1944, adopted and raised two children, a son Ray and a daughter Jill, and have nine grandchildren. Until his retirement in 1982 at the age of 62, Murray served 16 years as a deputy sheriff in Terrant County, where Ft. Worth is located.

And despite his late start in baseball, and limited time in the major leagues —Murray logged a total of seven years and 111 days, he said —his monthly pension is $3,131. "I'm comfortable . . . I can pay my debts."

Except for five or six skin cancers that Murray had removed shortly before our interview, his health is good. "I never felt better and had less," he quipped, "and I play golf three, four times a week." One of his local cronies is former Indians first baseman Eddie Robinson.

The highlight of his career, Murray said, "Was the playoff game in 1948, just being there and seeing Boudreau hit two homers and two singles (in four trips to the plate). What a game! I'll never forget that as long as I live.

"And what a team that was! I'm glad I was part of it, even if it was only a small part."

Though he has access to tickets for games played by the Texas Rangers in their new stadium, "The Ballpark in Arlington," close to Murray's home, he seldom goes.

"I played baseball from the time I was big enough to walk, but now that I'm out of the game, I don't miss it a bit," he said. "I did at first, but I got over it in a hurry, put it out of mind. I forgot it. The only thing I ever missed were the guys."

Why? "I can't stand to watch most of those s.o.b.'s that are playing today," he said. "They string out the games too long with their fiddling with those fancy batting gloves and stepping in and out of the batter's box to make sure everybody notices them.

"There are a couple of guys on the Rangers that I like, that kid (Rusty) Greer, the left fielder, the first baseman, (Will) Clark, is another, and the catcher, (Ivan) Rodriguez, I respect him. With the arm he's got, he's going to make it to the Hall of Fame. He reminds me of me. I could throw like that sitting on my knees," said Murray, and he chuckled again.

And if he had his career to do all over again? "I think I might fight a little harder for a job in the big leagues. A steady job. It's not that I was too easy going, it's that I was too hotheaded because I got up there (with the Indians) too danged late."

Then he repeated again: "Three years, eight months, two days, six hours and fifteen minutes."

They were what could have been—perhaps what *would have been*—Ray Murray's best seasons if World War II had not interfered, preventing him from reaching the Indians at an age when most players were making retirement plans.

THE 1948 WORLD SERIES, GAME 5

CHAPTER EIGHT

Larry Doby

"I'll always cherish the memory of Steve Gromek hugging me."

It happened in the heat of the 1948 pennant race, though Larry Doby steadfastly refuses to say exactly when, where, or even against which team, nor will he identify the offender, only that it was one of the most humiliating and degrading experiences of his life.

He slid into a base and was tagged out by an infielder who then spat tobacco juice in Doby's face, sneered and sauntered away.

To Doby, then the only black player in the American League less than a year after he followed Jackie Robinson in breaking baseball's color barrier, it also was every bit as degrading that—though seething with anger and resentment—he had to get to his feet and walk away.

"My reaction was that I wanted to beat the crap out of the guy, but I knew I couldn't, that I shouldn't," said Doby.

On other occasions that Doby remembers just as vividly, a certain member of an opposing team, a man in baseball's Hall of Fame, continually taunted the then-23-year-old outfielder by calling him one of the most vile names one could shout at a black man: "jigaboo."

Contrast both of those occurrences with one that took place on October 9, 1948, after Doby's home run off Johnny Sain gave the Indians and Steve Gromek a 2-1 victory over the Boston Braves in the fourth game of the World Series.

Gromek, a white man, impulsively, joyfully embraced Doby, and their picture was taken and published by virtually every major newspaper in the country the next day.

"Winning the World Series that year was the highlight of my career, but I'll always cherish the memory of Steve Gromek hugging me," said Doby. "It was completely, totally spontaneous; we just grabbed each other because we were so happy to win.

"As they say, God works in mysterious ways. Here's a white guy and an Afro-American guy who are put together and win a game, and when it's over they don't wonder, 'Should I not do this because I'm white and he's black?' or because 'I'm black and he's white?'

"No, they just do it, they just hug each other because they're happy, which made up for everything I went through. I would always relate back to that whenever I was insulted, or rejected by hotels. I'd always think back to that picture of Gromek and me. It would take away all the negatives."

Indeed, there were many "negatives" for Doby, who joined the Indians in 1947, exactly 81 days after Robinson played his first game for the Brooklyn Dodgers and, as he said, the three months that remained of that season were "the toughest time I went through in my entire baseball career."

Larry Doby

As did Robinson, Doby was forced to endure racial taunts and abuses by opponents—even by some teammates—through much of his 13-year major league playing career.

"It wasn't until about 1954 or 1955 that it got better, a *little better*," he said. "Chicago was still segregated when we (the Indians) won again (in 1954), and that also was the first year the team hotel in Tucson (Arizona) was opened to all of us in spring training.

"I've said this before and I'm saying it again: Baseball was not an all-American game until all Americans could play it as equals, which didn't happen for a long time."

Even a long time after the pioneer appearances of Robinson and Doby.

Doby went on to play in the major leagues for 13 seasons, for the Indians through 1955, and again in 1958, the Chicago White Sox in 1956 and 1957, and again in 1959, when he also played for Detroit,

He compiled a lifetime .283 batting average with 253 home runs and 970 runs batted in. He was a member of the American League All-Star team seven consecutive seasons (1949-55), twice led the league in homers, and was voted the Indians' "Man of the Year" in 1950 by the Cleveland chapter of the Baseball Writers Association.

Doby became the fifth player of the 1948 Indians to be elected to the Baseball Hall of Fame when he was voted in by the Veterans Committee on March 3, 1998. His four teammates who preceded Doby into the Hall were Lou Boudreau, Bob Feller, Bob Lemon and Satchel Paige, as well as owner Bill Veeck.

Doby also is a member of the Indians Hall of Fame. Doby was inducted into the Indians Hall of Fame, and the Cleveland Sports Stars Hall of Fame, and is one of five players whose number (14) has been permanently retired. Though he was retired in 1960 and 1961, Doby returned to uniform in 1962 when he and Don Newcombe were the first Americans to play in Japan.

He also is one of only four men to have played in both the Major League and Negro League World Series, as did Willie Mays, Monte Irvin and Paige.

But of all the recognition and honors Doby received, nothing meant more to him than that spontaneous, emotional embrace by Gromek, especially that it was captured for posterity on film.

"The picture was more rewarding . . . for me than actually hitting the home run (that won the game)," he said in his 1988 biography, *Pride Against Prejudice.* "It was such a scuffle for me, after being involved in all that segregation, going through all I had to go through, until that picture. The picture finally showed a moment of a man showing his feelings for me.

"But the picture is not just about me. It shows what feelings should be, regardless of differences among people. And it shows what feelings should be in all of life, not just in sports. I think enlightenment can come from such a picture."

Though he batted .301 with 14 homers and established himself as a bonafide major leaguer in 1948 when he 23 years old, it was a difficult and very lonely time for Doby, beginning with spring training in Tucson, Arizona.

Doby and his wife Helyn, whom he married in 1946, were not permitted to stay in the Santa Rita Hotel with the rest of the team, and for the next five or six years they would experience much of the same racial discrimination.

"All of it probably was tougher on Helyn. Even when she went to a game, she had to sit in the stands and listen to all that stuff," said Doby. That "stuff" were insults, taunts, even threats.

"But Helyn handled it because she knew the situation, and what it would be like. As for me, I refused to let it bother me. If I dwelled on those things, then I'd be a very weak person."

Later in his career with the Indians, as Doby admitted, "What really hurt me was when we'd take the kids out, maybe to a playground or something, and we were not allowed in because of the color of our skin. We'd try to find some kind of an excuse for the kids. We didn't want them to become bitter.

"As they grew older, they understood it better. But back then, our kids were young and didn't understand, and that's what hurt me so much."

Larry and Helyn Doby raised five children—Larry Jr., born in 1957, and daughters Chris, 1949; Leslie, 1954; Kimberly, 1958; and Susan, 1962. They have six grandchildren and four great grandchildren.

Doby's health is good now after undergoing surgery for the removal of a cancerous kidney on October 24, 1997.

Except for the fact that he was the American League's first black player, Doby arrived in Tucson in 1948 without great fanfare, based on his performance as a rookie, which was, to put it kindly, unimpressive.

Doby appeared in 29 games in 1947, all but one as a pinch hitter or late-inning replacement at first base (once), shortstop (once) and second base (four times). He batted .156 with five hits (four singles and a double) in 32 official at-bats, striking out 11 times—hardly the credentials of a budding star.

As then-Indians owner Veeck said in his 1962 autobiography, *Veeck As In Wreck*, "During that whole first year (Doby) was a bust."

Doby, who'd been leading the Negro National League with a .414 average and 14 homers, was a second baseman when the Indians purchased his contract for $10,000 from the Newark Eagles, but was told he'd be switched to the outfield in 1948.

"Before I went home that winter (1947-48) I was called aside by (coach) Bill McKechnie who said, '(Joe) Gordon is our second baseman, and he's going to be here for awhile, Boudreau is the manager and our shortstop, and it looks like (Eddie) Robinson is going to be our first baseman . . . have you ever played the outfield?'

"I told him no, but that I didn't care where I played, I just wanted to play. He suggested I get a book on playing the outfield and study it all winter.

"I got one that Tommy Henrich (of the New York Yankees) had written, and when I went to spring training I had a pretty good idea of what I had to do, though I'd never caught a fly ball in the outfield until I got to camp.

"Boudreau put me in right field and I played every game in spring training. A lot of people were skeptical about my ability because nobody was too sure how good the Negro League was. But I had a pretty good spring and opened the season in right field."

Though the Indians' 1948 spring training records are unavailable, Doby batted in the neighborhood of .340, according to newspaper accounts. Before breaking camp he was given a vote of confidence by Hall of Famer Tris Speaker,

Larry Doby

who'd played center field and managed the Indians when they won their only previous pennant in 1920.

"Doby is improving as fast as any ball player I ever saw," Speaker was quoted in the March 29 editions of the *Cleveland Press*. "I don't want to put the kid on the spot, but he could make it this year. He might not hit major league pitching, but he's got everything else."

And, on April 2, *Press* sports editor Franklin Lewis penned the following opinion: "The more alert and wiser observers realized that when the first game is played on April 20, the center fielder probably will be Walt Judnich, an old hand at the business.

"But W. Veeck, (vice president) H. Grabiner, L. Boudreau, or maybe all, know that Doby would be a capable asset this summer and he is being given every chance to prove his right to stick with the team. Before going further, let me say Doby has earned each chance."

Doby is the first to admit he wasn't a polished outfielder. "I made mistakes . . . I misjudged some fly balls, overthrew some bases, didn't charge some balls the way I should have . . . but I learned, and Speaker helped me a lot," he said.

When the season opened, the center fielder for the Indians was another veteran, Thurman Tucker. Doby started in right field, batted second and went 0-for-4 in a 4-0 victory over the St. Louis Browns.

Three months later—after clubbing a monster home run estimated at 550 feet in Washington on May 8, and upon recovering from a severely sprained ankle he suffered while making a spectacular catch, also against the Senators on June 27—Doby, then batting .286 with six homers, was installed in center field on July 15.

He remained there for the Indians for eight years, until he was traded by Hank Greenberg, who was then running the franchise, to the White Sox for outfielder Jim Busby and shortstop Chico Carrasquel on October 25, 1955.

Doby's relationship with Greenberg was, "OK," he said without elaboration. However, in an interview a few years ago, Doby's comments did not reflect well on Greenberg's judgment.

It was after Veeck had sold the Indians in November 1949 and Greenberg had taken charge of the franchise that Doby recommended that three players then in the Negro League be signed to contracts.

They were Hank Aaron, Willie Mays and Ernie Banks.

Later, Doby said he was told by Greenberg that the scouting reports on the three players were not impressive—that Aaron had a hitch in his swing, Mays couldn't hit a curve ball, and Banks was too slow to play shortstop.

All three were signed by other teams—and all three are now in the Hall of Fame.

Monte Irvin was another black player the Indians could have had. He was Doby's teammate with the Newark Eagles in 1947 and the owner of the team offered to sell Irvin to Veeck for $1,000. But Veeck declined, thinking that Irvin, then 28, was too old.

A Navy veteran of World War II who had been a four-sport star in high school in racially integrated Paterson, New Jersey, Doby was unprepared for the reception he received upon joining the Indians.

"I had never known segregation growing up," said Doby. "I lived in South Carolina until I was 12, and most of the kids weren't concerned with race. Then we moved to Paterson and I lived in a mixed neighborhood. Nobody ever called me a name. I never had a problem."

Prior to his first game with the Indians in 1947 against the White Sox in Chicago on July 5, Doby met with Veeck for about an hour, during which he was "coached" by the owner as to the exemplary standard of conduct expected of him.

"It was the first time I'd ever met him," said Doby. "He wanted to make sure I knew the rules.

"I had to be careful how I reacted to anything. I couldn't argue, not even turn around and look at an umpire who called what I might believe was a questionable strike. There could be no fighting—*absolutely* no fighting—and I was told it would be best if I didn't sign autographs for any Caucasian women over 15 because it might look like I was trying to get a telephone number.

"Veeck said it was the price I'd have to pay for being a part of baseball history, but all I wanted was to play. He also told me, and this was the most important thing I got out of our meeting, that we were in this together, that he was right there with me, alongside me all the way."

As reported in Boudreau's book, *Covering All The Bases*, Veeck also met with the players before Doby joined the team, telling them, "I understand that some of you said if a nigger joins the club, you're leaving. Well, you can leave now because this guy is going to be a bigger star than any guy in this room."

Further, As Veeck related in *Veeck As In Wreck*, "A couple of the (Indians) players made their objections known; I found faraway places to send them. Predictably, they were players of little talent and therefore the most threatened economically."

The players were never identified, but among those who were with the Indians in 1947 and not in 1948 were first baseman Les Fleming, outfielder George Metkovich and pitcher Bryan Stephens.

Later, during Doby's career with the Indians, and as both a player and manager with the White Sox, he and Veeck became close friends.

"Then, and to this day I regard Bill Veeck as my second father," said Doby. "He wasn't a man who had one set of values inside the church, and another outside the church, and he wasn't the kind who'd tell you something he didn't mean. He wasn't a hypocrite . . . he was one of the best men I've ever known, the greatest *humanitarian* I've ever known.

"After I'd been in the league for awhile, we went out together a lot. Bill liked jazz and so do I, and whenever there was someone in town like George Sharon or Dizzy Gillespie or Oscar Peterson, somebody like that, he'd call me and ask, 'You want to go?'

"We did that often, right up until the time he passed (in 1987)."

Obviously, the feeling was mutual between Doby and Veeck. In his book the late owner of the Indians said of Doby, "He was as close to me as any player I have ever known, although it took awhile before he would stop in the office to talk over his troubles. I am extremely fond of Larry and of his wife, Helyn, and their children."

Upon joining his new teammates in the clubhouse at Comiskey Park in 1947, Doby was introduced to each player by Boudreau as they were lined up in front of their lockers. Most of them shook his hand, though not all greeted him warmly. Those who did, Doby has said, were Gordon, Jim Hegan, Lemon and McKechnie.

"I wasn't scared or nervous," he said, "but I was lonesome . . . I was so very much alone."

Four players wouldn't shake Doby's hand, he said in this interview, although, on another occasion, he was quoted as saying there were six who refused. He declined to identify them, insisting, "I never will as long as I live . . . I don't want to dignify those people by mentioning their names."

But he also maintained that he did not, and does not dislike any of those who then—or since then—mistreated him.

"I am not prejudiced and I'm not a racist, and I'm not going to let anybody, regardless of how they treat me because of the color of my skin, cause me to fall into their category," he said. "I can honestly say there are a lot of people I don't and won't deal with, but that doesn't mean I don't like them."

And of those with whom Doby doesn't deal, it's simply a matter of, "When I needed them, they took an exit . . . now it's my turn to take an exit."

After that belittling experience in the clubhouse when he was introduced to his new teammates, they went out on the field and, Doby said, he was ignored—except by Gordon—when the players warmed up for the game against the White Sox.

"I stood there alone for several minutes while everybody played catch," he said. "Finally Gordon called to me, 'Are you ready? . . . let's go,' and threw me a ball."

Doby pinch hit in that first game, striking out against Earl Harrist in a 6-5 loss. It was reported in *Pride Against Prejudice* that several players, one of them Al Lopez, then a back-up catcher for the Indians, expressed relief that the rookie batted for pitcher Bryan Stephens.

Lopez, who would be Doby's manager with the Indians from 1951-55, and with the White Sox from 1956-57, was quoted as saying, "I'm glad that he didn't hit for me."

The two men did not share a close relationship in subsequent seasons. It was while Lopez was manager of the Indians that Doby was traded to the White Sox in 1955. And it was while Lopez was manager of the White Sox that Doby was sent to Baltimore on December 13, 1957, in a seven-player deal.

The day after Doby made his historical debut as the American League's first black player, another awkward situation arose, causing further embarrassment to him prior to a double header in Chicago.

Though Doby declined to discuss the incident, it was reported in his book that it developed after he'd been assigned to play first base in the second game.

Because Doby had never played the position, he did not own a first baseman's glove and was instructed to borrow one that belonged to Robinson.

Traveling secretary Spud Goldstein approached Robinson on behalf of Doby and reportedly said, "Would you lend your glove to Doby?" Robinson allegedly replied, "No, I won't lend my glove to no nigger."

"Persisting, Goldstein is supposed to have asked, 'Eddie, would you lend it to me?' With that, Robinson tossed his glove to Goldstein, saying, 'Here, take the glove.'"

The book continued: "Boudreau, in retrospect, and probably at the time, hesitates to judge Robinson negatively. '(Robinson) was upset maybe not as much with Larry as with me in replacing him at first base. He thought that Larry was a second baseman and an outfielder.' To add to Robinson's confusion about Doby's position, Boudreau had Doby working out at shortstop during infield drill before the first game of the double header."

Doby is quoted in the book, *Bill Veeck, A Baseball Legend,* by Gerald Eskenazi, as saying: "Joe Gordon or someone talked (Robinson) into letting me use the glove."

And Boudreau, in his book, *Covering All The Bases,* said, "Robinson told me that he lived in Baltimore during the off season and his neighbors would not appreciate his being on the same team as a Negro, but that he himself had nothing against Doby."

(In fairness, it should be said that Robinson has denied making the statements attributed to him, and in Chapter Ten of this book explains his version of the incident.)

It also should be reported that when Doby played first base that day—going 1-for-4 in the Indians' 5-1 victory—it was the only game of his 1,533 in the major leagues that he played the position.

It wasn't as bad for Doby on the field in 1948, though there still was much room for improvement. "When I'm living over here, and 24 other guys are living over there, how can it be a good situation?" he asked rhetorically.

"I mean, we're together for three, maybe three and a half hours for a game, and then I don't see them anymore until the next game. How can it be a good situation?" he said again.

"Sure, we were all focused on winning, and we made contributions—Boudreau, Gordon, (Dale) Mitchell, Lemon, (Ken) Keltner, myself—so, on the field, yes, it was OK, it was good . . . on the field.

"But how can anybody say we had great togetherness? I can't, though I realize we weren't brought there to be friends. We were brought there to play baseball. When I found a person who might object to being close to me, I let him be his own man. I did not infringe upon his privacy. I did not try to make friends with him."

Aside from the alleged lack of togetherness by the team, the 1948 season was a good one for Doby personally, though he also, on occasion, still had some problems.

He put together a 21-game hitting streak from late August into September, and the records also show that he delivered three game-winning hits: a grand slam against Washington that resulted in a 6-3 victory on September 15; a two-run homer in the bottom of the ninth to beat the Philadelphia Athletics, 5-3, on September 18; and, on October 2, he went 4-for-4 when the Indians won, 8-0, over Detroit to clinch a tie for the pennant.

And, after taking over as the regular center fielder, he also was outstanding defensively, especially on August 8 when the spotlight shined on Boudreau as the Indians swept the Yankees in a double header.

It was Boudreau's bases-loaded pinch hit that triggered an 8-6 victory in the opener, which was saved by Doby when he leaped high above the fence at the Cleveland Stadium to rob George McQuinn of what would have been a home run.

The Indians won the second game, 2-1, as Doby deprived Joe DiMaggio of a probable triple "with one of the most sensational sprints seen in this town since Tris Speaker roamed the pasture," according to Gordon Cobbledick in the *Plain Dealer* the next day.

That's not to say, however, that Doby was perfect in the field. He wasn't, specifically not on July 28, also at the Stadium. Doby failed to catch a fly ball that hit him on the bill of his cap for an error that allowed two runs to score and helped Philadelphia beat Lemon and the Indians, 2-1.

"I hadn't gotten used to wearing sunglasses," Doby explained, "and I didn't flip them down when I went over to left center to catch the ball. I lost it in the sun and, instead of ducking away from it, I just stayed there. The ball hit me on the bill of my cap, though it seems the media got more attention by saying it hit me on the head, so I just let it go at that.

"It was embarrassing, and I felt bad. But not because I got hit by the ball. Errors happen in baseball. If I'm going to dwell on that type of situation, I'm not going to be able to play the game. If you win, it's a different situation. We lost and that's why I felt bad."

And his off the field problems persisted because of the color of his skin.

Once, when the Indians played an exhibition game in Lubbock, Texas, Doby, who had been segregated from his teammates the night before and was not wearing his uniform, could not get into the ball park because he was black, according to *Pride Against Prejudice*.

"He went from gate to gate, trying to explain his situation, before Spud Goldstein arrived to confirm that Doby was, indeed, a member of the Indians. The rest of the team, meanwhile, had put on uniforms at the hotel and swept through the players entrance to the admiring shouts of local fans."

Mel Harder, then an Indians coach who observed first hand the abuse to which Doby was subjected, felt compassion for Doby, though there was little he could do to help the young black player.

"Going through Texas, and playing in cities like Nashville (Tennessee) and Birmingham (Alabama), and some of the things I saw and heard, I just couldn't stand. I felt really sorry for Larry. He had a lot of moxie, though, to handle the situation," said Harder.

Later that season, during a game in St. Louis where Doby often was the target of much verbal abuse and racial obscenities, he tried to climb into the stands in pursuit of a heckler. It would have been disastrous for him and, probably, black players who came along later, had he made it.

That was the only time Doby, or any of his teammates, or members of the media at that time, could remember his reacting in that extreme manner against a fan.

"I was lucky . . . I got stopped before I could get into the stands," he said. "I'm not sure who it was that stopped me, but it was good that they did."

When Veeck signed Paige as the sixth black player in the major leagues on July 7, 1948, Doby no longer was alone, although the two men were never buddy-buddy.

"I was glad to have Satch with us. He could still pitch . . . you don't win six games (Paige's record in 1948 was 6-1 with a 2.48 earned run average) if you can't pitch," said Doby. "I knew him from the Negro League, and we got along all right, but in all honesty, he had no influence over me. None at all."

Doby also admitted in *Pride Against Prejudice*: "I didn't like it when guys laughed at Satch's stories because I knew they were also laughing at Satch himself as a black man."

As for the two men pairing up together, Doby said, "Satch lived in different hotels (when the Indians were on the road). He never stayed where I stayed because he'd been around for a hundred years and knew everybody. He really wasn't allowed to do that, but he did. I think that's the reason he didn't remain with (the Indians) longer than he did (beyond 1949).

"It wasn't so much that Satch was a loner," as has been speculated, Doby said. "It's that he dealt with people, those he knew, and he knew an awful lot of people because he'd pitched in all the towns that we played in. He'd been in those towns long, long ago. Not just like two or three years . . . it was more like ten or twelve years previously. So all the black hotels that we lived in, he knew all the people, he was comfortable with them."

Doby wasn't close to Paige, he said, chuckling, "Because I abided by the rules. You can't have different rules for different people. Everybody has to go by the same rules, everybody has the same curfew, or should. That's the way it is, or should be."

Something else that Doby did not deny, though neither did he offer elaboration, was the physical intimidation he had to endure—brush back pitches, pitches thrown at his head, even pitches behind him, for various reasons, including the color of his skin.

"Everybody in the game gets thrown at, knocked down, because of situations," he commented.

"Did I get thrown at, knocked down because I'm an Afro-American? Well, only God and the person throwing the ball knew for sure," Doby answered his own question. "I can say, 'I think so,' or 'I don't think so,' but there's no way of knowing for sure."

Only once, late in his career, did Doby violate another of the cardinal rules established by Veeck, one that required him to turn the other cheek, to avoid physical confrontations with opposing (white) players at any cost.

It happened on June 13, 1957, when Doby, then playing for the White Sox, charged the mound in anger against a pitcher, Art Ditmar of the New York Yankees, he thought was trying to hit him. It's believed to have been the first baseball fight involving a black and a white player.

The possibility has been raised that the pitch might have been called by Elston Howard, a black player who was then the Yankees catcher, though Doby said he didn't know.

According to an Associated Press story that appeared in the *Plain Dealer*, "Ditmar was flattened by a sweet left hook to the chin by . . . Doby, who thought a wild pitch by the Yankee right hander was an intended duster.

"This started a wild melee into which the forces of both benches poured with two-fisted enthusiasm.

"After 28 minutes of punching, wrestling and hot oratory, order was restored and Doby and first sacker Walt Dropo, Chicago's two distance hitters, and New York's Billy Martin and Enos Slaughter were ejected."

Before peace was restored, Doby also brawled with Bill Skowron, and had words with Martin.

When asked if pitchers on his own team offered to "protect" Doby by retaliating in kind, he said, "Lem (Lemon) wasn't the kind of person to throw at anybody, I think that (Bob) Feller thought if he hit somebody he might kill him, and (Gene) Bearden was a knuckleball pitcher.

Larry Doby, an Indians coach in 1974, with catcher Dave Duncan.

then, at age 37, his skills were diminished after a two-year layoff and, while playing first base and the outfield, Doby batted only .225 with 10 homers.

When the season ended, that was it. Doby—permanently, this time—retired as a player. He purchased a tavern and also held a county job in New Jersey until returning to baseball in 1969 with the Montreal Expos, as a scout, then as a coach, first in the minor leagues then with the major league club.

In 1974, Doby accepted an offer to return to the Indians as a coach under then manager Ken Aspromonte. He did so in the hope of eventually becoming baseball's first black manager.

In an earlier interview, Doby said, "Word came to me that Cleveland might be making a change and would be interested in hiring an Afro-American manager. A person who was very close to me said it would be a good idea for me to go to Cleveland and learn the team," which he did.

The Indians did make a change in 1975, but not the way Doby hoped. Another Robinson, this one Frank, replaced Aspromonte, and Doby went back to the Expos. He was their minor league batting instructor in 1975, and returned as the Expos' first base coach in 1976.

And, when Veeck got back into baseball as the new owner of the White Sox in 1977, Doby rejoined him in Chicago.

"I don't know about the other guys (on the staff), although, after we got Early Wynn (in 1949), you never had to worry about somebody throwing at you on the day he pitched. He'd even the score every time. You could be sure of that."

Doby and Wynn were teammates with the White Sox briefly in 1959, Doby's last season as a player in the major leagues. After two years as a White Sox scout, Doby made a comeback in 1962. He received an offer he couldn't refuse to play in Japan—$30,000 plus traveling and living expenses, which was a very good deal at that time.

Doby signed and joined veteran pitcher Don Newcombe with the Chunichi Dragons of Nagoya as the first former American major leaguers to play in Japan. But by

Another of Doby's old friends, Lemon, was then manager of the White Sox, who finished third in the American League West that season, twelve games behind Kansas City. When the White Sox started badly in 1978, Veeck called Doby.

"He said we have to make a change and asked me if I wanted to manage. I said I did, though I hated to take the job from Lemon and wanted to talk to him first, which I did.

"Lem said, 'That's baseball . . . I'm your friend and I'll always be your friend, no matter what.' So I took the job."

At the time of the change, June 30, the White Sox were 34-40 in third place. They went 37-50 under Doby, finishing fifth.

"The last two months of the season we played about .500 ball and I thought that was pretty good, and that I'd get another opportunity, another contract," said Doby.

"But at the end of the season Bill called me into the office and said, 'We are not going to discuss this, I am just going to make a change,' that's all. All I could say was, 'OK.'"

The date was October 2 and their meeting was held in the same room in which they'd met 31 years and three months earlier, when Doby joined the Indians as the American League's first black player.

Of his dismissal by Veeck, Doby said in a 1994 interview, "I don't know to this day why he would not discuss it with me. I felt bad about it, of course, but I believed in Bill's integrity, his honesty, and I would never say anything bad about him.

"Now, if he had discussed with me some reasons why he didn't bring me back, then I might have found some fault with what he did. But we didn't discuss it. I remember him saying, 'Lawrence,' which is what he always called me, 'if we do (discuss it), we'll just sit here for hours and maybe we'll both wind up crying.' That was it."

Larry Doby, elected to the Baseball Hall of Fame in 1998.

Doby remained with the White Sox in 1979 as a roving batting instructor, but resigned at the end of the season, effectively ending his uniformed baseball career.

In 1980 he joined the New Jersey Nets of the National Basketball Association as their director of community relations, working under boyhood friend Joe Taub. It was a position Doby held until 1990 when then Commissioner Bart Giamatti urged him to return to baseball as an administrator in Major League Properties. And, since 1994, Doby also is a special assistant to American League president Dr. Gene Budig.

"I was happy to get back into baseball, though I didn't want to coach or manage again," Doby said then. "The way things are in the game today, I don't think I could handle those kids. I don't have the patience to do it.

"The discipline that was in place when I played doesn't seem to be there anymore. I couldn't see myself saying to a

player, 'I'm going to sit you down and fine you, blah, blah, blah.' And then he'd go upstairs and complain to the front office, or have the players union tell me I can't do this or that.

"Because of the money players are making today, and the rules that are in effect, you can't fine a guy enough to make it meaningful. It's all too different from the way it was when I played."

And because of that, Doby admits, "I'm concerned about the game, where it's headed, what's happening to it. I'm afraid that, in too many cases, the love of money has overshadowed the love of the game.

"We played because we loved the game. I don't think we realized what the money was, I think we were just happy and kind of surprised to be able to be paid pretty good to play a game that we loved. We didn't think in terms of it being work. Whatever the money was, we accepted it and were pleased to get it.

"But today, with the agents, if I give a player four million dollars and his statistics are the same as John Jones, then John Jones wants to get more. Salaries have become a source of competition among players and agents to see who gets the most, and that's not good."

Doby said his peak salary was $36,000 in 1956, after he hit .291 with 26 homers and 75 RBIs.

"One thing I wish is that more guys would think about those who are going to come along in this game after they are gone. Not too many do. Not enough of them do.

"It's like, when we first got into baseball, Mr. (Jackie) Robinson and me. They preached to us, 'If you guys mess up, others will not get the chance you're getting,' and that stuck in our minds.

"There were a lot of times I almost lost it, when somebody spit on me or called me a name or threw at me, but I knew I could not do anything about it without ruining it for the guys who would follow us."

Still, Doby said, in terms of racial relations, baseball has reason to be proud of the progress that has been achieved in the past half-century.

"I am telling you this from experience, from being personally involved, if all of our country had come along as far as baseball has, had made as much progress as baseball has in the last 50 years, this would be a much better country," he said.

"Fifty years ago there were two Afro-Americans involved in baseball, Mr. Robinson and me, and now we've got managers and coaches and front office people—in addition to a great many players—who are Afro-Americans.

"There's still a long way to go . . . on a scale of one to ten (in terms of progress), baseball is probably at a five, and being halfway there is pretty good, I think."

Larry Doby's home run in the third inning of the fourth game of the 1948 World Series sailed into the crowd in the right field stands at the Cleveland Stadium, giving the Indians and pitcher Steve Gromek a 2-1 victory over the Boston Braves.

Larry Doby Day at Jacobs Field in Cleveland on July 5, 1997, commemorating the 50th anniversary of his becoming the first black player in the American League, and the second (to Jackie Robinson) in the major leagues.

CHAPTER NINE

Steve Gromek

"The priest said . . . 'If it had been me, I'd be so happy, I would've kissed his black ass.'"

When Steve Gromek returned to his home in Hamtramck, Michigan in mid October of 1948, he was hailed as a local hero for winning Game Four of the World Series, 2-1, giving the Indians a three-games-to-one lead over the Boston Braves.

In that game, played on October 9 in Cleveland, Gromek scattered seven hits and beat Braves ace Johnny Sain, the National League's winningest pitcher with a 24-15 record that season.

Larry Doby's homer in the third inning provided the margin of victory.

And so, in the euphoric Cleveland clubhouse after the game, Gromek and Doby were photographed embracing each other. The picture appeared in virtually every major newspaper in the United States the next day.

Doby said he would "always cherish the memory of Steve Gromek hugging me (because) it was completely, totally spontaneous; we just grabbed each other because we were so happy to win."

Gromek also cherishes the memory of what happened that day, on the field and in the clubhouse after the game.

But he also remembers that not everybody in Hamtramck, a very ethnic suburb of Detroit, appreciated the emotion he displayed in the wake of the victory that was made possible by Doby, who'd been, only a year earlier, the American League's first black player.

Gromek chuckled as he reminisced about "some of the flak" he received from friends and acquaintances in Hamtramck, including—reportedly—even from the pastor of his Catholic church.

"I can talk about it now because the priest is gone and times are different," Gromek said as I visited him and his wife Jeanette in their new home in fashionable Shelby Township, Michigan, a few miles north of Detroit.

"The assistant pastor, who's also gone now, told me what happened," said Gromek. It took place the morning after Gromek and the Indians had beaten the Braves. The two priests were having breakfast and reading about the game.

As it was related to Gromek, "When the pastor opened the paper and saw the picture of me hugging Larry, he said to his assistant, 'Oh my goodness, look at this. Steve is kissing a black man. How could he do something like that?'"

Gromek said, "The assistant pastor looked at the photograph, read about Doby's home run, and said to the pastor, 'If I were pitching in the World Series and a black guy hit a home run to win a game for me, I'd kiss him, too.

"'In fact,' the priest said, 'Father, if it had been me, I'd be so happy, I would've kissed his black ass," Gromek said the assistant pastor told the pastor.

"Actually, I didn't kiss Larry, though I probably would have if the photographer had asked. What would be wrong

Steve Gromek

with that? We had just won a big game and we both were as happy as could be," said Gromek.

"It just looked like I kissed Larry because our faces were so close together. Here, I'll show you how it was," said Gromek, who embraced me the way he hugged Doby a half century earlier.

"See, I had my arm around his neck like this, and he had his arm around my waist. He squeezed me so hard I thought he'd break my ribs and—OK, I know it *looked* like I'd just kissed him—that's when the photographer snapped the picture."

Gromek also recalled the frosty reception he received from a friend—a *former* friend, he said—in the corner saloon near his home upon his return from the World Series.

"When I walked in there was a guy I'd played ball with in the old neighborhood when we were kids," said Gromek. "He ignored me and I asked the bartender, 'What's his problem?'

"I was told, 'It's that picture of you and Doby. He's upset about it.' When I asked why, he said, 'Don't ask me, ask him.' The guy said, 'Geez, you could've just shook his hand, you didn't have to hug and kiss him, did you?'

"We haven't talked since then," said Gromek.

There was something else about that fourth game of the World Series that Gromek vividly remembers—and which, in this case, does not reflect well on then player-manager Lou Boudreau.

It helped bring into focus a problem, either real or perceived, that Gromek had with Boudreau then, as well as in subsequent seasons.

"Let me tell you how I was picked to pitch that (fourth) game in the World Series," said Gromek, a spot starter-reliever whose record was 9-3 with a 2.84 earned run average in 38 games in 1948.

"Remember, (Bob) Feller lost the first game (1-0), then (Bob) Lemon and (Gene) Bearden won the next two (4-1 and 2-0). We were back in Cleveland and everybody thought Feller would pitch the fourth game.

"But Boudreau made a change. 'Instead of Feller,' Boudreau told us, 'I'm willing to sacrifice and pitch Steve (Gromek), then come back with Feller,'" Gromek quoted the manager.

"To me, the key word was *sacrifice*," said Gromek. "*Sacrifice* me in that game and come back with a strong Feller (in the fifth game)!

"You can ask anybody who was there, they'll tell you that's what Boudreau said. It really bothered me."

It also motivated Gromek.

"I said to myself, 'Hot damn! Sacrifice! And when I got home I told Jeanette, 'I'm pitching tomorrow,' and she said, 'That's great,' until I told her why.

"'Boudreau said he didn't want to pitch Feller because he was afraid he'd get beat, so he's going to sacrifice the game with me. How about that!'

"I was so mad when I went to bed that night, I could hardly sleep. I made up my mind I'd show him (Boudreau), that son of a gun."

Which he did—Gromek had a shutout until the seventh inning when Marv Rickert led off with a homer into the lower right-field stands on a 3-and-0 pitch. "He surprised me," Gromek said of Rickert's homer. "I thought he'd be taking, not swinging. I was just trying to get the ball in there for a strike."

Despite Gromek's masterful performance in the pressure-packed game, Boudreau's lack of confidence in him—at least in Gromek's opinion—didn't change.

"I never knew when Lou was going to pitch me, or pull me, or what," said Gromek.

"I don't know why he didn't have more confidence in me. Even before the World Series I pitched some crucial games, though I wasn't in the regular rotation, and we wouldn't have won the pennant without them. I kept myself ready, I was there anytime, any way Boudreau wanted to use me."

Gromek pitched out of the bullpen the first two months of the season and didn't start—or win—his first game until June 6, beating the Philadelphia Athletics, 11-1, in the nightcap of a doubleheader.

He also won the crucial second game of an August 8 doubleheader, 2-1, against Bob Porterfield and the New York Yankees, after Boudreau had limped off the bench to deliver a key pinch hit in an 8-6 victory in the opener.

That was the day most observers believe was the turning point of the season for the Indians.

"It seemed like every game I pitched was a big one," said Gromek, who went 3-0 against Philadelphia, one of four teams (with the Indians, Boston and New York) in contention for the pennant that season.

His lifetime record against New York was 17-10. "I was called a 'Yankee Killer,'" said Gromek, who won 123

Steve Gromek (left) embracing Larry Doby after Doby's home run won Game 4 of the World Series for Gromek.

games while losing 108 for the Indians and Detroit in a 17-year major league career that began in 1941 and continued through 1957.

Despite his contributions in 1948, Gromek continued as a spot starter-reliever the next two seasons, when his records were 4-6 and 10-7.

"That's why I was happy when Al Lopez replaced Boudreau in 1951," said Gromek. "I liked Lou, but it was obvious that he didn't have confidence in me, and I thought the change would be good for me."

It was, though not immediately; not until Gromek was traded to Detroit in an eight-player deal on June 15, 1953.

Gromek was a 19-game winner with nine losses and a 2.55 earned run average in 1945. When World War II ended and the servicemen returned to the major leagues in 1946, his record fell to 5-15 (with a 4.33 ERA).

Gromek takes umbrage at the suggestion that "wartime baseball" was not very good. "I'll grant you that some of the biggest stars were in the service, and that even a one-armed guy (Pete Gray) played that year (for the St. Louis Browns in 1945). But it still was pretty good baseball," he said.

"People say that about anybody who had a good year during the war (1942-45), that it was because all the good players were in the service.

"But how about Hal Newhouser? Everybody called him a wartime pitcher because he had two big years during the war (29-9, 2.22 ERA in 1944, and 25-9, 1.81 ERA in 1945). But don't forget, he had another great year in 1946 (26-9, 1.94 ERA) when all the stars came back.

"Newhouser was a helluva pitcher. He had great stuff. He's in the Hall of Fame, and he belongs there, though he should have made it a lot sooner than he did."

The only explanation Gromek offered for his losing record in 1946 was that, "It seemed like every time I pitched we'd lose by a run or two. If I gave up two runs, we'd score one. If I gave up four, we'd get three. And I was taken out for a pinch hitter a lot of times and didn't get a chance to be in the game if we did win.

"It was the same way for me back then as it was for Mickey Lolich with the (Detroit) Tigers when Denny McLain had his big years (31-6 in 1968, and 24-9 in 1969). The Tigers would score a lot of runs for McLain, but not many for Lolich (who was 17-9 and 19-11 in 1968 and 1969). That's the way it goes sometimes."

It also was in 1946 that Bill Veeck purchased the Indians (on June 21) and, even before they fell into sixth place in the eight-team American League with a 68-86 mark, 36 games behind the Red Sox, the new owner wanted to replace Boudreau as manager.

It was a chaotic season for the Indians as well as Gromek, who'd been classified 4-F by his draft board because, he said, "When I took my physical the doctor found a spot on my lung."

While the Indians improved to 80-74, good for fourth place in 1947, Gromek's record didn't. It fell to 3-5 in 29 games, all but seven in relief.

Though he didn't dwell on the subject, a knee injury he suffered in spring training undoubtedly was a reason for some of his pitching problems.

"It happened in batting practice," Gromek said. "I was pitching to (Ken) Keltner and he hit a ball through the box. It didn't hit me because I jumped out of the way, but I went down and twisted my (left) knee.

"I didn't think it was serious and kept pitching, but my leg ached like a toothache. Sometimes it hurt so much I'd be pitching and tears would come to my eyes.

"In those days you had to have five full years in the big leagues to qualify (become vested) for a pension and I didn't want to get sent out (to the minor leagues), so I kept on pitching."

Finally Gromek's knee got so bad that, when he was scheduled to start, or when it was likely he'd pitch in relief, he was given a shot of Novocain to deaden the pain. "By the time (the Novocain) wore off, my knee was really sore, but I kept pitching," he said again.

"When the season ended, I went to the front office and told them how bad my knee hurt and they told me to go home and rest it. Can you imagine that happening today?

"As I said, times were different then."

When Gromek reported for spring training in 1948 he was greeted with similar indifference. "They told me I was on my own, so what I did every day was run from one foul pole to the other, walk back and run again, back and forth, sometimes for two or three hours," he said.

Apparently it helped, though not immediately, and not completely.

"They didn't use me the first two months of the season," said Gromek, referring again to what he perceived to be Boudreau's lack of confidence in him.

"Then, when he did pitch me, it was always in an important game, a big game, a game we had to win. I'd go out to the mound thinking, 'I've got to win, I've got to win, I've got to win.' There always was a lot of pressure on me."

Of Gromek's 38 appearances, nine were as a starter, of which he won six, and four were complete games.

Ironically, as Gromek pointed out, the toughest batter he ever faced "was somebody most people don't remember or never heard of— a guy named Skeeter, Skeeter Webb."

Webb was a light-hitting (.219 lifetime average) infielder who, also ironically, preceded Boudreau as the Indians' shortstop. He played in the American League from 1938-48, and was the son-in-law of Steve O'Neill, who managed the Indians from 1935-37.

"That little son-of-a-gun (Webb) hit me like he owned me . . . I don't know why, he just did," said Gromek.

But that's not to say Gromek lacked respect for Joe DiMaggio and Ted Williams, the two greatest American League hitters of that era.

He especially remembers Williams. "I got him out the first 13 times I faced him, then he got me," Gromek said of Williams. "Oh, did he ever get me."

It happened after Gromek was invited to pitch batting practice prior to a benefit "all-star" game between U.S. Servicemen and American Leaguers at the Cleveland Stadium on July 7, 1942.

Williams, then still with the Red Sox (though he would spend the next three seasons in the Marine Corps in World War II), played for the American League team.

As Gromek recalled it, "Everybody else took four swings and got out of the batting cage, but not Williams. He stayed in there and hit against me for about five minutes.

"When I got through and sat down in the dugout, Williams came over to me and said, 'Skinny,' which is what he called me, 'you'll never get me out again.'"

It turned out that Williams was close to being right.

Two months later, on September 11, Gromek was called in to pitch against the Red Sox at League Park where the 40 foot high, concrete wall in right field was only 290 feet away—though some doubted that it was even that far.

He replaced Pete Center, who was working in relief of Jim Bagby Jr., with the bases loaded and Williams coming up.

"As I was warming up, Williams, who was standing alongside the plate squeezing his bat so hard that sawdust was almost coming out of it, hollered at me, 'Remember what I told you, Skinny.'"

Gromek did, of course.

"I don't recall what kind of pitch Williams hit, but whatever it was, he hit the ball so hard it went over the head of the first baseman (Eddie Robinson) so quick he couldn't get his glove up to catch it. The ball kept rising and hit high off the right field wall, then bounced all the way back to the infield.

Steve Gromek

"Two guys scored and Williams, who wound up on second base, yelled at me, 'Skinny, what'd I tell you!'"

And the Red Sox won, 15-2.

"Another time we were in Boston and I was hitting fungoes to the outfielders when Williams trotted by and asked, 'Skinny, are you pitching in this series?'

"I told him, 'No, I don't think so.'

"He said, 'Oh, that's too bad.'

"I asked why, and he said, 'Because I'm in a slump and you'd get me out of it.'

"He probably was right," said Gromek.

All of which might have been a factor in Boudreau's decision to start Bearden, not a well-rested Gromek, in the one-game playoff for the pennant in 1948, after the Indians and Red Sox finished the regular season in a tie.

"I don't know if I was under consideration to pitch that game. In fact, I'm sure I wasn't," said Gromek. "I think Lou and Joe (Gordon) and (coach Bill) McKechnie had decided on Bearden even before Newhouser got the last out in our last (regular season) game."

Detroit, with Newhouser pitching a five hitter, beat the Indians, 7-1, while the Red Sox won their finale against the Yankees, 10-5, leaving Cleveland and Boston tied.

When asked about Gordon's and McKechnie's input in the decision to start Bearden against the Red Sox with one day's rest, Gromek said, "Gordon was a team leader and was very close to Boudreau, and McKechnie had great influence over Boudreau."

He also said, "To me, the two best guys on the team were Gordon and (Allie) Clark."

The mention of Newhouser brought to Gromek's mind another anecdote. "Hal is one of my best friends, always has been," said Gromek.

"It's funny now, but when he pitched against us (in the final game of the 1948 season), I was saying to myself, 'He's my friend, but I sure hope he doesn't have his best stuff today.'

"But he did, although, in those days, (Newhouser) always had good stuff. He was in his prime.

"What's funny about it is that things were the other way around in 1954," said Gromek.

Then, Gromek was pitching for Detroit, and Newhouser was on the mound for the Indians, having joined them as a free agent after being released by the Tigers.

"I got even with Hal . . . well, sort of," said Gromek. "I beat him and the Indians (6-3, on April 24, 1954) in Detroit. I even got the first hit off him, a bloop single to left field, and while I was running to first base he kept yelling at me, 'You lucky so-and-so.'"

It was the last game Newhouser started in his 17-year major league career that began in 1939 and ended in 1955.

It also was in 1954, on September 18, a rainy and damp afternoon in Detroit, that Gromek faced the Indians again, this time pitching against Early Wynn, and was a 3-2 loser. It was the Indians' 107th—and pennant clinching—victory of the season.

Gromek's status under Boudreau in 1949 and 1950 remained the same as it had been in 1948; he continued as a spot starter-reliever, posting 4-6 and 10-7 records, and was a combined 14-11 the next two seasons under Lopez.

"I was glad when Lopez was hired because I thought I'd get more chances to pitch," said Gromek. "(Lopez) caught me a lot when he was with the Indians (in 1947) and I thought he knew me pretty well."

But it didn't turn out the way Gromek hoped. Mike Garcia blossomed in 1951 and went 20-13 after being given an opportunity in the starting rotation, along with Lemon, Feller and Early Wynn.

"Lopez told me in spring training, 'Steve, I know what you can do, but I've got to try this kid (Garcia). He's got a lot of promise, but if he doesn't do well, we're going to send him down and you'll get that (fourth) spot,'" Gromek said.

And when Garcia continued to do very well—he won 22 games in 1952 and was en route to 18 victories in 1953—Gromek was traded to the Tigers after making five appearances, four as a reliever with a 1-1 record.

The Indians received pitchers Art Houtteman and Bill Wight, infielder Owen Friend and catcher Joe Ginsberg, in exchange for Gromek and pitchers Al Aber and Dick Weik, and shortstop-third baseman Ray Boone.

Gromek said he also was glad to leave the Indians because the Tigers were his hometown team, which also was one of the reasons Houtteman, born and raised in Detroit, was angered by the deal that sent him to Cleveland.

"I heard that Houtteman complained, 'How the hell can the Tigers trade me for an old man like Gromek?,'" said Gromek, chuckling. "Bob Chakales (another pitcher who was with the Indians then), told me that he said to Houtteman,

'I'll make you a bet right now that Gromek wins more games for the Tigers than you do for us (Cleveland).

"So, the first time we went into Cleveland, Chakales told me, 'You'd better pitch good because I've got a hundred bucks riding on you.'"

As it turned out, neither pitched well that season—Gromek was 6-8 for the Tigers for a 7-9 overall record, and Houtteman was 7-7 for the Indians for an overall 9-13 mark.

It was with the Tigers the following season that Gromek enjoyed one last—and very satisfying—hurrah. He won his first seven starts and finished with an 18-16 won-lost record and 2.74 ERA for the sixth place Tigers, whose record was 68-86, 43 games behind the American League champion Indians.

"I pitched complete games in all but one of my victories, which is practically unheard of today," said Gromek. "Now starting pitchers go five, six innings and get out. If they go seven, it's considered good. In that respect, the game sure has changed."

In 1991, when he was 71, Gromek said he almost died, which is how he learned he was a diabetic.

Gromek was playing golf when he got sick. "I couldn't figure out what was wrong with me, except that I felt lousy," he said. "On the first tee, I hit my drive, finished the hole, then felt real weak. I didn't have any strength. I could hardly play the second hole and I told the guys I was with that I had to quit. I also had trouble seeing . . . I almost didn't make it home."

Jeanette picked up the story. "At first the doctor thought it was Steve's heart because he'd been diagnosed with an irregular heartbeat a few years earlier," she said. "They gave him a pacemaker and that's when they discovered there was a possibility it was diabetes.

"He was lucky. We all were lucky. His body was shutting down, but we got him to the hospital in time."

Now Gromek controls his diabetes with strict observance of a diet.

Steve Gromek and wife, Jeanette

He and Jeanette, who were married in 1946, raised three sons, one of whom, Brian, died of a cerebral hemorrhage on March 7, 1969 when he was only 17 years old. Their other two sons are Carl, born in 1948, and Greg, born in 1949.

All three were outstanding baseball players. "I think the youngest (Brian) might have gone on to be the best, but Carl and Greg were very good," said Gromek. Greg and Carl went to Florida State University on baseball scholarships, and earned law degrees.

Greg, a shortstop who was switched to pitcher, played in the Tigers' farm system for three years, reaching the Class AAA level before retiring. Carl was a second baseman. "They were a great double-play combination," said their proud father.

Tears welled in Gromek's eyes as he talked about Brian. "It was the first day of spring training for his high school team, March 3. He was just a junior and, when it happened, when he was stricken, he was running and told the kid he was with that he had a terrible headache.

"Then, all of a sudden, he collapsed. They called me and I rushed to the hospital. By the time I arrived there was no movement, nothing. It was terrible. They put Brian on life support and his brothers came home from college.

"By (March 7) there was no improvement, none at all, and we were told that if Brian lived, he would be a vegetable.

"The boys talked Jeanette and me into leaving the room, to go down and have some lunch, and it was while we were gone that Brian died."

Shortly thereafter, in honor of Gromek's late son, the Pony-Colt Baseball League in Birmingham, Michigan named its park the "Brian Gromek Memorial Field."

It also was a cerebral hemorrhage that Gromek's teammate, Don Black, suffered while batting against the St. Louis Browns at the Stadium on September 13, 1948. Black survived, but never pitched again.

"I remember it very well, and I remember Don Black very well," said Gromek. "I roomed with him in spring training that year. He was a good guy. I was in the bullpen when he collapsed at the plate. I don't remember if he swung at a pitch, or if he was just standing there in the batter's box, but the next thing we knew he was on the ground.

"They rushed him to the hospital and didn't think he'd live. But he did. Maybe his (aneurysm) wasn't as bad as my son's. I don't know.

"Later, Veeck had a night for him (on September 22) and gave all the proceeds to Black," said Gromek. A crowd of 76,772 jammed the Stadium for that game between the Indians and Red Sox, which Feller won, 5-2.

Black died eleven years later, on April 21, 1959, at age 43.

Speaking of Veeck, Gromek was reminded of his first unpleasant, then, surprisingly satisfying salary negotiations with the former Indians owner the winter of 1947-48.

"They cut me $2,500 (after going 3-5 in 1947) to $17,500, though Veeck said he'd give it back to me if I had a good season in 1948," said Gromek. "When the World Series ended, I just went home. I never wrote to Veeck, or said anything about the bonus. I just figured that was that.

"A little while later I got a call from Veeck. He said, 'Hey, how come I haven't heard from you? You want to get this (contract) thing settled?'

"I thought he was talking about my contract for 1949, and I told him, 'Well, I don't think your thing (offer) looks too good.' He said, 'Wait a minute. Let's get this other thing settled first. Didn't I tell you I was going to give you some money if you did well? That if you have a halfway decent season, I'd reimburse you (for the cut)?'

"And with that he said, 'I'm putting a check in the mail for you right now.' It was for $5,000, double the amount he cut me," said Gromek.

As for his contract for 1949, Gromek said he initially dealt with Rudie Schaffer, then the Indians business manager.

"When I rejected his first offer, he told me, 'I understand Bill gave you a nice bonus.' I said, 'Yeah, but it was just to make up for the cut I took last year. Now you want me to sign for the same amount. I'm not gaining anything, and I'm one of the guys who got you into the World Series.'

"He said he was sorry, but that was the best he could do. I told him to stick the contract up his you-know-what, and went home. Two days later my phone rang. It was Bill (Veeck) again. He said, 'Let's talk this over, I want to sign you right away. So I went back and he gave me what I wanted."

Gromek said the most money he made during his 17-year major league career was $21,000 in 1955, "after my big season" with the Tigers.

"The reason I got that much was because I had a clause in my contract that called for me to get a $2,500 bonus if I got traded. When I went to Detroit, they had to pay it, add the bonus to my salary for 1955. That's how it was that I made $21,000 that year."

As did Lemon, his former teammate, Gromek began his professional baseball career in the Indians' farm system as an infielder at Logan, West Virginia of the (Class D) Mountain State League in 1939. He had been signed by scout Bill Bradley, who played third base for the Indians from 1901-10.

"My bonus to sign," he said, "was a glove and a pair of shoes. I thought it was great. I just wanted to play," he said.

"Guess who pitched against me the first time I went to the plate at Logan?," said Gromek. Then, not waiting for a response, he said, "Stan Musial, who started his career as a pitcher, just the opposite of me. The (St. Louis) Cardinals switched him to the outfield, and the Indians made me a pitcher."

Gromek went on to play for Mansfield, Ohio in the (Class D) Ohio State League the latter half of 1939, and the following season for Fargo-Moorhead (Minnesota) of the

(Class D) Northern League, and Flint (Michigan) of the (Class C) Michigan State League.

"I was a good shortstop until I hurt my left shoulder swinging a bat. I was having a great game when I hurt it. I had a single, double and triple, and was going for the cycle, you know, a home run," he said.

"But I swung too hard and dislocated my shoulder. From then on I had trouble getting my left arm up to catch a fly ball or sometimes even to field a grounder, though my (right) arm was still good . . . I could still throw all right."

Gromek switched to the outfield, then was given a trial as a pitcher at Flint in 1941, and never left the mound. His 14-2 record at Flint earned Gromek a late-season call-up by the Indians and he pitched in nine games, two as a starter, winning one and losing one.

It was during that late-season trial with the Indians in 1941 that Gromek faced the Yankees the first time, an opportunity he said he owes to George Susce, then the bullpen coach—and which, he also said, helped establish his pitching credentials.

The date was September 14 in Yankee Stadium and, as Gromek remembered, "It was the eighth inning of the second game of a doubleheader. Joe Krakauskas was pitching and was getting tired. Jim Bagby and I were warming up in the bullpen and the call came from the dugout for a new pitcher.

"(Roger) Peckinpaugh was the manager then and wanted Bagby, but Susce told him, 'Take Gromek . . . he has good stuff today.' So I went in and retired all three guys I faced, one on a strikeout, and when I left the field it seemed like my feet weren't even touching the ground."

The Indians won, 5-2, when the game was ended after eight innings because of darkness and, as Gromek recalled, "Susce came up to me and said, 'Helluva game, kid.'"

"After that I always sat next to Susce in the bullpen. He'd tell me how to pitch to certain guys. Because he caught me in the bullpen, he knew my fastball was my best pitch, and if I had my good stuff, it would rise, you know, take off.

"Susce was right. One time I pitched against the Yankees and nobody made a ground ball out. All the outs were pop flies or strikeouts."

It happened on July 4, 1945 in the first game of a doubleheader in Cleveland.

The following spring, with Boudreau the Indians' new manager, Gromek took on a part-time job, in addition to being a young pitching prospect—and, in the process, probably helped his chances of making the team.

"Well, I guess you can say it was sort of a part-time job," he said.

"I was sitting in the lobby of the hotel one day and Mrs. Boudreau, Della, came over to me and asked, 'Steve, would you do me and Lou a favor?'

"She was the manager's wife and so, sure, I was willing to do her a favor. I asked her what, and she told me, 'We need a babysitter tonight. Our regular babysitter can't make it . . . would you watch our daughter Barbara until Lou and I get back to the hotel?'

"So I did. Maybe that's why I made the ball club that year," said Gromek, chuckling.

"Several years later, when I was with the Tigers at the tail end of my career, I was in a restaurant in Kansas City, where Boudreau was then the manager. It so happened that Lou and Della were in the restaurant, too, with Barbara.

"Della asked Barbara, 'Do you recognize this man?' She didn't, of course. So Della told Barbara that I was her babysitter 14 or 15 years earlier.

"Later, Barbara came over and apologized for not knowing me. I thought that was very nice."

Gromek was released by the Tigers in August of 1957 when his record was only 0-1 with an uncharacteristic 6.08 ERA in 15 games, all but one as a reliever.

The White Sox, then managed by Lopez, offered Gromek a job, "But it didn't work out," he said. "My back was bad . . . I had to hang it up."

But that didn't end Gromek's baseball career. Not quite.

Gromek took a job managing the Tigers' farm club in Erie, Pennsylvania, then in the (Class D) New York-Pennsylvania League.

"I hated it," Gromek said when asked if he enjoyed managing. "You've got to be a mother, father . . . everything to those kids when you manage in the minor leagues."

He even pitched in relief, 17 times without a decision. "I saved a game for one of the kids late in the season," he said. "When we got the last out and he got credit for the victory, he ran out to the mound, jumped on me and gave me a kiss, he was so happy to win his first professional game.

The Erie Sailors finished seventh that season and, when it ended, "That was it for me," said Gromek. "The Tigers asked me if I wanted to manage another year and I told them no, that I couldn't take any more. I would have liked to do some scouting, and the Tigers said they'd stay in touch, but nothing ever developed and that was it."

As Gromek reflected on his career, he repeated the question, "What would I do differently if I had it to do all over again?"

Then, after a brief pause, he said, "I'd try to come over here (to the Tigers) sooner than I did, although I had no control over that anyway.

"When they let me go in Cleveland, I came to Detroit and pitched great. Over there (with the Indians) I won about 90 games (actually 78) in 12 years, and I won 50-some (45) in less than five years here.

"Over there I always was in somebody else's shadow—Feller, Lemon, Bearden, Wynn, Garcia, you name it—but when I came to Detroit, I was a king, for a couple of seasons, anyway.

"But regrets? Only that I didn't get the opportunity to pitch more often over there."

And the high point of Gromek's career?

Now Gromek didn't hesitate.

"What else but the game I beat the Braves in the World Series?" he said. "How could there be anything but that?"

Which brought Gromek back to all that happened thereafter, including hugging Doby—maybe even kissing him—and, of course, the reaction by his parish priest, and friends in Hamtramck.

"Hey, I'd do the same thing all over again, and I'd enjoy it every bit as much."

Most assuredly, so would Doby.

And then, in parting, Gromek asked for Boudreau's telephone number. "I want to thank him again," he said, smiling broadly, "for 'sacrificing' that World Series game by pitching me instead of Feller."

WORLD SERIES VICTORY PARADE, 1948

CHAPTER TEN

Eddie Robinson

"Lou, you can have my glove and my uniform, too—I'm quitting."'

Eddie Robinson, a key member of the world champion Indians a half-century earlier, leaned back in his chair in the lounge at Wood Haven Country Club in Ft. Worth, puffed on his ever-present pipe and said it was time to set the record straight.

It had to do with a report that appeared in *Pride Against Prejudice*, the biography of Robinson's former teammate, Larry Doby, authored by Joseph Thomas Moore and published by Praeger Publishers.

The book said that Robinson had refused to lend Doby his glove —because of the color of Doby's skin—after the American League's first black player had been assigned to play first base in the second game of a doubleheader against the Chicago White Sox on July 6, 1947.

That was the day after Doby had joined the Indians from the Newark Eagles of the Negro National League where he'd been exclusively a second baseman.

Because Doby had never played the position, he did not own a first baseman's glove and was instructed by Manager Lou Boudreau to borrow one from Robinson, according to the book.

Robinson reportedly refused, saying, "I won't lend my glove to no nigger."

Then, again according to the book, traveling secretary Spud Goldstein asked Robinson, "Eddie, would you lend it to me?" and, it was written, "With that, Robinson tossed his glove to Goldstein" who, in turn, lent it to Doby.

"That's not true, that's not the way it was," said Robinson. "What happened was that I had been struggling . . . this was before Doby was signed, before his name had ever been mentioned.

"(Coach) Bill McKechnie came to me and said, 'Eddie, I know you're having a tough time (but) I feel you're going to pull out of it. Why don't you go in and talk to Lou and tell him that you realize you're having a tough time now, but you hope he'll stick with you.'

"So I went in and talked to (Boudreau) and told him what McKechnie suggested. He said, 'Don't worry, you're my first baseman,' and the next day (July 4) I hit two home runs in the first game of a doubleheader against Detroit. We won (13-6) and I really felt good."

Twenty-four hours later, Doby joined the Indians and struck out as a pinch hitter in a 6-5 loss to the White Sox in Chicago. The next day they were beaten again, 3-2, in the opener of a Sunday doubleheader in a game in which Robinson singled in four trips to the plate.

Eddie Robinson

Then, between games, "Lou walked over to me," said Robinson, "and said, 'Hey, Eddie, I want to borrow your glove. Doby is going to play first base.'

"He tells me this after just telling me a couple of days earlier, 'Don't worry, you're my first baseman.'"

And, making matters worse, in Robinson's mind, "Doby never played first base . . . he was always a second baseman. Joe Gordon (the Indians' regular second baseman) would have been happy to not play, but here Boudreau was, taking me out of the lineup after telling me not to worry.

"That's what was upsetting. It wasn't that Doby was black . . . it wasn't a racial thing at all.

"And, yes, I resented Lou for a long time after he told me what he did, about me being the first baseman, and then taking me out for a guy who'd never played first base.

"When a guy joins a ball club, whether he's white or black or whatever, and he's never played your position before, and the manager takes you out of the lineup for him to play in your place, sure, anybody would be upset . . . and I was."

Initially, after relating the story, Robinson said, "I'm not sure I want to put that on tape. I'd just as soon that not be in the book."

But a few minutes later he said, "Go ahead. Use it. And use this, too," urged Robinson, continuing the story of what he said "really" happened.

"After Boudreau asked to borrow my glove for Doby, I said to him, 'Lou, you can have my glove and my uniform, too—I'm quitting.'"

And with that, when the second game started, Robinson remained in the clubhouse, intending to shower and dress in street clothes—and leave—when McKechnie came in from the field.

"It was about the fourth inning and (McKechnie) said, 'Eddie, I know what this is all about. I know what's going through your mind. But what you and I know, it's not going to come out that way in the paper.

"It's going to look like you're doing this because of Doby being black. We know that's not the case, but it's not going to look that way in the paper. It's in your best interest, and for your future to put your uniform on and come back out (to the field).

"So I did, and that was it. The end of it, and McKechnie was right," said Robinson.

However, the other version of what happened in the clubhouse the day Doby played first base for the only time in his 10-year career with the Indians—the version that Robinson said is untrue—eventually surfaced and has been written and re-written often.

Robinson's explanation also tended to refute comments made by Boudreau in his 1993 autobiography, *Covering All The Bases,* published by Sagamore Publishing.

It was written that Robinson and Les Fleming, the other first baseman on the team in 1947, both of whom were Southerners, refused to shake hands with Doby when the latter joined the Indians.

Boudreau said in the book: "Robinson told me that he lived in Baltimore during the off-season and his neighbors would not appreciate his being on the same team as a Negro, but that he himself had nothing against Doby."

Robinson said he could not recall making that statement to Boudreau, nor did he remember being hostile toward the new player, or that he was unwilling to greet Doby with a handshake.

At the time the interview for this chapter was conducted in Ft. Worth, Doby was being honored by the Texas Rangers on the occasion of the 50th anniversary of his joining Jackie Robinson in breaking major league baseball's color barrier.

Doby was quoted extensively in the *Ft. Worth Star-Telegram* in a story that Robinson said he read.

"I know, it said there were six or seven guys who wouldn't shake his hand, and maybe that happened, I don't know. I can't say it's not true, but I don't remember it," he said.

"I don't even remember them bringing (Doby) around (to be introduced to everybody in the clubhouse). And if they had, I can't see myself refusing to shake hands with him, or anybody, for that matter.

"All I can tell you is that I had nothing against the man because he was black. I thought my relationship with Doby was OK. I think it's still OK."

Then Robinson volunteered, "Let me tell you this about Larry Doby. When I see all the accolades going to Jackie Robinson and not also to Doby, I don't think that's right. Doby was the first (black player) in the American League, he suffered through things just as Jackie did, and I think it should be a Jackie Robinson-Larry Doby tribute, instead of just for Jackie."

Eddie Robinson, 27 years old in 1948 and then no longer sharing first base with Fleming as they'd done the year before, was a major contributor in the Indians' drive to the pennant. He drove in 83 runs with a .254 average and 16 homers in what was his second full season in the major leagues.

Despite those statistics, Robinson was benched again for the Indians' most important game, replaced by another man who'd never previously played first base: Allie Clark.

"Well, the circumstances were different then," Robinson said of Boudreau's decision to install Clark at first base against the Boston Red Sox in the one-game playoff for the pennant on October 4.

"I could understand Lou's thinking, although, sure, I was still a little disappointed. Anybody in my shoes would have been disappointed.

"Lou said we were going to play all right-handed hitters (though left-handed hitting outfielders Dale Mitchell and Doby remained in the lineup), that we were going to shoot the moon," said Robinson.

The game was in Fenway Park where the 37-foot-high left-field wall—a.k.a. the "Green Monster"—315 feet from the plate, presented a friendly target.

"Allie might not have ever played first base, but he'd worked out there and Boudreau probably thought he'd have a better chance of getting a big hit than I would. "It was all right with me. I wanted to win and if Allie could help us more than me, that would be fine.

"I accepted it because Boudreau was the manager, and the manager is supposed to know what's best to do to win games."

Of his relationship with Boudreau, Robinson said, "I can't honestly say it was real good, but by then, any resentment I might have felt toward Lou (because of the July 6 incident involving Doby) was forgotten.

"Personally, I thought that Lou, being young, seemed to cater to the older players more than he did to guys like Mitchell and the younger fellows.

"But whether I was in the lineup that day (for the playoff game) or not, didn't make much difference," said Robinson.

As it turned out, Clark, batting second, went 0-for-2, grounding out both times, and in the bottom of the fourth, with the Indians leading, 5-1, Robinson took over at first base and singled in two official at-bats.

Robinson played every game in the World Series, going 6-for-20, and it was his eighth-inning single off Warren Spahn that drove in what proved to be the winning run in the Indians' 4-3 victory over the Boston Braves in the sixth and deciding game.

"We had great chemistry on that (1948) team, everybody meshed together, everybody did something, everybody contributed, which made it so good," said Robinson. "As far as I was concerned, we believed almost from the start that we had a chance to win it (the pennant), though there were other good teams in the league.

"The (New York) Yankees were good, and so were the Red Sox, though they got off to a terrible start. And the (Philadelphia) Athletics were right there until the last month or so of the season.

"I remember, after we won our first four games (over St. Louis and three in a row against Detroit), Gordon saying, 'Hey, we've got a chance to win this thing (the pennant).' I don't know if everybody believed him, but I did.

"I'd never been through a pennant race, but I believed Gordon because he was one of the leaders. He'd been through it with the Yankees (from 1938-46) before he came to Cleveland.

"(Bob) Lemon also was a leader on that team, if it's possible for a pitcher to be a leader. They both led by example, especially Gordon. Everybody respected him, looked up to him, admired him. He tried to keep everything lively and everybody loose, though it was tough on him.

"We roomed together on the road and one night in Philadelphia he said, 'Pennant races are fun, and they're not fun.' I asked him what he meant, and he said, 'It's the pressure. The pressure is really tough,' which it was, especially on him because of his role on the team."

Satchel Paige, the legendary black pitcher who was signed by Veeck on July 7, a year and two days after Doby made his debut with the Indians, helped ease some of the pressure, because of his personality, Robinson said.

"Satch went his own way, did his own thing, but he kept everybody loose. We all looked at him with awe," said Robinson.

"I never saw him pitch before he came to us, but he was a helluva pitcher, don't let anybody tell you otherwise. Even though he didn't have his blazing fastball anymore, he knew how to pitch, which made him so good.

"We wouldn't have won without Paige (he won six games and lost one) that year, although the same thing could be said about a lot of guys, in fact, just about everybody on the team.

"I had a lot of fun with Satch. We autographed a lot of baseballs that year and he used to say to me, 'Eddie, I'm not going to sign my name under yours because you write too pretty.'

"In those days," continued Robinson, "you tried to let people read your name, let them know who signed a ball, not like today. Now you get an autographed ball and you don't know who the hell signed it. I don't know if (today's players) do that on purpose or not."

When he talked about Gordon and Lemon being leaders on the team, Robinson also cited McKechnie, then 61, as having great influence over Boudreau.

McKechnie, nicknamed "The Deacon," was one of the veteran coaches—Muddy Ruel was another—that Bill Veeck insisted that Boudreau add to his staff. They replaced two of Boudreau's longtime friends, Oscar Melillo and George Susce. Mel Harder, who retired after the 1947 season, his 20th as a pitcher for the Indians, was the team's third coach.

Of the three, McKechnie, because of his extensive experience, was closest to Boudreau, Robinson said.

McKechnie previously managed Newark (New Jersey) in the old Federal League in 1915, and Pittsburgh (1922-26), the St. Louis Cardinals (1928-29), Boston Braves (1930-37), and Cincinnati (1938-46) in the National League, before joining the Indians in 1947. Four of his teams won pennants, the Pirates in 1925, the Cardinals in 1928, and the Reds in 1939 and 1940. McKechnie also coached for Boudreau in 1949, and the Red Sox in 1952 and 1953, then retired, and was elected to the Hall of Fame in 1962.

Robinson had great respect for McKechnie and, based on comments attributed to the coach in a March 25, 1948 article in the *Cleveland News*, the veteran coach felt the same about the first baseman.

"I haven't pulled for many ball players the way I'm pulling for that Robinson. There isn't a better, cleaner living kid in the game," McKechnie was quoted in the story penned by sportswriter-columnist Ed McAuley.

When Robinson was asked if he thought that McKechnie and Gordon influenced Boudreau to start Gene Bearden in the playoff game against the Red Sox, he said no.

"Regardless of how I felt at the time about being benched for Doby, and then for Clark in the playoff game, I had a lot of respect for Boudreau," said Robinson. "He was a helluva guy, a great player and, considering his age (31 in 1948), did a good job of managing in a tight pennant race.

"Lou was his own man and, while I think he would listen to Gordon and McKechnie and the coaches, I'm sure he made his own decisions. That's all I can tell you about that."

Robinson was more eager to talk about two games in 1948 that he vividly remembers—the doubleheader against New York at the Stadium on August 8.

It was the day the Indians swept the Yankees, 8-6 and 2-1, and is generally acknowledged to have been the turning point of the season. Those two victories kept the Indians in first place, .006 percentage points ahead of Philadelphia, and increased their lead over New York to two games, and to two and a half over Boston.

That was the time Boudreau limped off the bench to deliver a bases-loaded pinch single in the seventh inning of the opener, scoring two runs and overcoming a 6-4 deficit. Steve Gromek pitched a masterful game to win the nightcap with eighth inning relief help from Ed Klieman.

Boudreau and Gromek received most of the credit, but the Indians probably would not have won either game without Robinson's contributions.

He hammered three homers that day, two in the first game, the second coming in the eighth inning with a runner aboard, breaking the 6-6 tie. Then, in the fifth inning of the second game, Robinson delivered his 13th homer of the season, accounting for the Indians' margin of victory.

"You're right, Boudreau got most of the ink, but he should have, coming off the bench the way he did," said Robinson. "That didn't bother me. We won the game . . . two of them, in fact. That was the big thing."

Robinson's first homer, a two-run shot that preceded Boudreau's dramatic pinch hit in the seventh, ended an 0-for-15 slump for the handsome first baseman who, at the time, was being booed by many of the 73,484 fans in the Stadium.

Robinson had incurred their wrath in the fifth inning of the opener by dropping a pop foul for an error that helped the Yankees score two unearned runs.

When asked if those three homers in the two victories over the Yankees represented the highlight of his career,

Robinson paused momentarily to re-light his pipe, smiled and said, "No . . . the highlight of my career was winning the pennant and World Series (in 1948)."

Two months later, on December 14, 1948, Robinson was traded to the then-Washington Senators in a deal that, he said, pleased him.

"I was happy. I didn't like playing in Cleveland because I didn't like that Stadium. I was married to a girl from Baltimore at that time, and in Washington, I was close to home," he said.

Robinson's dislike of the Stadium was based primarily on the fact that it was so huge—"It definitely was not a hitter's park," he said, which brought up the subject of the outfield fence that Veeck had installed after he purchased the franchise in June 1946.

Reportedly, the groundskeepers, Emil Bossard and his sons, Harold and Marshall, were instructed to make the outfield fence portable so that it could be moved in or out, closer to the plate or deeper, depending on the opposition.

That is, if the team coming in had a bunch of long ball hitters, the Bossards—in the middle of the night, under the cover of darkness— would move the fences back. If it was a weak-hitting team the Indians would be playing at that particular time, the fences would remain in place, closer to the plate, supposedly giving the home team an advantage.

"I don't know about that, how often the fences were moved," said Robinson, "although I remember one time, in 1947, a little guy hit a home run against us. The next day, probably Veeck, said, 'If that little (bleep) hits a home run, the fence has got to go back,' and it did."

Shortly thereafter a rule was instituted that prohibited outfield fences being moved after Opening Day.

The deal that sent Robinson to the Senators, which so greatly pleased him, proved to be a very good one for the Indians. They received pitcher Early Wynn and first baseman Mickey Vernon for Robinson and pitchers Ed Klieman and Joe Haynes.

And, as it turned out, Robinson didn't get to spend much time in Washington; the trade began an American League odyssey in which he played for eight teams, including two stints with the Indians, through 1957, after which he retired as a player.

In 1,315 games in 11 seasons (and parts of two others) Robinson batted .268 with 172 home runs and 723

RBIs, and appeared in two World Series, with the Yankees in 1955 as well as the Indians in 1948.

Robinson was dealt to the White Sox on May 31, 1950; to the Philadelphia Athletics on January 27, 1953; to the Yankees on December 16, 1953; back to the Athletics, then located in Kansas City, on June 14, 1956; and to Detroit on December 5, 1956.

He was released by the Tigers after 13 games on May 17, 1957, signed with the Indians, for whom he played 19 games and was released again on June 29, 1957, then joined Baltimore as a player-coach the final month of that season.

Robinson's best years were 1951, 1952 and 1953, when he drove in 117 and 104 runs for the White Sox, and 102 for the Athletics. His best batting average was .296 in 1952, a year after he socked a career- high 29 homers.

But Robinson's career in baseball didn't end when he finished the 1957 season in Baltimore. Not by a long shot.

When he retired from the Orioles as a player, all he did was trade a uniform for a white shirt and a desk—and he's still involved with the game at the executive level.

Robinson began in the Orioles' front office in 1958, went to the then-Houston Colt 45s in 1962, to the Kansas City Athletics in 1966, in 1967 to Atlanta where he became general manager in 1972, and to the Texas Rangers as general manager from 1977 through 1982, after which, for the next three years, he did special assignment scouting and personnel evaluating for the Yankees.

"I've worked for so many guys . . . guys like Bill Veeck, George Steinbrenner, Paul Richards, Charlie Finley, Judge Roy Hofheinz, Ted Turner, Brad Corbett . . . I'm thinking about writing a book," he said. "I'd call it, 'The Men In My Life.' I'd have a helluva lot to tell."

Then he said, unnecessarily, "I love baseball . . . it has been my life."

It all began for Robinson in 1939 when he played for Valdosta, Georgia in the (Class D) Georgia-Florida League. He got a $300 bonus to sign and a salary of $150 a month but, as Robinson said, his career almost ended before the season was halfway through.

"The manager called me in one day and said, 'Eddie, I've got to tell you, we have another first baseman coming in.' I told him I was very disappointed to hear that, and asked him to please hang in there with me," said Robinson.

"I was probably hitting only about .220 at the time, but the manager told me, 'It's not your hitting, it's your fielding . . . you've got to learn to pick up those throws in the dirt.'

"Well, I worked at it, and worked at it so much I think I probably could pick up those bad throws with my eyes shut."

It saved Robinson's job—and career, for that matter—though he batted only .249 that season and, he said, "My salary was cut fifty bucks, to $100 a month . . . but I didn't care, I just wanted to play ball."

Robinson improved to .323 at Valdosta in 1940, was promoted to Elmira, New York of the (Class A) Eastern League where he hit .295 in 1941, and blossomed in 1942 while playing for Baltimore, then in the (Class AA) International League, hitting .306 with 27 homers.

World War II interrupted Robinson's career as he served in the Navy the next three years. He returned to Baltimore, which was still in the minor leagues, in 1946 and hit .318 with 34 homers and 123 RBI. It won him, not only a promotion to the Indians, but also the International League's "Most Valuable Player" award.

Interestingly, one of the players he beat out for MVP honors was Jackie Robinson, whose .349 batting average for Montreal was highest in the league.

When asked the obvious question, Eddie Robinson said, "There were no incidents involving Jackie (Robinson) that I can recall. It was strange for everybody (having him in the league) because it had never happened before, but our club (Baltimore) just more or less accepted him. I don't remember that any of our guys yelled things at him, or gave him a bad time."

Both Robinsons went to the big leagues the next year, though a broken ankle in August, the result of a foul ball off his own bat, prematurely ended Eddie's season in 1947 with a .245 average, 14 homers and 52 RBIs in 95 games.

Now Robinson walks with a slight limp, the result of a World War II operation to excise a tumor from his leg, and also because of what he calls "gimpy" knees. The still ruggedly handsome former first baseman is president of Eddie Robinson Enterprises, Inc., a company he started in 1986.

At the time of the interview for this chapter, Robinson was scouting and evaluating personnel for two major league clubs, the Red Sox and Minnesota Twins.

"This is the thirteenth year I've been in business and teams that I've worked for have won three World Series," he said.

As a scout, how would he evaluate the young Eddie Robinson who helped the Indians win the World Series a half century ago?

"I'd give myself very good grades," said the old Eddie Robinson. "I was an above average hitter for power and average, and an above average fielder. But I was a below average runner and, though I had a below average arm, it was good enough for being a first baseman."

If he compared himself to anyone playing today, who would it be? "Will Clark or Tino Martinez," replied Robinson, "which would mean I'd be worth five or six million dollars a year, a lot more money . . . a *helluva lot more* than I ever made."

Robinson's peak salary, he said, was $18,000 in 1950. He was paid $6,000 by the Indians in 1948, plus $6,772 as his share of the World Series prize money.

Robinson's second wife, Bette, whom he married in 1955, is an international trader and also operates her own business, "Robinson Exports," out of their home located on the grounds of the Wood Haven Country Club.

Eddie and Bette raised three sons, Marc, born in 1959, Paul, born in 1961, and Drew, born in 1963, and also have five grandchildren. Paul followed his dad into baseball; he is an area scouting supervisor for the Anaheim Angels. He pitched in the Philadelphia Phillies minor league system one season, but suffered an arm injury and was released.

Tragedy touched the lives of Eddie and his first wife, Elaine. They were married in 1943 when Robinson was in the Navy and their first child, a daughter, Robbie Ann, died in 1946 when she was two years old.

"Robbie Ann was a darling little girl . . . she developed a brain tumor and was in a coma for a month before she passed away," said Robinson. "It was very traumatic, very difficult, knowing there was nothing we could do."

Robinson also has a son by his first wife. Eddie III was born in Cleveland in 1948, and was a wide receiver and kicker at California Lutheran College. He was drafted by the Pittsburgh Steelers, though he didn't stick with them, "He wasn't big enough for the NFL," said Robinson. He and Elaine were divorced in 1950.

Before the interview ended, Robinson made clear his concern about the future of baseball.

"I don't have any idea where it's going, except that I know it's out of control," he said. "Now the union (the Major League Players Association) just about runs the game.

The only things the clubs absolutely control are their staffs and the minor leagues.

"When (the clubs) start giving untried players, high school players, $10 million (as the Arizona Diamondbacks did in signing an amateur player in 1996), it tells you they absolutely don't know what they're doing. What it tells me is that they have a lot of money and too many of them are trying to keep up with the Joneses.

"It's OK for a rich club to spend a lot of money to sign a player, but it shouldn't carry over to clubs that don't have a lot of money, which is happening with free agents and in arbitration.

"And the agents . . . they're really smart. In my day, if you had a good year, it didn't mean (bleep). You had to have at least two good years back-to-back to establish yourself. Then you could demand some money.

"But today (players) can go to arbitration and, if they've had a terrific year, they match that with some guy who might have been in the big leagues ten years, but their numbers are similar so they want the same money.

"Baseball has gotten itself into this fix and, frankly, I don't know where it's going to end," Robinson said again.

"Ten years ago I said, '(Bleep), there's no way the game can survive if these things continue to happen.' But it has (survived) and those things are still happening. Big corporations like Disney and Budweiser are getting in and they can afford to spend the money.

Eddie Robinson

"It's got to end somewhere, but I don't know where, or when, and I worry about it.

"Anyone who loves the game, has to worry, same as I do."

CHAPTER ELEVEN
. . . .

Bob Lemon

"We were uninspirable . . . we felt we were going to win all the time.'"

When he was strong, fully rested and, as he says, "bright eyed and bushy tailed," Bob Lemon was awful. Awful as a pitcher, that is.

"Probably because I felt so good, I had a tendency to overthrow the ball and my sinker didn't sink. And when that happened, I usually got jocked," said the former pitcher, coach and manager who still does some special assignment scouting on the west coast for George Steinbrenner and the New York Yankees.

Lemon, like his former teammates, no longer is the robust and athletic man he was during a Hall of Fame career that began in 1938 when he was —as everybody thought then—a power-hitting third baseman at Oswego, New York of the Class C Canadian-American League.

Now Lemon uses a cane to get around, though he does so, he said, "Only because it makes it easier. I have poor circulation in my legs."

Still a heavy cigarette smoker, Lemon shrugged and said, "What the hell. As old as I am (78 in 1998), why should I quit now, after all these years?"

Since suffering a mild stroke in 1996, Lemon also has a minor speech impediment that causes him to slur some words.

"Yeah, yeah, I know you think I've been drinking, but that's not it," he said with a chuckle as we talked in my hotel room near the airport in Los Angeles where Lemon insisted we meet. "It's easier for me to find you than to give you directions to my house."

Lemon still lives in Long Beach, California with wife Jane, whom he married in 1944.

They still grieve the loss of their youngest son, Jerry, who was killed in an automobile accident in Arizona in 1978.

As Lemon said, "It's something you never get over."

Jerry Lemon, then 26 and fresh out of the Army, was driving to Phoenix to visit his brother Jim. The accident happened in the desert between Palm Springs, California and Phoenix. "Jerry dozed off, ran off the road and hit a tree," said Lemon, softly, sadly, no longer smiling.

Jim, the Lemons' middle son, born in 1950, is principal of a school in the Phoenix area. Their oldest child, Jeff, born in 1948, lives near his parents in Long Beach where he works for the Santa Fe railroad. Jim and Bob have given their parents five grandchildren.

Now some 40 pounds heavier than the 187 he weighed in 1948 when he blossomed as a major league pitcher, the still ruddy-faced Lemon remains on the payroll of George Steinbrenner's New York Yankees as a scout for the team he managed for parts of four seasons (1978-82).

And he's still quick with the quip.

Bob Lemon

"Hey, Meat," he called me by his favorite pronoun—Meat, as in Meathead —"if George wants me to do this, I do this. If he wants me to do that, I do that," said Lemon, who also piloted the Kansas City Royals from 1970-72, and the Chicago White Sox in 1977 and 1978.

Lemon won the American League Manager of the Year award in 1971 when the Royals, in only their third year of existence, finished second in the western division.

But then, as Lemon said, he "got dumb in a hurry," and was fired when the Royals fell to fourth place a year later.

Lemon again was voted A.L. Manager of the Year in 1977, after taking over the White Sox, but apparently got "dumb" again and was replaced after 74 games in 1978 by former Tribe teammate Larry Doby.

And again, Lemon wasn't out of work for long.

Only three weeks, after which his relationship with Steinbrenner began.

Steinbrenner hired Lemon to take over for Billy Martin for the final 68 games of 1978. He led the Yankees to a 47-20 record and a final-day first-place tie with the Boston Red Sox, then a victory in a one- game playoff for the pennant, and beat Los Angeles in the World Series.

Then, in Steinbrenner's version of managerial musical chairs, after 65 games in 1979—and in the wake of the tragic death of Lemon's son—Martin replaced Lemon with the Yankees in fourth place with a 34-31 record.

Two years later, in the second half of baseball's strike-shortened season of 1981, Steinbrenner brought Lemon back to take over for Martin. Under Lemon the Yankees beat Oakland in the A.L. Championship Series, but lost to the Dodgers in the World Series.

Lemon continued as the Yankees skipper in 1982, but lasted only 14 games (six victories, eight defeats), after which he was "re-assigned" by Steinbrenner.

Despite being fired—or, more kindly stated, *re-assigned* or even *replaced* —several times by Steinbrenner, Lemon bears no animosity toward the man known throughout baseball as "The Boss." Quite the contrary, in fact.

"I like working for George. He treated me OK, and he's still treating me OK," said Lemon. "I always got along with him, and I still do. I get a paycheck every month.

"The big thing with George is just that he wants to win. He buys a winner and he pays for a winner. He jumps on guys who don't hustle, who don't play hard . . . and he's definitely more a player's boss than a coach's or manager's boss.

"Everybody knows George has an ego that won't quit. He likes to see his name in the papers, whether what's written is good or bad.

"But that's the worst thing I can say about him—and that's not bad."

When asked if Steinbrenner interfered much with the on-field management of the Yankees, Lemon chuckled and replied, "No. But

Bob Lemon

(Al) Rosen did. And when you see Rosie, you can tell him what I said."

Rosen, another of Lemon's former teammates with the Tribe, was general manager of the Yankees at the time.

"Rosie would call and tell me that George wanted me to do this or that. Then he'd say, 'Don't get pissed off at me, I'm just the damned messenger.' And when I still argued with Rosie, he'd get pissed off at George himself, and tell me, 'Do whatever the hell you want, but this is what The Boss wants you to do. I'm just delivering the message.'"

That was more than 15 years ago and Lemon has long since lost his managerial aspirations.

"I liked it (managing) then, when I was doing it, when everybody got along all right. But things are too different now," he said. "The animals are running the zoo. It's not the same. Now, a manager is expected to motivate his players, which, to me, is ridiculous.

"Why should somebody need to be motivated to make a million dollars?" Lemon wanted to know. "Isn't a million dollars enough motivation?"

Lemon's motivation was just to play—and stay—in the big leagues, which is the reason he switched from third base to the outfield, and then to pitching.

And if he hadn't, if he had not established himself as one of the best pitchers in baseball in only his third full season on the mound, it's doubtful the Indians would have won the pennant and beaten the Boston Braves in the World Series in 1948.

That was the year Lemon's record was 20-14 with a 2.82 earned run average, the first of seven 20-victory seasons (in the next nine) that led to his 1976 election to the Hall of Fame. His 13-year major league career totals: 460 games, 350 as a starter, 207 victories, 128 losses, 3.23 ERA

"What would I have done if I had not switched to pitching?" Lemon repeated the question. "I don't know . . . but I probably wouldn't have lasted long in baseball."

He was considered a decent hitter and good fielding third baseman in the minor leagues, from 1938 through 1942, before going into the U.S. Navy for three years during World War II.

Bob Lemon with Lou Boudreau.

Still, Lemon wasn't given much chance of winning a job with the Indians when he reported for spring training in 1946.

Ken Keltner was then in his prime as the Tribe's third baseman, so Manager Lou Boudreau switched Lemon to the outfield because of his strong arm and impressive minor league credentials.

Lemon opened the season as the Indians' center fielder and was outstanding defensively. It was his sensational, game-saving catch that preserved Bob Feller's 1-0, Opening Day victory over Chicago.

But offensively, it was something else. Lemon hit only .180 with one homer in 55 games in 1946, and by mid-season he was benched, except as a late-inning defensive replacement.

"If I had learned to hit the change up, it might have been different," he said. "Bill Dietrich (of the White Sox)

got me with it on Opening Day. Hell, I'd run half way to the mound trying to hit it, that's how bad it was.

"I could hit anything else they threw, but not the change up, and the word got around pretty quick. Pretty soon, that's all I saw. Fastball out of the strike zone. Curveball out of the strike zone. Then a change up."

Soon thereafter Mel Harder, then still a pitcher for the Tribe, and Hall of Fame catcher Bill Dickey of the New York Yankees, made an impact on Lemon's career.

While his bat had fallen silent, Lemon had pitched some batting practice for the Indians, which caught the eye of Harder. He also recognized Lemon's strong arm and was aware that the weak-hitting third baseman-turned-outfielder had done some pitching when he and Dickey were stationed together in the Navy.

When the Yankees played the Indians in June, Boudreau sought out Dickey, whose playing career was winding down, and asked about Lemon.

Dickey highly recommended Lemon as a pitcher and Boudreau and Harder began another conversion of the third baseman-turned-center fielder.

Lemon went on to make 32 appearances on the mound, all but five as a reliever, the rest of the 1946 season. Though he won only four and lost five games, Lemon's ERA was a sparkling 2.49, and from then on there was no doubt about the position he'd play in the future.

In 1947, Lemon's record improved to 11-5 in 37 games, 15 as a starter, under the tutelage of Harder, who became the Indians pitching coach in 1948.

"Once Lemon realized that he did not have to throw as hard as he could to get batters out, he became a good pitcher, a winning pitcher," said Harder.

And a Hall of Fame pitcher.

But first, except for an interesting twist of fate, Lemon almost was "lost" by the Indians.

It happened in 1946, shortly after Bill Veeck bought the Indians and, of course, before Lemon showed the potential for becoming a winning pitcher.

Under the impression that Lemon would never amount to much with the Indians, Veeck verbally agreed to sell the third baseman-outfielder and erstwhile pitcher to the Washington Senators for the waiver price, which was then $7,500.

The deal Veeck made with Senators owner Clark Griffith was that the sale of Lemon was not to be announced until the next afternoon, in deference to *The Plain Dealer*, Cleveland's morning newspaper.

However, when Griffith prematurely leaked the news a day early that he was going to buy Lemon, Veeck angrily called off the deal because the papers hadn't yet been signed, even though Lemon and his wife were packed and ready to leave for Washington.

That non-sale of Lemon—as well as Veeck's subsequent cancellation of his plan to trade Lou Boudreau to the St. Louis Browns for shortstop Vernon Stephens in November 1947—led to the remark for which he is often credited, to wit:

"Sometimes the best deals are those you don't make."

It was shortly thereafter, on July 2, 1946, that Lemon won his first major league game as a starter, a 4-2 victory over the Browns.

Lemon further established himself as a major league pitcher in 1947, going 11-5 as the Indians finished fourth, and reported for spring training in 1948 as the No. 2 starter behind Bob Feller.

The then-27-year-old right hander immediately proved that he was no fluke—and that Harder's and Dickey's judgment was sound—by beating Detroit, 8-2, with a six-hitter in the second game of the season, and racking up a 9-3 record by June 11.

Then, on June 30, Lemon hurled a no-hitter against the Tigers, beating them, 2-0, for his eleventh victory in 17 decisions.

As Boudreau commented later, "When you take part in a no-hitter by one of your pitchers, it's something you never forget, especially the key plays. I'll always remember Lemon's for another reason—because it was such an important victory for us. We were in first place but Philadelphia and New York were breathing on our neck, and Boston was right behind them."

In his no-hitter, Lemon struck out four and walked three, and the Tigers came close to hits only twice. In the fourth inning, George Kell shot a line drive to left field that Dale Mitchell hauled in with a leaping, one-handed grab near the wall at Briggs (later Tiger) Stadium in Detroit. An inning later, Keltner went behind third base to back hand a bounder off the bat of Hoot Evers and threw him out by half-a-step at first base.

Lemon got the only runs he needed in the first inning when the Tigers committed two errors, one by Kell, the other by shortstop Johnny Lipon, Boudreau's double and a long fly (the sacrifice fly rule was not in effect then) by Hank Edwards.

"I wasn't even aware that I had a no-hitter going, although I thought it was funny, really strange, that nobody would talk to me in the dugout the last couple of innings," said Lemon, who finally realized in the ninth that he was working on a gem.

He went on to easily retire the final three Tigers—pinch hitter Vic Wertz on a bounder back to the mound, Eddie Mayo on a strikeout, and Kell on another grounder to Lemon.

The victory raised Lemon's record to 11-6 and gave rise to speculation that he had a shot at becoming the first pitcher to win 30 games in one season since Dizzy Dean in 1934.

He didn't make it; Lemon said, "I ran out of gas in September."

Until then, however, Lemon was something very special. Including his no-hitter, he pitched a league-leading ten shutouts, helping to keep the Indians in or around first place throughout the season.

"We thought all along that we could win, though it got a little hairy at times," said Lemon.

It was a confidence that had its genesis in spring training, according to Lemon, even though the Indians were coming off a disappointing season in 1947 when they finished in fourth place, 17 games behind the Yankees, with an 80-74 record.

"We had a good spring in Tucson (Arizona) . . . the cowgirls were all cowing and everything was perfect. Everything jelled for us," he said.

The cowgirls were all "cowing?"

"C'mon, Meat," responded Lemon, again calling me by his favorite pronoun for a friend and winking as he said, "You know what I mean."

Lemon acknowledged that the Indians really caught fire on August 8 when an injured and taped-up Boudreau delivered a clutch pinch hit in the opener of a doubleheader against the Yankees that scored two runs, tied the game and led the Indians to two victories.

Lemon had a front-row seat for Boudreau's heroics. "I was on second base, a pinch runner for Allie Clark, when Lou put himself in the game," said Lemon.

"I was surprised because the man was hurting. I thought he had a broken toe (it was a badly sprained left ankle, as well as bruises of his right shoulder, right knee and right thumb) because he was soaking his foot in a bucket of ice the whole game, until he went up to hit.

"I think we all just took for granted that Lou would come through. He was having that kind of a season."

When asked if the Indians were inspired by Boudreau's dramatic hit, Lemon chuckled and said, "Hell, we were uninspirable . . . we already had all the inspiration we needed. That's what kept us so loose, all of us, all season. When we went out on the field we felt we were going to win all the time."

After registering his 20th victory by beating the Browns, 9-1, on September 11, completing another sweep of a doubleheader that kept the Indians in third place, three games behind Boston, Lemon failed to win his last four starts, taking the loss in three of them.

However, while Lemon struggled, rookie Gene Bearden and Feller, rebounding from a slump, each went 4-0 and the Indians won 12 of 15 games from September 12-29, including seven in a row, to regain first place by two games over both the Red Sox and Yankees.

When Lemon's troubles continued into the next game, October 1, a 5-3 loss to the Tigers, the Tribe's lead over Boston and New York shrunk to one game with two left to play.

Bearden came through again to beat the Tigers, 8-0, on October 2, to clinch a tie, but Hal Newhouser, long a Tribe nemesis, bested Feller, 7-1, in the regular season finale, while Boston was beating New York, 10-5.

The loss to the Tigers left the Indians and Red Sox deadlocked with identical, 96-58 records, forcing a one-game playoff the next day in Boston.

"I swear, that's the best stuff I ever saw Newhouser have," Lemon said of the future Hall of Famer who would pitch for the Indians in 1954 and 1955. "Funny thing is, I don't think he even wanted to pitch that game. I guess it was a matter of pride with him, to pitch well and beat us that day."

But Lemon claimed that nobody in the Cleveland clubhouse panicked.

"It was like Satch (Satchel Paige) said. 'We just gotta go out and get 'em tomorrow. We gotta beat the Red Sox, and then we gotta beat them Braves.' He was right."

Bob Lemon (left) with Joe Gordon.

After the loss to the Tigers, Boudreau held a clubhouse meeting and told the players that Bearden was his choice to pitch against the Red Sox the next day.

"I've heard tell that (Johnny) Berardino jawed (argued) with Lou, that Bearden, being left-handed, would have trouble in Fenway Park, but it was no big thing," said Lemon.

"I think (Joe) Gordon summed it up best. He said, 'Lou, you got us this far, we might as well go along with you for another game.'

"That was it. No argument. Boudreau called the shot."

Could Lemon have pitched the playoff game? Did he want to?

"I could have, I think, but Boudreau picked Bearden," said Lemon. "Like Gordon said, he (Boudreau) got us that far, why change?"

En route by train to Boston for the all-or-nothing game the next day, Lemon said the Indians were confident they'd win . . . they even did some celebrating, including Bearden, who had the assignment to face the Red Sox the next day.

"My dad was with us and the next morning he comes up to me and asked, 'Are you pitching today?' I said, 'No, Bearden is, but don't tell anybody. Lou (Boudreau) wants to keep it a secret until game time.'

"My dad said, 'Bearden? Why Bearden?' I asked, 'Why not?' and he says, 'Geez, we had to put him to bed last night. That's why.'"

And why did Bearden have to be put to bed the night before he would pitch the most important game of the season?

"Because he was gassed, for chrissake, that's why," said Lemon.

Boudreau always put a new baseball in the locker, under the cap of the pitcher who was to start the game for the Indians. And because he wanted to keep his choice of the starter for the playoff game a secret until the last minute, he put new baseballs in the lockers of Bearden, Bob Feller and Lemon.

It kept the Red Sox guessing until the last minute.

As Lemon testified, "Vince Orlando, who was the clubhouse guy for the visiting team, saw a ball in my locker and, I'm sure, went running to the Red Sox to tell them that I was going to pitch," he said.

"But then he saw a ball under Feller's cap and told (the Red Sox) that it wouldn't be me, it would be Feller.

"And when he saw a ball in Bearden's locker, he didn't know what the hell was going on, which is what we wanted them to think.

"When the game started (and Bearden was announced as the Indians pitcher) Feller and I were in the bullpen warming up—and we warmed up for seven innings as Boudreau had said, 'We'll use everybody, if necessary.'"

Fortunately for the Indians, it wasn't necessary.

Neither Feller nor Lemon was needed as Bearden was masterful. He pitched a five-hitter, Boudreau went 4-for-4 with two homers, Ken Keltner delivered a three-run homer, and the Indians won the pennant with an 8-3 victory.

Two days later, the Indians squared off against the Boston Braves in the World Series—but first, they celebrated the franchise's first pennant in 28 years.

"Oh, did we ever," chortled Lemon.

And, in the ensuing revelry, the Indians almost lost their second-string catcher, Joe Tipton—and, for that matter, Lemon, too—as the pitcher somewhat sheepishly confirmed.

It was an incident that was not reported until later, because, as Lemon said, "The writers in those days didn't write everything that happened. Not like today. But it was no big thing, anyway."

What happened, according to Lemon, was that, "Tipton said something to Keltner about some money Joe had lost in a poker game. Something like that. They got into yakking at each other and I told Joe, 'What the hell, you'll have six grand coming (if the Indians win the World Series), so whatever you lost in the poker game couldn't mean that much.

"It was something like that, anyway, and Joe got pissed off. He popped me in the ear and I hit him back. In the mouth. That's all there was to it."

The squabble between Tipton and Keltner, and then Tipton and Lemon was not an indication of trouble within the ranks of the Indians, Lemon insisted.

"Naw, nothing like that," he said. "Oh, Tipton would get gassed sometimes and get kind of porky, but not bad. Once in spring training he got gassed and said something to

Bob Lemon (left) with Bob Feller.

Jim Fridley. First thing you know, Fridley knocked Tipton on his ass.

Bob Lemon (left) and Warren Spahn, rival hurlers in the second World Series game, pose in the locker room before taking the field.

*Bob Lemon (left)
"teaching" Ronald Reagan
how to pitch for the movie
"The Winning Team," in
which Reagan played Hall
of Fame pitcher Grover
Cleveland Alexander.*

"But Tipton wasn't a bad guy. We didn't have any bad guys on that team."

Lemon said the attitude of the Indians going into the World Series was no different than what it had been during the season.

"We didn't know how to act because most of us had never been in a World Series. Joe Gordon was the only one who ever did (with the Yankees in 1938, 1939, 1941, 1942 and 1943). We just felt like it was another game, or another seven games," he said.

Actually, only six games.

With Feller on the mound in the opener, the Indians lost, 1-0, because of a disputed decision by National League umpire Bill Stewart on a pickoff play at second base.

Several years later, Phil Masi, the Braves player who scored the game's only run, admitted that he should have been called out, not safe, and also that Stewart had confided that he blew the call, that Feller's throw to Boudreau in the eighth inning was on the mark and on time.

Instead, Masi scored on a subsequent single by Tommy Holmes and the Braves prevailed.

The Indians came back to win four of the next five. Lemon beat the Braves and Warren Spahn, 4-1, in a route-going performance in Game Two, and was credited with the World Series-clinching victory, 4-3, with eighth-inning relief help from Bearden in Game Six.

Ironically, Lemon thinks that Stewart's ruling that cost Feller a possible victory, helped the Indians—and Lemon—win the next game.

In what he once described as his "most memorable game," Lemon said then, "I know it hurt Feller, but it might have turned out good for me and the Indians. If it hadn't happened, I might not have won the next day and we might not have won the World Series.

"I was in trouble, on the ropes in the first inning of the second game, and Boudreau got the bullpen up. The Braves got one run in, then had runners on first and second and only one out. I knew I'd be out of the game if I didn't get the next man, and it was killing me. No pitcher wants to be knocked out of a game in the first inning, especially in the World Series.

Hank Greenberg negotiating a contract with Bob Lemon.

"Before I made a pitch to the next batter, we tried the pickoff at second again. The same one that Feller and Boudreau worked—but didn't get the call—in the first game.

"But this time the umpire, an American Leaguer (Bill Grieve) called the runner (Earl Torgeson) out."

Then Lemon struck out the next batter to escape further damage, and the Braves didn't score again.

"The funny thing, the thing that made it so ironic," continued Lemon, "is that Feller's pickoff, the one that wasn't called and cost him the game, helped make mine work. All the hell we raised because we thought Stewart blew the call for Feller, I think made the umpires more alert, more aware that we might try it again.

"And because I got Torgeson at second, I got out of the inning instead of being knocked out of the game. I stayed out of trouble the rest of the way, and we won."

The Indians got two runs in the fourth on Boudreau's leadoff double and singles by Gordon and Larry Doby; another run in the fifth on Dale Mitchell's single, a sacrifice bunt and Boudreau's single; and one more in the ninth, when

Jim Hegan reached on an error and Bob Kennedy delivered a two-out single.

"If my pickoff didn't work and the Braves got some more runs, maybe they would've won, not only that game, but the whole Series," added Lemon, which was the reason he said that game was "more memorable" to him than even his no-hitter against the Tigers earlier that season.

Lemon's success in the World Series tended to belie his explanation that he'd "run out of gas" in September, causing him to fail in his final four starts of the regular season.

There was a difference, he said. "By the time we were playing the Braves, it was cooler. And, don't forget, it was the World Series. I guess I was inspired, whatever the hell that means."

Indeed, whatever the hell that means, Lemon obviously continued to be inspired, although it seems that not enough of his teammates were.

While the Indians and their fans had to wait six years for another pennant, Lemon continued to be one of the best pitchers in baseball. He led the A.L. with 23 victories in 1950, and 23 in 1954 when the Indians won a league-record 111 games (but were swept in the World Series by the then-New York Giants), and was a seven-time member of the All-Star team.

Finally, in 1957, the third baseman-turned-center fielder-turned-pitcher crashed, failing for the first time in 11 major league seasons to compile a winning record. Lemon won only six games while losing 11, with a very uncharacteristic 4.60 earned run average.

He underwent elbow surgery during the winter of 1957-58 and returned for another season, but it would soon be over for Lemon.

With Bobby Bragan then the Indians manager—who would be replaced on June 26 by Lemon's buddy, Joe Gordon—the former ace opened the 1958 season in Cleveland, but failed to win a game (losing one) in 11 appearances.

Lemon agreed to return to the minors, to San Diego of the Class AAA Pacific Coast League, where his record was only 2-5. When the season ended, so did Lemon's playing career.

"Actually, my arm was OK . . . it was the rest of my body that fell apart," he quipped.

It was during Hank Greenberg's regime (1950-57) as general manager of the Indians that Lemon reached his peak salary, $55,000 in 1956.

While conceding, "I liked Hank," Lemon also acknowledged that their relationship was not always idyllic. Especially not in December 1954, after Lemon had gone 23-7 with a 2.72 earned run average.

"That's when Hank ran for the woods," said Lemon, meaning that Greenberg was unwilling to consider a raise for the pitcher. "He sent me the same contract for the same money, $50,000, I made the year before. He wouldn't talk to me about a raise. He wouldn't get into any deals with me.

"Finally I said to Greenberg, 'If you buy me a new car, I'll sign for what you're offering.' Hell, the car I wanted was only about $1,000, or something, and I knew he could get it from Bob Kennedy," who worked for a Ford agency during the off-season.

Kennedy had been Lemon's teammate with the Indians from 1948 until he was traded in April 1954.

"Greenberg said OK, but I'll be damned, the car he got me was a little old Nash, like they drove the pitchers in from the bullpen. He probably got a real good deal on it.

"I told him, 'Hank, I'll get killed on the damned freeway driving a car like that.' My whole family couldn't even fit

in it. I called Kennedy and told him to bring me the car I wanted, and to take the bill to Greenberg.

"When Kennedy did, Greenberg hit the damned ceiling. He made it sound like I got a Cadillac, or something.

"All I got was a Ford. A Ford convertible, with everything on it," said Lemon, chuckling at the memory.

"But Hank got over it and we were good friends," until Greenberg died in 1986.

Lemon remained out of baseball in 1959, but got bored "selling insurance." He returned to baseball as a coach for the Indians in 1960, but left at mid-season, joined the Philadelphia Phillies in 1961, then went to work in the front office of then-Los Angeles Angels in 1962.

"My boss was Roland Hemond (now senior executive vice president of the Arizona Diamondbacks) and one day he called me into the office," related Lemon. "I thought, 'Uh, oh, what did I do wrong now?'

"Roland asked me if I wanted to manage Hawaii (in the Pacific Coast League). I jumped at it," and so began a new career for Lemon that almost brought him back to Cleveland in 1967.

He managed in the minor leagues for the Angels through 1966, when he was named Manager of the Year at Seattle, and was one of two men under consideration to replace the fired Birdie Tebbetts as manager of the Indians.

Joe Adcock got the job and, later, then General Manager Gabe Paul said that his decision to bypass Lemon was his "biggest mistake" in a baseball career that spanned nearly half a century.

Lemon returned to the Angels as a coach in 1967 and 1968, and in 1969 managed Vancouver in the Pacific Coast League, the top farm club of the Seattle Pilots. He began the 1970 season as a coach for the Royals and, on June 9, replaced Charlie Metro as manager. He later managed the White Sox and Yankees until, in 1982, he decided "the animals are running the zoo."

Obviously not one to mince his words, Lemon recalled an earlier occasion when he spoke his mind, and paid for it, after the Royals blew a game in 1972.

"I was pissed off the way we played," said Lemon. "I said to somebody in the press room, 'When this (season) is over I'm going to some island and open up a bar and the first sonofabitch who comes in and even mentions baseball, I'll throw his ass out,'" said Lemon.

Lemon didn't intend for Ewing Kauffman, then the owner of the Royals, to hear the remark, but he did.

And, with three days left in the season, Kauffman fired Lemon.

So, then, if Lemon had it all to do over again, would he take back the remark that got him fired?

"Hell, no," he replied. "There's nothing I'd do different."

Or say? "No. Nothing."

OK, how would Lemon like to be remembered?

"That I was a fair manager," said Lemon, meaning an unbiased manager, not mediocre.

And how would he like to be remembered as a pitcher?

"That I was awfully brave to go out there with the stuff I had. And lucky."

So were the Indians.

Lucky that, back there in 1946, Lou Boudreau and Mel Harder, decided to give a third baseman-outfielder named Bob Lemon a chance to pitch.

Bob Lemon

CHAPTER TWELVE

Gene Bearden

"I didn't throw many spitballs, just enough to make 'em think about it."

Everybody thought it was a fluttering knuckleball that vaulted Gene Bearden into national prominence in 1948 when he pitched the Indians to the pennant.

Bearden won 20 games that season, the most important of which was an 8-3 victory over the Boston Red Sox—*with one day's rest!*—in an unprecedented one-game playoff for the American League pennant.

And if there'd been a Cy Young Award then, the 28-year-old rookie probably would have been the American League winner by acclamation.

Without a doubt, that all-or-nothing playoff for the pennant was the most significant—and pressure-filled—game the Indians had played in nearly three decades, and Bearden was the toast of Cleveland's baseball fans who had waited since 1920 for their team to return to the World Series.

But now the truth is out.

It also was a spitball that helped Bearden achieve the spectacular success he enjoyed in 1948 when his brief major league career suddenly peaked, but then declined almost as swiftly as had been his meteoric ascension as one of the best pitchers in baseball.

The once-Hollywood handsome left hander, blind in one eye since 1987, the result of a cataract operation "that backfired on me," with his gait slowed because of a 1976 hip replacement, still makes his home in Helena, Arkansas with his wife, Lois, whom he married in 1946.

Bearden is deeply involved with the American Legion amateur baseball program in Arkansas and, perhaps because of it, he didn't immediately, or even *willingly* confess to the secret he'd kept hidden for nearly half a century.

Instead, Bearden played word games when the subject was broached.

"Did I throw spitters?" he asked, rhetorically.

Then, doing his best to keep a straight face, Bearden said, "Why, spitters are illegal . . . and unsanitary. You know that."

When pressed for an answer, Bearden asserted, "I ain't going to tell you," though he eventually did, but still with a degree of circumvention.

"Hell, everybody who ever pitched has tried to throw a spitter," he said.

Does that mean he did, too?

"Well," Bearden said, before a lengthy pause, "yes, me, too," he admitted.

"I didn't throw all that many, and I never got caught. But I guess after nearly 50 years, it's OK to say I did.

"I had a pretty good (spitball), but my knuckleball was my best pitch. I had a decent slider, too, though nobody ever gave me credit for having one, and my fastball wasn't all that bad either.

"But it was my knuckleball that got me where I went. I threw it harder than most guys, probably 80 or 85 (miles an

Gene Bearden

hour). It had a downward rotation that made the ball drop when it got to the plate," said Bearden.

"When I threw a spitter, it would run away from a right-handed batter, something like a screwball, and I also could make it go down, depending on how I threw it."

Bearden said he "loaded up" the ball "with sweat from the back of my neck," and insisted, "It was no big thing. I didn't throw many spitballs, just enough to make 'em think about it, to put it in the batter's mind. That's what pitching is all about."

Apparently Bearden made the batters do a lot of thinking in 1948 as he came from virtually nowhere to claim the third spot in the Indians' rotation, though he didn't get his first start until May 8, the twelfth game of the season.

"I was beginning to think I'd never get to pitch . . . it seems every time Boudreau would schedule me to start, we'd get rained out," said Bearden.

The Indians opened the 1948 season on April 20 with a 4-0 victory over St. Louis at the Stadium, but thereafter, for the next 19 days until Bearden got his chance to show what he could do, they were idled by four rainouts and five open dates.

When he finally did get to pitch, Bearden allowed only three hits in beating the Washington Senators, 6-1, with ninth-inning help from reliever Russ Christopher.

"I'll never forget that game," he said. "Next to the play-off game, it was the most important in my life. It was also my second greatest baseball thrill."

For seven innings, Bearden and the Indians clung to a 1-0 lead against the Senators' Sid Hudson. Then, in the eighth inning, "Larry Doby hit the longest and one of the prettiest homers I have ever seen, up against the megaphone in Griffith Stadium," he said.

The Indians took a 6-0 lead into the bottom of the ninth, when Bearden, apparently too eager to wrap up his first major league victory, lost his control. After retiring the first two batters, he walked the next four and needed help from reliever Russ Christopher to get the last out, and the Indians prevailed, 6-1.

Bearden went on to win three straight and six of seven through June 8, and with a 13-7 record, beat Detroit, 10-1, on September 10, the first of seven consecutive victories through the October 4 playoff game against the Red Sox.

Six of Bearden's 20 victories were shutouts, and he

was the American League's earned run leader with a glittering 2.43 average in 37 games and 229 2/3 innings.

Bearden's outstanding pitching continued in the World Series. He hurled another five hitter (and got two of the Indians' five hits himself) to beat the Boston Braves, 2-0, in the third game. Then he stalked out of the bullpen in relief of Bob Lemon in the eighth inning of the sixth and deciding game to save a 4-3 victory.

Though he was hailed as a hero, Bearden sloughed off the praise, saying that he almost was a "bum" instead.

"I was given credit for putting out a fire (when he replaced Lemon in the eighth inning with the Indians leading, 4-1, and the bases loaded with one out), yet I never was hit so hard in all my pitching career.

"The first batter, (Clint) Conatser, hit a ball more than 400 feet to center. It was a high knuckler that didn't drop. It was almost gone (for a home run) when Thurman Tucker finally caught up with it for the second out. A run scored after the catch, and then Phil Masi blasted the left-field wall with a long double, scoring another run and our lead was cut to one run.

"I thought Boudreau was ready to yank me, instead he came over and said, 'OK, Gene, keep chucking. You'll stop 'em. And if you don't, you'll pitch tomorrow anyway.

"The next batter, Mike McCormick, drove the guts out of the ball. It was hit viciously, right at me. I had no choice. I had to stop it or get killed. I stopped it and the inning was over. But if it had hit me, or gone past me, the runners on second and third would have scored and the Braves would have won.

"Then in the ninth I lost Eddie Stanky on a walk. Sibby Sisti was sent in to sacrifice (but) his attempted bunt popped into the air, a few feet above him and Jim Hegan, who caught it , turned it into the neatest, prettiest double play I ever saw.

"So we won the Series. By my great pitching? Nonsense. I was lucky, pure and simple—those outs were hard smashes. A slight change in the direction of any of them, and a seventh game would have been necessary.

"Was I a hero? Well, they said I was. But I know I was almost a bum."

Making Bearden's ascension to prominence even more noteworthy is the fact that he wasn't Bill Veeck's first choice—Spec Shea was— when the Indians acquired him in a five-player trade with the New York Yankees on December 6, 1946.

Gene Bearden (right) hugs his battery mate, Jim Hegan, in the Indians' dressing room after the rookie lefthander set the Boston Braves down, 2-0, with five hits and gave the Cleveland club a 2-1 lead in the World Series.

In his 1962 autobiography, *Veeck As In Wreck,* the man who owned the Indians from 1946-49 called Bearden the "wild card" in the deal with the Yankees that also brought pitcher Al Gettel and outfielder Hal Peck to Cleveland, for second baseman Ray Mack and catcher Sherman Lollar.

"I'm not going to say that I thought Bearden was going to be anything special (but) he was the biggest surprise I've ever had in baseball," said Veeck, whose bid for Shea was rejected by Larry MacPhail, then general manager of the Yankees.

Shea went on to become a very effective pitcher for the Yankees and Washington from 1947-55, but there's little doubt that, without Bearden in 1948, the Indians would have failed for a 28th consecutive year to win the third pennant in franchise history.

As recounted by Veeck, he accepted Bearden in place of Shea upon the advice of Casey Stengel, then manager of the Yankees' Oakland farm club in the (Class AAA) Pacific Coast League.

Bearden had gone 15-4 for Oakland in 1946 and Veeck said he'd been told by Stengel, "If MacPhail is crazy enough to give (Bearden) up, grab him."

It also was Stengel who—again as reported by Veeck—in effect caused Bearden's rapid decline as one of baseball's best pitchers.

After being elected the Indians' "Man of the Year" by Cleveland's baseball writers in the wake of his remarkable performance in 1948, Bearden won only eight of sixteen decisions in 1949.

When his record fell to 1-3 in 14 games in 1950, the Indians, then under the command of Hank Greenberg, Bearden was sold on August 2 to Washington for the then-$10,000 waiver price.

And three years later Bearden was back in the minor leagues, never again to regain the brilliant major league stature he'd once known.

In those five seasons from 1949 through 1953 he pitched for Detroit, the St. Louis Browns and Chicago White Sox, in addition to the Indians and Senators, winning a total of 25 games and losing 31. It gave him an overall major league record of 45-38, with a 3.96 earned run average in 193 games in six-plus seasons.

Though it is adamantly denied by Bearden, the popular theory regarding his downfall as expounded by Veeck in his book follows:

"I wonder if anybody has ever made the connection between Gene's quick decline in 1949 and the fact that Casey Stengel, his old manager at Oakland came up to manage the Yankees that same year.

"Casey knew something about Gene—or at least suspected something—that he had been warming over in the back of that craggy mind of his. Bearden was a knuckleball pitcher, the only pitch he needed when he was right. Most knuckleballers, to be effective, have to keep the ball low. Gene's knuckleball was especially effective because it broke down very sharply, which made it impossible to hit for any distance.

"From watching him as often as he had, Casey had the distinct impression that Gene's knuckler usually dipped below the strike zone after it broke, which meant that Gene was totally dependent upon getting the batter to swing. He instructed Yankee hitters to lay off Bearden's knuckleball until there were two strikes against them.

"He was right. Bearden would fall behind the hitter and have to come in with his very ordinary fastball or curve or, even worse, start his knuckler up high. That kind of information gets around the league with the speed of light, and Bearden was through."

To which Bearden responded, somewhat testily: "I've heard that story a thousand times and it's not true. It's baloney. I'm not one to make alibis, and I'm not making one now. But the truth is, I got hurt in spring training (in 1949), and it affected me for a long time.

"I pulled a hamstring in my right leg real bad and got all messed up. Anybody who's ever pulled a hamstring knows what I'm saying. I didn't pitch for a couple of weeks, and when I tried to come back I couldn't stride right.

"My leg was a little better by the time the season started so I pitched and won three games. Then I pulled (the hamstring) again. I still pitched, but I couldn't get back in the groove I'd been in, and I never did. Fact is, sometimes I still have trouble with that leg, even after all those years."

Then Bearden conceded, "In a way, there might have been some truth to what Casey was supposed to have said. When you don't stride right, and I couldn't because of my leg, your release point is different. It's what caused me to walk more batters in 1949 (an average of 6.5 a game), than

I did in 1948 (an average of 4.1 a game). But batters laying off my knuckleball had nothing to do with it.

"I don't like to make excuses, and I'm not making one now," Bearden said again. "What happened to me was just one of those things that happens in baseball that can't be explained."

Bearden went from the Senators to the Tigers in April 1951, to the Browns in 1952, and to the White Sox in 1953, after which he was let go and returned to the Pacific Coast League.

Bearden said he had "a couple of big seasons" in the P.C.L., but nobody from the major leagues called to offer him a job.

"I went something like 12-6 for Seattle (in 1954), then the next two years (1955 and 1956) I think I was 17-3 or 17-4, and 15-5 for San Francisco, and I know I had a winning record, I won more than I lost as a pitching coach at Sacramento (in 1957 and 1958), but I guess everybody in the big leagues thought I was too old, so I just packed it in and came home.

"Baseball is a business, you know, and if you're in it long enough, you learn to take the ups with the downs."

And, to paraphrase Bearden, also the "downs"—of which he subsequently had many—with the "ups."

The Indians had plenty of both ups and downs in 1948, and Bearden's memories of that dramatic season are vivid and mostly pleasant.

"We had a great bunch of guys," he said. "We knew we had a good team, but I don't think anybody was sure we could win (the pennant) until that day in August, when Lou (Boudreau) pinch hit against the Yankees."

That was August 8 and Boudreau, who wasn't in the lineup for a doubleheader against New York that day because of an assortment of injuries, limped to the plate to bat for Thurman Tucker. The bases were loaded with two out in the seventh inning and the Indians trailing, 6-4, against the Yankees' ace reliever, Joe Page.

Boudreau singled for two runs, tying the score, and the Indians went on to sweep the doubleheader, 8-6 and 2-1.

"After that it was, if we lost, forget it, we'd get 'em tomorrow— and most of the time we did," said Bearden. And most of the time he was a key factor, winning eleven of his last 15 decisions down the stretch.

"We knew how to play the game, and we played it together, we were close, not like today. There doesn't seem to be any camaraderie in baseball. Back in my day you'd see eight, ten, twelve guys going out together to eat and talk baseball.

"But it doesn't seem to be like that today. It looks like everybody is playing for himself, probably because there's so much money out there.

"Everybody has an agent, everybody walks around with a brief case, and everybody reads the *Wall Street Journal* and the stock market, instead of *The Sporting News*, like our guys did.

"If the guys I'm seeing on television are worth the money they're getting, players like Ted Williams and Joe DiMaggio and Bob Feller, all the real good ones of my day, would own the ball clubs if they were playing now."

After that 1948 season, Bearden might have owned at least part of the Indians. Instead, he was paid $36,000, the most he ever made in the major leagues in one year.

"I'm for guys making as much money as they can. But the way things are going, it's getting out of hand, and that's a crying shame. Some guys in the game today, all they do is sit on the bench and eat sunflower seeds, get hundreds of thousand dollars a year and think they deserve more money.

"And if you're a pitcher, you can't pitch inside or the batters will come out after you."

Did they in Bearden's day? "You've got that right, but they never got far because Mr. Hegan (Indians catcher Jim Hegan) would stop them before they got halfway."

One who tried was Dave Philley, an outfielder who played for the White Sox in 1948, and became a member of the Indians in 1954.

"Mr. Philley didn't like it that I was pitching him tight and started out (to the mound), but didn't make it," said Bearden, chuckling. "Mr. Hegan made sure of that."

Bearden had pitched Philley "tight"—or as he subsequently admitted, even tighter—to "protect" Larry Doby who,

Gene Bearden (left) rejoices with Lou Boudreau (center) and Ken Keltner after the Indians beat the Boston Red Sox, 8-3, in the one-game playoff for the 1948 American League pennant. Bearden pitched a five-hitter, Boudreau cracked four hits, including two home runs, in four trips to the plate, and Keltner smashed a three-run homer.

as the American League's first black player in 1947, was the target of much verbal abuse and taunting by opposing players.

"I had thrown the ball tighter than tight to Mr. Philley, actually behind him, and I guarantee it wasn't a knuckleball either," said Bearden, chuckling again. "That's the way we protected Larry against the guys who gave him a bad time. They usually got the message. If they didn't the first time, we kept telling them."

Obviously, Philley was one of the players Bearden thought was too abusive toward Doby.

"You've got that right again," he said. "There were a couple who were pretty bad in St. Louis, too." Who? "(Bob)

Gene Bearden's pitching form was photographed in this sequence of pictures during the Indians' 8-3 victory over the Boston Red Sox in the playoff for the 1948 American League pennant.

Dillinger and (Al) Zarilla. But we handled them in our own way. We threw behind them, sometimes even between their legs."

As for Satchel Paige, who joined the Indians in July of 1948, Bearden said, "Ol' Satch was a damn good pitcher, don't believe anybody who said he wasn't. A lot of guys thought Veeck signed Satch as a gimmick, just to sell tickets, but he did a helluva good job for us.

"People say we couldn't have won without me, or without Lemon or (Bob) Feller or Boudreau, but they could say the same thing about Ol' Satch. And he also was good for Doby."

Certainly, the highlight of Bearden's season was his victory over the Red Sox in the playoff game that gave the Indians the pennant, after which he was carried off the field by his joyous teammates.

Though he'd pitched two days earlier, shutting out the Tigers, 8-0, on October 2 to clinch at least a tie for the pennant, Bearden was Boudreau's choice to face the powerful Red Sox in Fenway Park, a notoriously difficult place for southpaws.

But, according to Bearden, "It wasn't anything special. Hell, I was in the bullpen in case they needed me the day after I beat the Tigers," when Feller lost to Hal Newhouser, and the Red Sox were beating the Yankees to forge the tie and force the playoff.

"I figured it would be Lemon who'd start in Boston, or maybe Feller. He'd be ready. He had only pitched three innings, and (Feller) handcuffed the Red Sox last time he faced them. I'd been throwing in the bullpen the last few innings of the game against the Tigers until the batboy came out and said, 'Lou wants you to go into the clubhouse right away.'

"I was there when everybody filed in . . . nobody was happy and they showed it, though Boudreau was very calm. He ordered the clubhouse door barred and told the policeman to stand outside and, under no circumstances, allow anyone in.

"Then he told us that he thought I should pitch (against the Red Sox) and if I had anything to say, that I should say it then.

"I said, 'OK.' That was it."

As for Johnny Berardino's reported argument with Boudreau against starting a left hander in Fenway Park, Bearden said, "That didn't bother me. (Berardino) just wanted Lou to look up our (starting pitchers) records in games in Boston that year."

They showed that Feller, Lemon and Bearden all were 1-1 in Fenway Park, Ed Klieman had won two games in relief (of Don Black and Gettel), Christopher, was 0-1 (in a game started by Paige), and spot starters Sam Zoldak and Steve Gromek both were 0-1.

Bearden's earlier victory over the Red Sox in Fenway Park was a 2-0 shutout on June 8 and, as he said, "Any time you pitch a shutout in that park you ought to get the Statue of Liberty (as a reward)."

Was he nervous, with so much at stake in the playoff game?

"Hell, no," said Bearden. "It didn't bother me. How could any of us be nervous after going through a season like we did? Besides, we probably were all too tired to be nervous. But we also were mad because we had lost to the Tigers.

"I was more nervous the first game I started (against Washington on May 8). I had waited so long to pitch. We kept getting rained out and I kept getting pushed back."

But if Bearden and his teammates weren't nervous before the Indians played the Red Sox for the pennant, that apparently was more than could be said about Veeck and his right-hand man, Vice President Hank Greenberg.

"When I went out to warm up, Boudreau was at the corner of the dugout arguing with Veeck and Greenberg," said Bearden. "They were raising hell with Lou because he was going to play (Allie) Clark at first base. I don't think they were mad because I was pitching; they just wanted (Eddie) Robinson to play first base.

"Finally I heard Lou say, '(Clark) is going to play first base . . . you can fire me if you want, but it will have to be after the game,' and that's the way it was left."

And before Bearden made his first pitch, Clark approached him in the dugout. "It's something else I'll never forget," said the old pitcher, chuckling.

"Allie said to me, 'Don't you dare throw over here and try to pick somebody off first base. Remember, I never played here before.'"

The game became anti-climactic in the fourth inning when the Indians broke a 1-1 tie with four runs, three of them coming on a homer by Bearden's roommate, Ken Keltner. "I knew then we'd win," said Bearden. "It gave everybody a lift." Then Boudreau hit his second homer of the game in the fifth, increasing the Indians' lead to 6-1.

The Red Sox retaliated in the sixth with Bobby Doerr's two-run homer, but Bearden never lost his cool.

"I had tunnel vision . . . I didn't see anybody that day but Jim (Hegan)," said Bearden.

Single runs by the Indians in the eighth and ninth made it seem easy as Bearden blanked the Red Sox the final three innings.

Birdie Tebbetts, who would become manager of the Indians in 1963, made the last out of the game on a grounder to Keltner, after Bearden himself threw out Doerr, Billy Hitchcock prolonged the suspense by coaxing a walk and Billy Goodman struck out.

Bearden said "about 85 percent" of his pitches in that game were knuckleballs.

How many spitters?

"I ain't saying . . . I've probably already said too much," Bearden replied, good naturedly.

After the game, of course, nobody got fired. Everybody celebrated, including Veeck and Greenberg, both of whom congratulated Boudreau.

Bearden said he had great respect for Boudreau. "He was fair . . . he was right out front with everybody. You always knew where you stood with him.

"Everybody used to say that Lou was a 'hunch manager,' and maybe they were right. That was the reason he used Clark instead of Robinson at first base, maybe even why he started me instead of Lemon or somebody else.

"But playing his hunches must have been OK, at least in 1948, because we sure won a lot of games."

While Bearden also made clear his respect for Veeck— "I was crazy about Bill," he said—he did not share the same opinion of Greenberg.

"I didn't like Greenberg worth a damn because of the way he treated everybody, not just me," said Bearden. "He thought he was better than everybody else."

When asked if he'd ever argued with Greenberg, Bearden replied, "I don't argue with people, I just tell them what I think."

So, then, did Bearden ever tell Greenberg what he thought?

"Yes. It was sometime in 1949 or 1950, after Veeck had left (sold the Indians). I told Greenberg that everybody couldn't be a Hall of Famer like he was, that he ought to learn how to treat people. That was it. Just a clash of personalities, between him and me."

It's only *partially* accurate to call that crucial victory over the Red Sox the "highlight" of Bearden's career, he said.

"Because of the importance of the game, how much it meant, it's something I'll always remember, sure."

Gene Bearden is shown autographing the cast on the broken ankle of Boston Braves outfielder Jeff Heath after Bearden beat the Boston Red Sox in the playoff for the 1948 American League pennant. Bearden's teammate, Johnny Berardino, is at the right in the photograph.

"Winning the pennant was the culmination of a whole lot of hard work and a lot of dreams for all of us. When you work all your life toward a goal, and then you reach it, you figure, 'This is what I set out to do when I was just a kid,' which I did, when I was 12 years old.

"I used to listen to the St. Louis Cardinals on the radio down here (in Lexa, Arkansas). That's when they had Pepper Martin, who was my favorite player, and Dizzy and Daffy Dean . . . when they were the old 'Gashouse Gang.'

"I used to tell myself, that's what I'm going to do when I grow up, play in the big leagues, play in the World Series, and I was one of the fortunate few. I got to know what it was like to be on top," if only for a little while.

But there also were two other "big thrills" that Bearden said he'll always cherish.

One of them was, "Just putting on a major league uniform for the first time (in 1947), knowing that I was one of 25 guys on one of only sixteen teams . . . that was really something."

Another was winning that first game in Washington.

It was a gem, as reported by Harry Jones in the May 9, 1948 editions of the *Cleveland Plain Dealer:*

"Gene Bearden, a gangling southpaw with a devastating knuckler, pitched a truly remarkable game in his first start as a major leaguer, allowing but three scratch hits and losing a shutout only by one out in the ninth inning as the Indians defeated Washington, 6-1."

Something else that makes that game so memorable to Bearden was that Doby hit a two-run homer that Bearden said he can still see flying out of Washington's old Griffith Stadium.

"There's always all that talk about how far (Mickey) Mantle used to hit them, but the home run that Doby hit over the center-field fence that day had to go 550 feet," said Bearden. "I don't know where it landed, but it had to be a 20-dollar ride in a cab."

It all began for Bearden as a first baseman at Moultrie, Georgia in the (Class D) Georgia-Florida League in 1939 because, as he said, "I could always hit." The Yankees gave him a $250 bonus to sign.

"We had a bunch of rainouts early in the season and needed an extra pitcher," said Bearden. "The manager wanted to know if anybody could pitch, and I told him I'd try. The first ball I threw hit the batter right on the neck. But then I was OK, and after that I was a pitcher.

"I used to mess around with a knuckleball when I was a kid, and at first (at Moultrie) I used it as a change up, an off-speed pitch. But then I got to really working with it and it turned out to be real good for me."

Bearden spent the next four seasons in the minor leagues, and joined the Navy in 1943 during World War II, which almost ended his baseball career.

In July of 1943, Bearden was a machinist's mate aboard the ill-fated cruiser, U.S.S. Helena, which was sunk in the South Pacific by a Japanese destroyer.

Bearden was in the ship's engine room when the ship was struck by a torpedo and suffered a severe knee injury and a month later underwent extensive surgery in a naval hospital in Jacksonville, Florida. He tried to keep the injury a secret, even after his knee was healed, fearing it would jeopardize his baseball career.

"I didn't want anybody to get the idea that I wasn't strong enough to pitch," he said.

"'I didn't know what to do. I had learned a trade in the Navy, but baseball was the only thing I had known. Finally, I ran across a doctor who said he might be able to patch me up well enough, which he did. He was quite a guy. He worked with me four months," Bearden was quoted in an article in the *Cleveland Plain Dealer* on May 9, 1948, the day after he won his first major league game.

When asked in this interview about his wartime injuries, Bearden shrugged and said, "Our ship was sunk. I was injured, but not enough to kill me. I was lucky, but anybody who got home was lucky.

"If I had my way about it, nothing more would ever be written about my experiences in the Navy. I was just another sailor, luckier than many, because I met up with a doctor who, to me, was the best orthopedic surgeon in the business. His name was Dr. Weiland. I don't remember his first name."

Two years after the U.S.S. Helena was sunk, Bearden was back on the mound in 1945 for the Binghamton (New York) Yankees of the (Class A) Eastern League where his 15-5 record earned a promotion to Oakland. Under Stengel in 1946, he was 15-4.

"I learned more from Casey than anybody in baseball," said Bearden. "He was like a second father to me. Everybody thought he was a clown, but the man knew baseball. I was sorry to leave him when I was traded, but I knew the

Yankees had a couple of left-handers (pitchers) and the Indians didn't have any, so I figured I'd get a good chance in Cleveland."

But he didn't in 1947. "They (the Indians) had so many pitchers in camp that spring, I don't know how many. They were looking at everybody, and in order to be able to pitch good, you've got to pitch a lot," which Bearden didn't.

He opened the season in Cleveland but didn't get into a game for 25 days. Finally, on May 10, he made a brief appearance in relief against St. Louis, facing four batters, only one of which Bearden retired. He gave up two hits and a walk for an 81.00 ERA.

Five days later, on the May 15 roster cut down date, Bearden was demoted to Baltimore, then the Indians' top farm club in the (Class AAA) International League.

But not without a fight.

As Bearden was quoted in the *Cleveland News* on January 31, 1949:

"I was told to report to Baltimore on option. Spud Goldstein, the traveling secretary, told me the news.

"'I'm not going,' I said. Spud seemed shocked. 'You can say you don't want to go, but don't say you're not going.'

"'I'm not going,' I repeated. 'Then you'd better see Boudreau,' said Spud.

"I went to Lou's room. (Coach) Oscar Melillo was showing him a card trick. Lou told me to sit down. Finally he asked, 'What's on your mind?'

"'Spud tells me I'm going to Baltimore.' Lou said, 'That's right. We've got to cut the squad now, but if you have the stuff I think you have, you'll be back with us very soon.'

"I said, 'I'm not going.' He said, 'What do you mean, you're not going?'

"I said I wasn't . . . and when Lou saw he couldn't persuade me, he said, 'You'd better go back to Cleveland and see Bill Veeck. This is a problem for him,'" which Bearden did.

"I told Bill I didn't want to play in the International League, I wanted to go back to Casey (Stengel) on the Coast (P.C.L.) which then was the next thing to the big leagues.

"Bill was very understanding. He told me to go to Baltimore and talk to the manager, Tommy Thomas," which Bearden did, but to no avail.

He spent the next eleven days in Baltimore, pitching three games, taking the loss in two of them, and staged another rebellion. "I told them if they didn't send me to Oakland, I was going home," which was then in Long Beach, California.

"Three days later I was pitching again for Casey who, I guess, called Veeck and got me back. I never did know how. Maybe (Oakland) made a deal with Baltimore, or whatever. It cost me a $500 fine, because I had jumped the Baltimore club, but I didn't care.

"I just wanted to pitch, and as long as I wasn't going to pitch in Cleveland, I wanted to pitch for Casey," said Bearden.

It proved to be the turning point in Bearden's career.

He won 15 games in a little more than three months, finishing the season with a 16-7 record. That winter Bearden pitched—and again pitched very well—for Culiacan in the Mexican League, and was in excellent shape when he reported to the Indians the following spring.

The rest is history.

Bearden became the brightest of stars in the baseball galaxy, although—unfortunately for him and the Indians—it was for only one brief season.

"Ah, but what a wonderful season it was," said Bearden, to which his teammates and thousands of Indians fans could—and undoubtedly would—add a fervent, passionate "amen."

Before our visit ended, I opened, with some reservation, one last subject for Bearden's comment: movie actress Shelley Winters. It was back in 1950, during spring training in Tucson, Arizona, that Bearden was rumored to be involved with the then-slim, svelte, blond Ms. Winters, who was in Tucson filming the movie, "Winchester 73."

According to Louella Parsons, a syndicated gossip columnist at the time, Ms. Winters took a liking to Bearden, and that the two had begun a relationship. It was strongly denied by Bearden in a first-person article under his byline in the March 2, 1950 edition of the *Cleveland News*.

Bearden said, "I may be crazy, but any person who has seen and knows (my wife) Lois, and can imagine me giving her up for anyone, is even crazier. I can only say what I've said repeatedly since the story was printed: There's absolutely nothing to it. My one ambition is to stop it as quickly and definitely as possible.

"But I'm terribly upset, because when I try to explain the situation to some people, they just laugh. I don't know whether they think I'm lying, or whether they think it's perfectly all right for a married man to go around the country making love to other women.

"I'm especially anxious for the people in Cleveland to know the truth. That's why I jumped at the opportunity . . . to speak out today.

Gene Bearden

Bearden acknowledged in the article that he had met the movie star, and that he had dinner with her while emphasizing that "several other people" were there, and that, "I wasn't alone with her for a minute. I never have been alone with her."

Then, he said, "I did make one mistake, I guess. A couple of photographers from Cleveland arrived in advance of the main party and asked me out to dinner. I called Miss Winters and invited her to join us. We ate together—and that was that. At no time was I alone with the girl," he said again.

But still, even nearly a half century later, the report persists, to the great consternation of Bearden.

When pointedly asked about his alleged affair with the movie star, Bearden said, "Nothing to it . . .nothing to it."

Gene and Lois Bearden, who celebrated their golden wedding anniversary in 1996, raised three children, a daughter, Gene (who spells her name the same as her father does) born in 1950, and sons Gary, who came along in 1948, and in 1949, Shea, which was Lois's maiden name.

Upon his return from professional baseball, Bearden worked as an on-air personality and sports director for Helena radio station KFFA for four years, and later was part owner of an automobile agency until 1993 when he invested in, and now manages a mini-storage facility.

Though his activities now are limited, Bearden's health is "pretty good for an old guy," which obviously is true.

As general manager, manager and coach of two American Legion teams, both called the "Helena Redbirds, Post 41," for more than 30 years, Bearden works with boys aged 15-16 and 17-18. At the time of our interview he was preparing for postseason tournaments, hoping his teams would win a third Arkansas state championship and advance to national competition.

As it turned out, both reached the regional finals before they were eliminated.

"It's very time consuming, but also very satisfying," he said of his volunteer work. "It keeps the kids busy and out of trouble. I try to teach them responsibility and teamwork, to make them feel good about themselves.

"And it's worth it to me because I grew up playing Legion ball, which helped me get to the top, for a little while, anyway," added Bearden, somewhat ruefully.

How time consuming? "You figure it out," he replied. "Our teams start with tryouts as soon as the weather breaks in the spring, we practice or play seven days a week, and each of the teams play about 70 games a year.

"We have clinics, teach the kids fundamentals . . . but the big thing is that we keep them out of trouble.

"The way I look at it, for all of the stuff I've learned over the years, this is my way of giving some of it back. These are all poor kids and we're in a very depressed area."

Helena is located in Phillips County, about 110 miles from Little Rock. "We're pretty low on the totem pole," he said. "Farming is the big thing and, you know, farming doesn't pay much. We've got two or three chemical plants, but that's about the only industries that we have."

Not only is it time consuming for Bearden, it's also expensive—it costs him "about $3,000 to $4,000 a year" as a partial sponsor of his teams.

"I scrounge around and dig up as much equipment as I can, the (American Legion) post donates a little bit, Al Rosen used to send me a lot of stuff when he was still in baseball (with Houston and San Francisco) before he retired in 1993, and I reach into my pockets a lot."

Then, before our visit ended, I asked Bearden again if he can still throw the knuckleball that made him famous.

"No, sir. Those days are gone, long gone," he said.

And what about the spitball?

"I keep telling you, spitters are illegal . . . unsanitary," and Bearden chuckled again.

CHAPTER THIRTEEN

Al Rosen

"We were like the Three Musketeers, you know, one for all and all for one."

Al Rosen vividly remembers the time he was standing under a shower in the Indians locker room and was startled to hear Walt Judnich, then one of the team's veteran outfielders, shout, "We are a team of destiny! A team of destiny!"

The date was September 19, 1948, and the Indians had just swept a doubleheader from the Philadelphia Athletics in front of 75,382 fans in the Stadium. It boosted them to within a half-game of the first place Boston Red Sox with ten games remaining.

No wonder Judnich was pumped.

Only 12 days earlier, after splitting a doubleheader with the Chicago White Sox on Labor Day, the Indians were third, 4 1/2 games behind the Red Sox, and the experts were saying a miracle was necessary for them to get back in the race.

By a miracle or whatever, the Indians won 11 of their next 13 games, convincing virtually everyone that Judnich was right, that they were indeed "a team of destiny."

"I was startled when Judnich yelled, but I can't say I was surprised. I'd seen enough of those guys to know. They were unbelievable," said Rosen. "That team had an aura about it. It was really something."

Rosen referred to the 1948 Indians in the third person because, at the time, he was a rookie, having joined them only three weeks earlier, in the wake of what he called "a monster season" in the minors.

Rosen hit .327 with 25 homers and drove in 110 runs for Kansas City, then in the (Class AAA) American Association, missing the batting championship by two percentage points, and was voted "Rookie of the Year."

On August 23, the last day of the season, Rosen got hurt sliding into second base. The Indians summoned him to Cleveland for an examination. "They also put me on the 25-man roster, which was a terrific thing for me," he said. "It made me eligible for the World Series, if the Indians got that far."

They did, as Judnich believed they would, catching the Red Sox on September 22, overtaking them four days later, though they faltered on October 3, then won the pennant with an 8-3 victory in a one-game playoff in Boston on October 4.

Rosen, who would become a longtime star for the Indians, batted only five times in five games during the final month of 1948, and went to the plate just once as a pinch hitter against the Boston Braves in the World Series.

"It was in the fifth game (an 11-5 loss) and my claim to fame, my *only* claim to fame in that World Series, was that I was the only pinch hitter out of four or five (actually three) who hit the ball. I popped out, but the others struck out," said Rosen.

Now retired after ten years as a major league player and executive with the New York Yankees, Houston Astros

Al Rosen is congratulated by Larry Doby after a home run in 1949.

and San Francisco Giants, Rosen lives in a posh gated community in fashionable Rancho Mirage, California with his second wife, Rita.

They've been married 26 years and have five children—Al's three sons: Rob, an attorney, Jimmy, also an attorney and talent agent, and Andy, a musician, and Rita's daughter Gail, a communications specialist, and son David, who is the umpires' room attendant at Candlestick Park in San Francisco—and two grandchildren.

Rosen's first wife, Terry, whom he married in 1952, took her own life in 1971. "She had been sick for many years. She was living in Philadelphia and in treatment there, and finally decided she couldn't handle it anymore," said Rosen without further elaboration.

Of all the surviving members of the World Championship Indians team of half-a-century ago, Rosen probably is in the best physical—and financial—condition. He said he walks 2 1/2 miles every morning and swims in his backyard pool, then plays golf "every day of the week."

In January 1980, Rosen underwent coronary bypass surgery and, since then, "I've changed my lifestyle. Instead of steak and potatoes, I now eat a lot of fish and vegetables," he said.

"I was very lucky. I was a runner in those days and I was having a lot of trouble with my left shoulder. I didn't run for two or three weeks and when I started again and still had the pain, I went to the doctor. He thought it might have been a form of tendinitis and injected me.

"But it didn't get any better and, when I still didn't have any relief, the doctor suggested I go to a cardiologist, which I did. I had an angiogram, which showed a blockage, that (the left anterior descending coronary artery) was about 99% blocked.

"The doctor wanted to do surgery right away and, when I asked the alternative to surgery, he said, 'One morning the newspaper will say that Al Rosen, while having dinner with friends last night, dropped over dead from a heart attack.' He pointed out it was not something from which you have a series of heart attacks. When you have a heart attack from the kind of blockage I had, you die.

"So I had the operation. Right away. I was lucky," he said again.

Despite his limited time with the Indians in 1948, Rosen was around the "team of destiny" long enough to regard it as one of the best of all time.

He was, however, diplomatically evasive when asked to compare it with the 1954 Indians, of which Rosen was the physical and emotional leader.

In 1954 the Indians set an American League record with 111 victories, but were ingloriously swept in the World Series by the then-New York Giants.

"I think we had a better pitching staff (in 1954), maybe the best in the history of baseball, and the manager (Al Lopez) was the best I've ever known. But that 1948 team had the greatest *esprit de corps* of any club ever, which was one of its strengths. Those guys would not be denied. They never quit. They never gave up," said Rosen.

Those Indians of 1948 also were a hard-living, fun-loving group, which Rosen also readily acknowledged, though not unkindly.

"Believe it or not, just about everybody was half in the bag on the train going to Boston the night before the playoff game the next afternoon," said Rosen.

It was, then, logical to ask what the Indians were celebrating.

They'd just lost the regular-season finale, 7-1, blowing a golden opportunity to win the pennant, dropping them into a tie with the Red Sox and forcing an all-or-nothing playoff.

"Those guys were like the Three Musketeers, you know, one for all and all for one, except there were more than three, there were a lot of them," Rosen said of his 1948 teammates.

"Going to Boston on the train that night, each table in the dining car had champagne and three or four bottles of booze on it. The whole thing was amazing. It was like everybody *knew* we were going to win. No sweat. I'd never seen anything like it.

"After I went to bed, Gene Bearden woke me up about one o'clock and asked me, 'Did you ever play first base?' I said, 'No', and he said, 'Well, you're playing first base tomorrow.' I got cold chills. I couldn't sleep the rest of the night.

"The next morning, when our train arrived in Boston and we got to the (Kenmore) hotel, Boonie (Ray Boone, another rookie on the team) and I went right away to Fenway Park. I had to know if Bearden was right."

He wasn't. Allie Clark, an outfielder, would play first base.

"I wanted to play, but not first base, and, to tell you the truth, I was relieved," said Rosen when Clark's name, not his, appeared on the lineup card.

"I guess (Manager Lou) Boudreau considered me, but probably thought that Allie, who'd been with the team all year, would perform better under pressure than some bush-ass rookie like me."

Then—to offer additional insight into the personality of the "team of destiny"—after the Indians beat the Red Sox, 8-3, they staged an even wilder celebration. This despite the fact that two days later they would open the World Series against the Braves, also in Boston.

It was during the team party that Bob Lemon and Joe Tipton got into a fight, and later that night Joe Gordon squared off against an obnoxious fan.

"Joe and I were in the hotel bar and a guy came up and hit me on the shoulder," said Rosen. "He said, 'Al Rosen, what the hell are you doing here?'

"I had no idea who he was and, before I could react, Gordon asked the guy, 'Hey, are we bothering you?' The guy said, 'No, you're not bothering me,' and Gordon said, 'Well, you're bothering the hell out of me,' and decked him. Knocked him right over a table.

"Joe shouldn't have done it, and if somebody did something like that today, he'd probably be sued. But that's the way those guys were . . . like I said, like the Three Musketeers, one for all and all for one."

As for the Tipton-Lemon bout, Rosen said, "I don't know why they got into it, except that Tipton didn't like (Ken) Keltner, who was Lemon's friend. I guess Tipton said something to Lemon about Keltner and Lemon got mad. But it was no big thing. Tipton got into a lot of fights. He was always like that."

Rosen had his problems with Keltner, too, for one simple reason.

Keltner, who broke in with the Indians in 1938 and, in 1948, at the age of 32 knew he was nearing the end of his career, understandably regarded Rosen, then 23, as a threat to take his job.

According to Rosen, Keltner made known his feelings during a game against Washington.

"Benny—Benny Beltner, as everybody called Keltner—was hitting in tough luck, you know, hitting the ball hard but right at somebody," Rosen recalled the incident. "This particular night he hit a sinking liner to left center and the Senators center fielder, Gil Coan, raced over and made a great catch.

"When Keltner got back to the dugout everybody was saying, 'Tough luck, Benny,' so I did, too. He looked at me, nobody else, and said in a real loud voice, 'Tough luck, my ass, you bush bastard.'

"I never backed up to anybody, but I decided then and there that this was no way for me to get started with those guys. I wasn't going to take any of Keltner's crap, but I also knew it was up to me to stay out of his way, which I did."

On another occasion, later in his career, Rosen made crystal clear his unwillingness to "back up" to anybody. It took place in Yankee Stadium, against the team the Indians in Rosen's era always seemed to be battling for the pennant.

According to Rosen, a key member of the Indians claimed he couldn't play that night, complaining of a sore muscle in his leg as he lay on the trainer's table. Rosen stalked into the room and, with sarcasm dripping from his voice, said, "In big games, big men play."

The player on the table cursed at Rosen, who responded, "Look at (Mickey) Mantle. He plays every day on a worse leg than yours."

More profanity between the two men ensued and, with that, Rosen said, "I've been kidding you, and it's obvious that you're not kidding me. I think it's best that you not say anything more to me, and I won't say anything more to you."

As Rosen turned to leave the trainer's room, he said the other player called him a "yellow, no good son of a bitch."

Rosen wheeled around and threw a punch. And another. So did his teammate. It took trainer Wally Bock and a couple of players to pull them apart.

"Nobody calls me yellow," Rosen said of the incident. How about "no good son of a bitch"?

"Well," he said, "a lot of guys called me that . . . but don't ever call me yellow."

Rosen started the 1949 season with the Indians as an extra man, but played in only 23 games, 13 as a pinch hitter, going only 7-for-44. On July 3 he was optioned back to the minors, this time to San Diego, then in the (Class AAA) Pacific Coast League, where he batted .319 in 83 games, while Keltner was completing his career with the Indians.

Keltner's average fell to a low of .232 while sharing third base with several others, including Boudreau, Bob Kennedy and Johnny Berardino, and was released at the end of the season.

Al Rosen

He caught on with the Red Sox in 1950, which is when Rosen returned to the Wigwam again, this time to stay—in a starring role—for the next seven years.

After Rosen hung up his spikes in 1957—prematurely, he admits in retrospect, and with a trace of regret—he remained in Cleveland in the brokerage business with Bache & Co., one of the country's leading investment firms.

He had attended the University of Florida for a year, and then the Navy assigned him to the V-12 program at Miami (Florida) University. After being discharged, and following the 1946 season, Rosen, needing only two semesters, went back to Miami to earn his degree in business.

It was while he worked for Bache that his love of baseball got the best of Rosen again.

"From the time I could walk, baseball was all I ever thought about," he said. "I'm sorry I quit when I did, because I realize I could have played longer."

Rosen's love of the game was the motivation when he, along with then-Clevelander George M. Steinbrenner III, tried

to buy the Indians in 1971. The franchise was owned by Vernon Stouffer and was awash in red ink.

"I was on the Indians board of directors and went to spring training, but my involvement was limited," said Rosen. "George (Steinbrenner), who was not in baseball then, was my friend and always had an abiding interest in sports.

"I got a call one day and was invited to attend a meeting with some prominent Cleveland businessmen, among them Art Modell (who owned the Cleveland Browns in the National Football League), Sheldon Guren (then president of U.S. Realty), Eddie DeBartolo (who owned Thistledown race track and whose son would buy the San Francisco 49ers of the NFL), and others."

Rosen said that Howard Metzenbaum (who would become a U.S. Senator), and Ted Bonda (who would later become owner of the Indians), also were involved.

"It was a very interesting meeting. DeBartolo owned some land (in the southeastern part of Greater Cleveland) that he called the 'Golden Triangle.' He wanted to build a sports complex that would include a new stadium. (DeBartolo) wanted to move his race track there, and Modell also was ready to go there with the Browns.

"The Indians were the missing link. If they were included, along with the Browns, who would have gone, and DeBartolo's race track, this big complex would have been complete.

"George (Steinbrenner) and I lined up some people, he became the leader, the spokesman, and we got into negotiations with Stouffer to buy the Indians' franchise which, we thought, came down to a handshake agreement.

"The price was to be $8.3 million, though the deal also included forgiveness of $300,000 that the Indians had borrowed from the station that televised the team's games, so the bottom line was $8.6 million.

"While we were in Steinbrenner's office waiting to wrap up everything, Marsh Samuel (who then owned a public relations firm) was downstairs with the media to make the official announcement because the word was out that we were buying the club.

"Stouffer finally called from Scottsdale (Arizona) where he had a home. He was three sheets to the wind and told us no deal. We were shocked because we thought we had the club. Then Stouffer sold it to Nick Mileti for $10 million worth of paper, which wasn't worth a nickel."

As a result of the failed deal that aborted DeBartolo's plans for a new sports complex—which would have led to the abandonment of Cleveland Stadium in the mid-1970s and, probably, kept Modell and the Browns in Cleveland—Steinbrenner put together a group that purchased the Yankees in 1973 for $10 million.

Four years later, Rosen joined Steinbrenner as president of the Yankees, a job he held for only about a year and a half.

"I had problems with George, and George had problems with me," was Rosen's explanation for leaving the Yankees.

"My problem was that he was too dictatorial," said Rosen. "He gave me responsibility, but not authority, and probably was the biggest second guesser I ever met in my life. A very difficult man.

"And yet, I could probably call George Steinbrenner right now and say, 'George, I need $100,000,' and he'd probably not say a word and send a guy with the money.

"But working for him, and being his friend are two different things. That's what I told him when I left (resigned) the Yankees in July 1979. I said, 'George, I'd rather be your friend than work for you.'"

It was in 1978, during Rosen's tenure with the Yankees, that they finished in a tie with Boston for the pennant, after Lemon replaced Billy Martin as manager for the final 68 games.

They played the Red Sox in a winner-take-all game on October 2 —ironically, two days shy of the 30th anniversary of the 1948 playoff for the pennant between the Indians and Boston.

Both times the Red Sox won the coin toss for the home field, which reminded Rosen of another Steinbrenner anecdote.

"I was in the American League office and Haywood Sullivan (then general manager of the Red Sox) was on the phone," Rosen related the story. "I told him, 'You call it, Sully,' but he said, 'No, you're right there, Al, you call it because you can see it.'

"I told Sully, 'Actually, I hope you win it because we can beat you up there.' I think our record in Boston that year was 7-0, but we were only 3-4 against the Red Sox at

home, though George, of course, wanted the game in Yankee Stadium.

"We lost the flip and I had to call George and tell him. He asked me, 'What did you call?' I told him, 'Tails,' and he said, 'Dammit! What do you mean you called tails! Don't you know that the probable odds are that heads comes up more often?'

"True story," said Rosen, "and that's George Steinbrenner for you."

As it turned out, New York beat the Red Sox, 5-4. Yankees shortstop Bucky Dent, who hit only four home runs all season until then, popped a fly into the nets atop the "Green Monster" in left field for a three-run homer in the seventh inning, wiping out a 2-0 deficit. Then Reggie Jackson homered in the eighth to account for the winning run.

Though Rosen had no job upon his departure from the Yankees in July 1979, he was hired as general manager of the Astros before the season ended, and remained in that position for six years. Then he joined the Giants as their president and general manager in September 1985.

Under Rosen, the Giants won the National League West Division championship in 1987, and the N.L. pennant in 1989.

Rosen finally—irrevocably, this time—retired from the game he loved since he was old enough to walk, when his friend, Bob Lurie, sold the Giants to Peter Magowan after the 1992 season.

When Rosen, then 17, entered as a "walk on" at Thomasville, North Carolina of the (Class D) North Carolina State League in 1942, he was paid $90 a month. "I didn't care how much I would make, I just wanted to play baseball," he said.

At the time, Rosen was deeply troubled because of his Jewish ancestry, according to comments attributed to him in Hank Greenberg's biography, *The Story Of My Life*, published in 1989:

"I grew up in a neighborhood (in Miami) that was a real melting pot . . . I was the only Jew (and) I had my problems. I can still remember in Miami, no Jews or dogs allowed in apartment buildings. A sign right on the wall."

For a long time Rosen felt he was discriminated against because of his heritage. It was a subject that arose as we discussed his climb through the minors, as well as the problems experienced by teammate Larry Doby, who preceded Rosen with the Indians as the second black player to break major league baseball's color barrier in 1947.

"Larry had it tough, no doubt about it," said Rosen. "I wasn't with the Indians when Doby first came up, but it wasn't much better for him for several years, and I was very much aware of it from my own perception. After all, I was a Jew, and while Hank (Greenberg) had been there (in the major leagues), there weren't too many others.

"But I always felt that, if Larry had a little different personality, if he'd had the same personality that, say, Luke Easter had, there'd be no doubt he'd be in the Hall of Fame. Depending on his mood, Larry could be sullen, arbitrary, or happy, friendly.

"The bottom line is that Larry did a terrific job. He came out of an all-white high school (in Paterson, New Jersey) where he was a star athlete in all sports and didn't really know, he didn't have any way of knowing, what he was going to be up against, which was pretty rough.

"I know I heard racist remarks, probably not as bad as Larry, but they were there for me, too, because I was a Jew."

Rosen caught the Indians' attention early, when he batted .307 at Thomasville. However, before he could hit, throw or catch a baseball in 1943, Uncle Sam beckoned. Rosen entered the Navy, earning a couple of battle stars during World War II.

Discharged with the rank of Lieutenant (junior grade), Rosen, in 1946, returned to baseball, resuming his climb through the minor leagues by hitting .323 at Pittsfield, Massachusetts of the (Class C) Canadian-American League.

It earned him a promotion in 1947 to Oklahoma City of the (Class AA) Texas League where he was even better, batting .349 with 25 homers and 141 RBI, which led to Rosen's first face-to-face meeting with Indians owner Bill Veeck.

"With about three weeks left in the Indians' season (in 1947), they recalled me and said I should join them in New York," said Rosen, though he was puzzled by the route they gave him. "I was instructed to fly into Chicago and meet Veeck at the airport, then go to New York.

"I arrived in Chicago about six in the morning and Veeck took me to breakfast. We talked and then he gave me a check for $1,000. It was the first time in my life I ever had that much money."

Upon joining the Indians for the final three weeks of the season, Rosen went 1-for-9, mostly as a pinch hitter in

seven games, and reported to Tucson, Arizona the following spring with high hopes.

High hopes that soon were dashed.

Despite playing well in spring training, Rosen said he wound up on "loan" to Kansas City. "I was a third baseman and, not only was Keltner still playing well, he also was one of Boudreau's best friends."

As for his relationship with Boudreau, Rosen said, "To this day I don't know that I was ever one of Lou's pin-up boys. I'm just not sure how the chemistry worked between us. He and I never had much to say to each other, and I didn't have the same feeling for Boudreau that I had for Al Lopez."

Being optioned to Kansas City was odd because that farm club in the (Class AAA) American Association then had a working agreement with the Yankees, while the Indians' top minor league team then was Baltimore in the (Class AAA) International League.

"The reason I was sent to Kansas City was that the Indians had made a deal with the Yankees for a pitcher named Charlie Wensloff. Part of it was that I would play for Kansas City that summer. It was pretty obvious that the Yankees wanted a good look at me," said Rosen.

But it also was obvious, based on Veeck's $1,000 gift to Rosen, that the Indians weren't going to let him get away.

Still, being sent to Kansas City bothered Rosen.

"I thought it was a pretty cruel thing to do to a player," he said. "There you are, in an organization where you know the people because you've been with them and played with a lot of the guys, and then they send you somewhere else, really loan you somewhere else."

Apparently, it also bothered Baltimore.

"If you did a little history on that, I think you'd find that Baltimore was very upset that I wasn't going there, that the Indians were sending me to Kansas City."

It ruptured Baltimore's relationship with Cleveland. The next year the Indians made San Diego their top farm club and Baltimore worked with another major league organization.

Rosen swallowed his disappointment and fashioned another big year, which the Indians, including Boudreau, could not ignore—and which got him to Cleveland in time for the stretch run for the pennant and to be eligible for the World Series.

By then, too, Greenberg had become an integral part of the Indians organization, first as a minor stockholder, then as Veeck's right-hand man, and finally, from 1950-57, as general manager.

Despite the fact that Greenberg had been one of Rosen's favorite players—really, one of his *idols* —as the young Jewish boy was growing up in Miami, the two men did not get along well during the years they were together in Cleveland.

In Greenberg's biography, Rosen made clear his great admiration for the Hall of Fame slugger, who died in 1986:

"I was aware of Hank Greenberg from the time I was a boy . . . I had two favorite players, Greenberg and (Lou) Gehrig. Those two I always watched. But Greenberg particularly because he was chasing Babe Ruth's (home run) record in 1938—I was fourteen years old then —and there was a consciousness of his being a Jew."

Rosen also was quoted:

"Greenberg was to Jewish ball players what Jackie Robinson was to blacks. I'm not trying to draw an analogy between the problem the blacks have and the Jews, but there were problems nevertheless. Whenever people don't come to grips with that, there can be a real problem. And Greenberg went through a great deal and he paved the way for people like me."

However, in subsequent articles and in our interview, Rosen admitted they had a serious falling out during Greenberg's eight-year tenure as the Tribe's general manager.

"The most money I ever made as a player was $42,500 in 1954, after my big year," said Rosen, who hit .336 with 43 homers and 145 RBI, missing the Triple Crown by one percentage point, and won the A.L. MVP award.

"Then, that winter Hank cut me $5,000 because I didn't have as good a year as I did in 1953," said Rosen.

His resentment was understandable. It was in 1954 that Rosen, in his words, "was off to another monster season" and, on April 25, was asked by Lopez to move from third base to first.

Al Rosen, a rookie in 1948, won the American League's Most Valuable Player award in 1953.

"Al said they were trying to get a first baseman and, until they did, would I mind moving over? Here was the most valuable player in the league being asked to move to a new position for the good of the ball club," said Rosen.

He did. He played first base for 30 games. It was during that time, in a game against Chicago on May 31, that Rosen broke the index finger on his right hand, though the injury was not initially diagnosed as a fracture.

"I got hurt because I switched from one position to another after I was requested—*requested!* —by the manager to do so, which I agreed to do . . . can you imagine a player doing that today?" he asked rhetorically.

"I played eight games before a doctor even looked at my hand, though it hurt like hell. I soaked it. Every night. But I played. Every game.

"In today's world, the minute a player gets hit, out of the game he comes, the doctors examine him, they take x-rays, and he doesn't play again until he's OK.

"During a trip to Philadelphia (June 5-7) we had an off day and I spent it with a friend. He picked me up and, when he saw my finger, he took me to a hospital. They took x-rays and saw that my finger was fractured.

"I returned to Cleveland and didn't play for a week or so, until one night (June 15, in a game against Washington). I was on the bench and we were losing in the eighth inning. We loaded the bases and needed a pinch hitter. Lopez looked at me. I said, 'Sure, sure,' and I got a hit that won the game.

"The next night, the same thing. Lopez asked me to pinch hit in the seventh inning (of a tie game against the Senators) and I got another hit. Not only was it a hit, it knocked the pitcher (Maury McDermott) out of the game. It hit him on the kneecap and he had to be replaced."

Rosen's hit resulted in a three-run uprising, and the Indians added another run in the eighth to win, 5-1.

After those two key pinch hits, and with his finger tightly taped, Rosen returned to the lineup part time at first base, even once at second base because he still had trouble throwing a ball.

Finally, on June 29, Rosen was able to return to third base, with Vic Wertz, who had been acquired in a trade with Baltimore, installed permanently at first base.

"Though I played every day, I never fully recovered (from the broken finger) until the next season and my career went downhill," he said. "We won the pennant, but it was a miserable year for me personally."

Rosen wound up hitting an even .300 with 24 homers and 102 RBI in 137 games, considerably less in all categories than his 1953 MVP season. and Greenberg used it as justification for cutting Rosen's salary to $37,500.

It got even worse in 1955, which began for Rosen with an automobile accident in Florida two days before spring training . "I was rear-ended by a guy doing about fifty miles an hour," he said, which resulted in a severe whiplash injury.

That started what Rosen called "another miserable season," and ended with a career-low batting average of .244.

It was slightly better for Rosen in 1956, when he hit .267, but, as he said, "I saw the handwriting was on the wall, that Hank (Greenberg) was going to trade me.

"When (Greenberg) told me he had a deal worked out with the Red Sox, I said, 'No, I'm retiring,' and I did. Greenberg tried to talk me out of it, but couldn't. My salary by then was down to $32,500, and he wanted to cut me to $27,500 to play in 1957."

Rosen went to work for Bache, but "got the itch" the following spring to play some more.

Even during our interview in Rosen's home, as he sat in his paneled den adorned with his MVP plaque and photos of the highlights of his splendid career, he said, "I wish I had continued (playing) a few more years . . . I believe I could have."

He almost did, back there in February 1957, when Veeck, acting, he said, as Greenberg's emissary, offered Rosen $40,000 to return to the Indians for another season. "We—Hank and I—were still like two big horned rams butting heads all the time," said Rosen, which is why Veeck intervened.

So did Kerby Farrell, who had replaced Lopez as the Indians' new manager. "Kerby was very flattering," said Rosen. "He said he really needed me, that I would be a big help to him, that I'd be team captain. I flat-out told Kerby no.

"But then I got this urge and, well, one thing or another . . . I was in pretty good shape because I had been working out . . . and I decided I'd do it, un-retire.

"I called my boss at Bache and he said not to worry, that my job would be there when I got back, that I should have a good year, and all that. I was supposed to go to Daytona Beach (Florida) where the Indians had spring training for their farm clubs, get in shape and join the Indians for the last week on the road, prior to opening the season.

"Then I got a call from Veeck. I'll never forget it. He said, 'Al, you better call High Henry (Greenberg). He's on the warpath.' I said, 'About what?' Veeck said, 'Just call him.' When I did, Greenberg said, to the effect, 'You are going to get $27,500 and not a cent more. Nobody is going to tomahawk me.'

"I said, 'Hank, it sounds like you don't care whether I play or not.' He said, 'I don't.' I said, 'OK, I won't.'"

And with that, Rosen remained retired, his playing career ended after ten seasons in the major leagues with a lifetime batting average of .285, 192 homers and 717 RBI in 1,044 games. He was a member of the A.L. All-Star team four times, every year from 1952-55.

Rosen and Greenberg remained at odds for more than 20 years. "We never talked," Rosen said, "until sometime in the late seventies or early eighties. I was with the Astros and we were in Los Angeles, playing the Dodgers. I ran into Hank and said, 'Don't you think it's about time?' and we had, well, not a tearful, but an emotional, you know, reunion."

In retrospect, Rosen said there were two things he'd do different if he had his career to do over again.

"First, I would sit down after I broke my finger in 1954 and not play again until it was healed, completely healed," he said, holding up his right hand to display the still disfigured first joint of his index finger. "My finger affected me the rest of the season, and I'm reminded of it because arthritis has set in and it pains me often.

"Second, I wouldn't have quit (retired) when I did," he said, despite his problems with Greenberg. "I should have played at least one more season . . . I know I could have. When I think about it, I had five years (1950-54) that were about as good as anybody could put together."

He was right, despite some disparaging remarks attributed to Greenberg in his biography. It was during their contract negotiations in the winter of 1953-54, after Rosen had won the MVP award and was seeking a raise—a contract in the $55,000-$60,000 range—that Greenberg said, according to quotes attributed to Rosen in the book:

"Let's see. You just completed your fourth year in the big leagues.' I said, 'Yes, Hank, four years.' And he said, 'Let's see what I did in my fourth year.' And he opened up the top left-hand drawer in his desk and he had a little green book that had all his records in it. I'm not sure that my numbers are right, because I can't remember all the numbers, but he said, 'How many homers did you hit?' I said, '43.' I think that year he hit more than that. Then he said, 'You knocked in what?' I said, '145.' He said, 'You hit what, .336?' I said, 'Yes, Hank.'

"Well, he had better numbers than me in every category. When I walked out of there I felt like I'd had a bad year. He reduced me to ashes. It was absolutely devastating. At any rate, we came to an agreement ($37,500 with a $5,000 bonus).'"

The following year, again as recounted in the book, Rosen quoted Greenberg as saying, "'Remember, we gave you the $5,000 bonus' (in 1954). I said, 'Well, if you're going to talk about bonuses, what about my moving from third to first?' I reminded him that in 1940 he had moved from first to left for $10,000 (for Detroit).

"He said, 'Yes, but that was me and this is you.'"

All of which brought us around to the current state of the game, as baseball continued in its attempt to recover from the devastating aftereffects of the 1994 strike by the Players Association that cut short the season and aborted the World Series.

Al Rosen

Rosen winced as he said, "It's incomprehensible what some players are getting, even some college kids who have never played a game of professional baseball. There is a lot of money floating around baseball, but there also are a lot of clubs that are losing money.

"I have a real problem with the future of baseball. In fact, I have a problem contemplating the future of sports in this country 25, 50 years from now. Neither you nor I will be around, but I don't think there is the kind of money out there to keep things going as they are now."

It was during the strike of 1994 that Rosen said, "When I played in the major leagues the owners were an avaricious bunch who created the situation that exists. In my era a player was only a chattel, nothing more than a piece of property that was used—and *abused*—by ownership.

"But now the players have the upper hand and are abusing, not only the owners, but also the fans."

Rosen remembered those comments. "The strike ended (in 1995), but the problems persist," he said, softly, even sadly.

"I don't know . . . I just don't know."

CHAPTER FOURTEEN

Ray Boone

"It was a working man's team, a bunch of blue-collar guys."

When it all began for Ray Boone as a 24-year-old Indians rookie in 1948, he was confronted with several weighty decisions that would have a significant bearing on his professional baseball career.

First, he didn't know if he still was a catcher, as he'd been since high school and in three minor league seasons, or a shortstop, the position to which he'd been switched—*temporarily*, he thought—in a desperation move by his minor league manager the preceding season.

More importantly, Boone didn't know if he wanted to be a catcher or a shortstop.

Then, Jim Hegan was only 28 and well established behind the plate for the Indians, and player-manager Lou Boudreau was the regular shortstop.

Did he want to compete with two other young catchers, Joe Tipton and Ray Murray, to play behind Hegan? Or would he prefer to serve as understudy to Boudreau, then in the prime of his career and headed for the Hall of Fame?

"I remember Boudreau calling me aside during the final week of spring training and saying, 'I've got one spot left on the roster, do you want it?'" Boone said as we talked in the living room of his home in El Cajon, California, a suburb of San Diego.

"Lou told me I could either back him up at shortstop, or they'd send me out (to the minor leagues)."

In effect, Boudreau said to Boone, "Do you want to try to beat me out of a job? Or do you want to go back to catching, in which case there's no guarantee you'll even get to the major leagues?"

Imagine being asked that question by the man who was then acknowledged as the best shortstop in the world.

Boone said he pondered his options, then told Boudreau he wanted to stay with the Indians, choosing to be a shortstop, not a catcher.

"Lou said, 'OK,' and that was it," said Boone.

But then, "Along came Hank Greenberg telling me I was crazy. It wasn't that he thought I should continue to catch, but that I should go somewhere and play every day.

"'You shouldn't be sitting on the bench up here . . . let me send you to Triple-A,' Greenberg said. But I told him no, I wanted to stay with the big club."

Greenberg was then in charge of the Indians' farm system and player development.

Boone stayed with the Indians for three weeks into the season, sitting on the bench watching Boudreau—as well as Hegan.

"By then I was getting pretty antsy. I went to Greenberg and told him I'd changed my mind," said Boone. "He told me, 'It's about time you wised up,'" and on May 4 the Indians sent Boone to the Hollywood Stars of the Pacific Coast League.

Ray Boone

But that created another dilemma for Boone—and, as it turned out, also for Indians owner Bill Veeck.

Hollywood, then managed by Jimmy Dykes, was an independent Class AAA minor league team. The Indians' top farm club then was Oklahoma City of the Class AA Texas League.

After two weeks, during which he played well at shortstop and was hitting around .325 for Hollywood, Boone was informed that the Indians wanted to send him to Oklahoma City, which would have represented a demotion.

It also would have been a violation of a major league rule then in effect.

"Dykes wanted to keep me," said Boone. "He told me I didn't have to go, that I could refuse the assignment. He said, 'I'll call the commissioner and tell him you're playing well for me, that I'm more than satisfied with your work here, and as long as I am, the Indians won't be allowed to send you down.'"

Whereupon Bill Veeck entered the picture.

"Bill called me and said, 'Ray, the people (owners) at Oklahoma City have been killing me since we sent you to Hollywood. They've been counting on getting you back, they want you . . . would you please agree to go down there for me?'

"Then he said, 'When somebody does me a favor, he gets it back twofold, trust me,'" said Boone.

So Boone agreed to go to Oklahoma City—and, less than four months later, Veeck lived up to his promise.

"Bill returned the favor more than twofold," said Boone, who was recalled by the Indians in late-August, making him eligible for the World Series.

Now semi-retired, although, as he says, "I still do some scouting for the (Boston) Red Sox," Boone and his wife Patsy, a recovering cancer patient, live in a mobile home park. They have three children, a daughter, Stacey, and two sons, Bob and Rod. Their neighbor across the street is former Indians manager Dave Garcia, and a few houses down the street lives the mother of Graig Nettles, a Tribe third baseman from 1970-72.

Though his playing days are far behind him—Boone ended his career in 1960 after 13 years in the major leagues with six teams—he revels in the accomplishments of his son, Bob, and grandsons Bret, Aaron and Matthew.

They comprise the first three-generation family to play major league baseball.

Bob was a catcher for the Philadelphia Phillies, California Angels and Kansas City Royals from 1972-90. He managed Tacoma in the Pacific Coast League (1992-93), was a coach for Cincinnati (1994), and was manager of the Royals from 1995 until July 9, 1997, when he was replaced by Tony Muser. (Ironically, Muser was one of 12 future major leaguers signed by Ray Boone as a scout for the Red Sox.)

Bret, a second baseman, was a fifth-round selection in the 1990 amateur draft by Seattle, played for the Mariners in 1992 and 1993, and was traded to Cincinnati in November 1993.

Aaron, a third baseman, was a third-round pick in the 1994 draft by Cincinnati, and made it to the major leagues in 1997.

Matthew, also a third baseman, was chosen in the third round of the 1997 draft by Detroit, and is now playing in the minor leagues.

Ray Boone's other son, Rodney, was a catcher in the Royals and Houston farm systems from 1972-75.

As Reds General Manager Jim Bowden told the elder Boone, "'I'll tell you why we drafted Aaron. I went to our scouting director and asked him how he liked the kid. He said he never saw him play (at the University of Southern California), but I told him to draft Aaron for one simple reason.

"'I'm a genes man,'" Boone said he was told by Bowden.

When the patriarch was asked who among the Boone clan was the best, he was understandably evasive.

"Well," he started, "Bob was a good player . . . I probably was a better hitter, but his forte was his ability as a catcher. As he always said, 'The one thing that kept me in the lineup was my glove. Without that mitt, I'm on the bench.'"

OK, so which one of his grandsons is best?

"Well," Boone started again, "right now that's hard to tell because there is so much potential in all of them."

So, will they be better than their grandfather was?

"Probably," said Boone—though that's saying plenty.

Ray Boone's lifetime major league batting average was .275 in 1,373 games. He led the American League with 116 RBIs while playing third base for Detroit in 1955, and drove in 114 runs in 1953, when he was traded by the Indians to the Tigers in an eight-player deal on June 15.

The Tribe received pitchers Art Houtemann and Bill Wight, infielder Owen Friend and catcher Joe Ginsberg for

Boone and pitchers Steve Gromek, Al Aber and Dick Weik.

Though it does not rank as one of the Indians' best deals, it was a good one for Boone. He became one of the best third basemen in the league after being switched to that position by Detroit, and made the American League All-Star team in 1954 and 1956.

Leaving the Indians was good for Boone because, as he said, "It was difficult to be the heir apparent to Boudreau, as great and as popular as he was. It was tough for me in Cleveland, but I harbor no resentment against Boudreau or the club.

"The one thing I wish is that the Indians would have given me a shot at third base, though I can understand why they didn't."

Ken Keltner was the Indians' third baseman in 1948, he and Al Rosen shared the position in 1949, and Rosen was the regular through 1956.

Though Boudreau had a career year in 1948, he became overweight—leading some scribes to derisively call him "the fat manager"— and his ability slipped in 1949. It gave rise to speculation that Boudreau held Boone back, that he resisted giving the young shortstop playing time.

But Boone denies that was the case. "In all honesty, and in fairness to Lou, I can say he helped me . . . he encouraged me . . . he did nothing to hurt me."

Boone, who started scouting for the Red Sox in 1961, suffered what he called a "mild" heart attack in January 1997, a few days after serving as an instructor in the Indians "Fantasy Camp" at Winter Haven, Florida.

"We went to Orlando to visit Bret," he said. "About three in the morning I woke up with chest pains, and was soaking wet with perspiration. It was a heart attack, but only a mild one. I'm on some medication, but there was no damage. I'm fine now."

Boone's wife Patsy, a former professional swimmer, underwent surgery for ovarian cancer in 1994. "The prognosis (for her complete recovery) is good," said Boone.

Ray and Patsy grew up in the area, and he was a star at (San Diego) Hoover High School where he was preceded by five years by Ted Williams.

Ray Boone

When Williams returned to San Diego in the winter during the early years of his career, he'd take batting practice at the school playground. Boone, who was still a student, said that he and three of his buddies would "shag" for Williams, while the playground director, who had played some minor league baseball, pitched.

"Ted would give each of us 50 cents, which we thought was pretty good, and if other kids came up to shag with us, we'd chase them away, telling them, 'Mr. Williams just wants us four to shag for him,' whether it was true or not."

But it wasn't until 1951, nine years after Boone embarked upon his professional baseball career, that he finally said more than "Hi" and "Thanks, Mr. Williams," to the future Hall of Famer.

"I wanted to talk to Williams in 1948, after the Indians recalled me from Oklahoma City and he was in Cleveland with the Red Sox," said Boone. "I was playing catch on the side before a game one day and Ted was in the batting cage. I remember thinking, 'Maybe I should go over and tell him that I went to Hoover High School, too, same as he did.'

"But I didn't . . . I thought he might say, 'So what? Who cares?' or something like that, and I don't think I even said hello to him until, I guess it was 1951.

"We were in Boston and I hit two home runs in a game at Fenway Park. The next day, after I made the third out of an inning, I rounded first base, headed for my position at shortstop, and as Ted trotted in from left field he said to me, 'They can't get old Hoover High guys out, can they?'

"I was so thrilled . . . I can close my eyes and still hear Ted saying that to me."

It was an emergency situation—not of Boone's doing—that presented the opportunity for him to play shortstop for the first time at Oklahoma City in 1947.

Boone was signed by the Indians out of high school in 1942, and played at Wausau, Wisconsin of the Class C Northern League where he batted .306 and was voted by the local media as the rookie most likely to succeed.

But before Boone could capitalize on that performance, he served almost three years (1943-45) in the Navy during World War II.

"I figured I'd be drafted, so I enlisted, and because of my baseball background I was stationed right here in San Diego as a boot camp drill instructor," said Boone. He also was involved in the athletic program, "putting up ball fields, organizing intramural games, and stuff like that," and played on the camp baseball team.

One of Boone's teammates in the Navy was another Indians farmhand, a then-third baseman named Bob Lemon, who would become a star pitcher, help Cleveland win the pennant and World Series in 1948, and be inducted into the Hall of Fame in 1976.

Discharged in March 1946 with the rank of Specialist Second Class, Boone was assigned to the Wilkes-Barre, Pennsylvania club in the Class A Eastern League. He batted .258, and continued to impress the Indians with his catching ability and, especially, his strong arm.

It earned him a promotion to Oklahoma City where he began the 1947 season sharing the catching duties with Murray, another who would spend time in Cleveland in 1948.

While in the process of hitting .264 in 130 games at Oklahoma City, Boone was approached late in the season by

Manager Pat Ankenman, who'd played briefly as a shortstop in the National League.

Ankenman told Boone that he was in desperate need of improvement at shortstop. The situation was so bad, in fact, that Ankenman was considering putting himself in the lineup, though he was 35 at the time.

"Would you give it (shortstop) a try?," Ankenman literally pleaded with Boone, who, with some reluctance, agreed.

"But only to give it a try," he told the manager.

"Actually," said Boone, "we had shortstops coming and going all season, six of them, I think. I played the last 22 games (at shortstop) and though I didn't start so well, I guess I did OK for a guy who'd always been a catcher."

In his first game at the new position for Oklahoma City, Boone committed three errors—all in one inning.

But, as he said, "When the inning was over and I headed for the dugout, everybody in the park stood up and applauded for me, because they knew I had never played short before.

"When the season ended, that was it. I didn't think anything more about it. I figured it was only a temporary move."

However, on the first day of spring training in Tucson, Arizona, the next season, Boudreau called Boone into his office. "Lou said they'd had pretty good reports on me, and asked if I wanted to continue playing shortstop," said Boone. "If I didn't like it, Boudreau said I could always go back to catching.

"I told Lou that I wanted to stay at short . . . I considered it kind of a fun position compared to catching."

The rest is history, at least after Boudreau again talked to Boone several weeks later about remaining with the Indians as their back-up shortstop.

It's interesting, as Boone pointed out, that his son Bob's career began just the opposite. Bob Boone started as a third baseman with the Phillies, who then had Mike Schmidt, another future Hall of Famer, playing at the Triple-A level.

As the elder Boone said of his son, "It's an example that Bob uses a lot of times, the importance of being in the right place at the right time, which he was in 1972."

Andy Seminick and Doc Edwards, two former catchers who then were instructors for the Phillies, suggested that Bob be switched to catching because of the presence of Schmidt, who was then breaking in with the Phillies at third base.

"When they recommended that Bob go behind the plate, he called and reminded me that I'd always told him to do whatever it took to get to the big leagues," said Ray. "So Bob did. He made the switch, and it got him to the big leagues pretty quick (in September 1972)."

Ray Boone's bat—along with Veeck's fulfillment of the "twofold" favor he'd promised—also got the converted catcher to the big leagues pretty quick in 1948.

As Boone said, "I had a great year at Oklahoma City." He hit .355 and led the Texas League, though he didn't have enough plate appearances to win the batting championship.

The reason Boone didn't was because the Indians recalled him in late August, though he didn't play in his first game until September 3 when he replaced Boudreau midway through the first game of a double header, which the Indians won, 7-0, over St. Louis.

Boone batted only five times (with two hits) after being promoted by the Indians, and once as a pinch hitter in the World Series (when he struck out) for Walt Judnich in the 11-5 loss to the Boston Braves in the fifth game.

But it marked the beginning of a fine major league career for the new shortstop.

Boone's memories of the 1948 Indians, and the pressure-packed, final month of the season are absorbing, coming as they did through the eyes of a then-rookie.

"I could tell in spring training that they were a special group of guys . . . it was a working man's team, a bunch of blue-collar guys. Some had a lot of mileage on them, but they were all pros," said Boone.

"Nobody had an ego, not even the guys who should have, like (Ken) Keltner and (Joe) Gordon, not even (Bob) Feller, and certainly not Lemon.

"But, back then, in spring training, I'm not sure many guys, maybe not anybody, thought they'd win the pennant for one simple reason: they didn't know Gene Bearden was going to be a 20-game winner.

"In fact, in spring training and during the first three weeks of the season when I was with them, we had only two starting pitchers, Feller and Lemon, and Boudreau was trying to find, not only someone to fill the third spot in the rotation, but a fourth as well."

As for Larry Doby, the second black player to break baseball's color barrier the previous season, Boone said, "It never occurred to me . . . the racial thing. When I was a kid growing up, I lived in a real integrated neighborhood in San Diego. I played with black guys, Mexicans, Hispanics, Italians. I never even knew there was a racial problem."

Boone admitted, however, "There were times I felt sorry for Larry because some guys in the league gave Larry a tough time, and fans, too, the things they yelled at him.

"But not on our team, not that I can recall. Like I said, our guys were a bunch of blue-collar guys and I don't think it mattered what anybody was, as long as they did their job."

In his recollection of the hectic final month of the 1948 season, which began with the Indians in third place, one game behind Boston and percentage points behind New York on September 1, Boone said, "Every day was like being in a pressure-cooker, right up to the last game.

"Being a rookie, I probably felt the pressure more than anybody, especially going into that last game (on October 3, a 7-1 loss to Hal Newhouser and the Tigers). Nobody expected Newhouser to pitch because he only had a couple, three days' rest. But he did, and he pitched a helluva game (to beat Feller).

"I'm sure Newhouser didn't volunteer . . . the Tigers probably just said to give him the ball and (Manager Steve) O'Neill did. In a game like that you go with the best you've got, especially if you're an old timer like O'Neill. That's what he did. He went with his best.

"I'm also sure that, knowing Newhouser, he would have tried just as hard to beat his high school team as he did against us, because he was that kind of a competitor."

The Tigers knocked Feller out of the box in the third inning when they scored four runs, they added two more off Steve Gromek in the fifth, and Newhouser had a shutout until the ninth.

"All through the game we're watching the scoreboard to see what was happening in Boston," said Boone. "We knew if New York beat Boston, we'd still win the pennant."

But the Red Sox prevailed, 10-5, creating the deadlock that would be broken the next day in Fenway Park.

"After we lost to the Tigers and the Red Sox beat the Yankees, I'll never forget Boudreau coming into the clubhouse and saying, 'Well, pack up, now we've got to go to Boston.'

"That's all. Just, 'Pack up, now we've got to go to Boston.'"

The overnight train ride was, as Boone confirmed, "a wild one," which was strange, considering that, in reality, the Indians had nothing to celebrate.

"Well, I guess the thing about it, it was sort of a *release*," said Boone. "A release from the pressure everybody had been under. Six months of it."

He denied that anybody on the team was "satisfied" that they'd had a good season no matter what the next day would bring.

"Hell, no, that wasn't it," said Boone. "I just think that everybody was relieved. But I'm also sure that nobody thought we were going to lose the next day, either."

The Indians didn't, as Bearden pitched one of his best games to beat the Red Sox, which launched another subject: Boudreau's choice of the rookie left-hander to pitch the most important game of the season —actually, the most important game an Indians team would play in more than two decades.

"When Lou told us it was his recommendation to start Bearden, who had pitched well that season but had never done much of anything before that, instead of two future Hall of Famers (Feller and Lemon), I was surprised," said Boone. "I think a lot of guys were. If it had been my call, I wouldn't have started Bearden.

"But I guess Lou factored everything in, that Bearden had pitched well against Boston, and he was a 19-game winner until then.

"After Boudreau told us that his choice was Bearden, Gordon seconded it," said Boone. "Maybe they'd talked about it previously, I don't know. But as soon as Gordon spoke up, that was the end of it. Boudreau was the manager, but Gordon had a lot of influence. He was one of the leaders on the club.

"We were told to keep it a secret, and when we walked out on the field at Fenway Park everybody in the press corps wanted to know who was pitching, Lemon or Feller or who. It was funny. All we could say was, 'I don't know . . . ask Lou.'

"It was a real con game, especially when it came time to warm up and all three guys—Lemon, Feller and Bearden—walked out of the dugout and went to the bullpen.

"As it turned out, of course, Boudreau was right. Bearden did a helluva job, so I guess Lou knew what he was doing."

Boone also talked about the reaction of Eddie Robinson when the lineups were posted and Allie Clark was penciled in at first base, a position he'd never previously played.

"Eddie was in tears," Boone said of Robinson's reaction. "Nothing against Clark, but I couldn't blame Robinson

for being upset. He'd played first base all season and then we get down to the last game with everything on the line and somebody else is in his place."

Robinson got in the game in the bottom of the fourth inning, singled in two trips to the plate and scored the Indians' final run in the ninth inning of the 8-3 victory.

And then the fun began. "Oh, man! the party we had that night was really something," chortled Boone.

"When we showed up for the workout the next day you wouldn't believe how hungover some of the guys were.

"Boudreau came into the clubhouse and said, 'There are three cabs waiting outside . . . you, you and you get into one . . . you, you and you get into another . . . and you, you and you take the third one. Get over to the spa and sweat out the booze.'

"Remember, the World Series started the very next day," said Boone, declining to name those who Boudreau identified as "you," and sent to the sweat boxes.

"Let me just say that a lot of guys were really hungover," he said again.

But if the pennant party adversely affected the Indians, it didn't show. They won the World Series in six games.

And then came a celebration to end all celebrations on the train returning to Cleveland, after Lemon, with relief help from Bearden, beat the Braves, 4-3.

"Bill Veeck took off his wooden leg, filled it with booze and passed it around," said Boone.

Why? "Who knows . . . Bill couldn't tell you himself. He was feeling absolutely no pain.

"When we got close to Cleveland, Veeck made the train stop every ten or fifteen miles or so, and handed out champagne to people who were outside, welcoming us home.

"By the time we got to Cleveland, got off the train and into cars for the parade (to downtown) we all looked terrible. Our clothes were soaked with booze and none of us had anything clean to wear because, when we left Cleveland after the fifth game, everybody said, 'Don't bring a suitcase . . . just a shaving kit, we're going to wrap this thing up right away.'

"That's how confident we were that we'd win," said Boone.

He was voted a quarter share of the World Series prize money which, for Boone, amounted to nearly $1,700.

But it was the championship ring that he coveted even more than the money—and which, in Boone's mind, completed the "twofold" favor that Veeck had promised nearly four months earlier.

It's one of four championship rings owned by Boone, the other three given to him by the Red Sox, the team for which he has scouted since 1961, after they won American League pennants in 1967, 1975 and 1986.

The most money Boone made during his playing career was $32,500 in 1956, after he hit .284 with 20 homers and his 116 RBIs were the most in the American League.

Perhaps because his grandsons are able to cash in on the wild escalation of salaries in professional sports—the average salary in the major leagues in 1997 was close to $1.4 million—Boone doesn't seem to be as critical of the situation as are most old timers.

"Well, first of all, it shows you how much money there is in baseball," he said. "When you stop and think about it, my thirty-two-five ($32,500) was pretty good for those days, considering how little teachers and (school) coaches were making.

"And the same concerns that are being expressed now were raised back there ten, 15, 20 years ago. Remember when Gene Tenace got $250,000 to sign with the (San Diego) Padres as a free agent? Man! Everybody thought that was outrageous. But look what's happened since then.

"My biggest problem with what's happening now is trying to understand how any team can give a kid $10 million, you know, the college guy the (Arizona) Diamondbacks signed after San Diego screwed up," said Boone.

It was a reference to the contract won by U.S. Olympic team first baseman Travis Lee, who was drafted by the Padres, but wasn't tendered an offer early enough and was declared free to sign with any organization. The expansion Diamondbacks made Lee the offer he couldn't refuse.

The other expansion team, Tampa Bay, was equally generous to a pair of untested schoolboy pitchers in 1997. The Devil Rays gave $10.2 million to right hander Matt White, and $3 million to left hander Bobby Seay.

"Do I worry about the future of baseball?" Boone repeated my question. "No, not really. It will always be here

Ray Boone

. . . it's too great a game. And if the money is out there—which it must be, otherwise the salaries wouldn't keep going up and up and up—well, the players should get their share."

All of which led to the inevitable question: If Boone had his career to do all over, what, if anything, would he change?

First, he replied, "Only one thing. I'd start playing shortstop sooner, in high school, or in American Legion ball. I wouldn't get behind the plate. I wouldn't be a catcher."

Then Boone corrected himself. "Something else I'd do, I'd work harder, which is not to say I didn't work hard. But I realize I could have done more to improve myself. When my day was over, it was over.

"But I look back at the way Ted Williams pushed himself and, I'm told, the way Hank Greenberg did, and I know I could have done more, should have done more. I wish I had.

"But then, the bottom line is that I took a Hall of Famer's place, so I must've had something going for me."

CHAPTER FIFTEEN

Bob Kennedy

"When we were in Cleveland, it was like being in Camelot."

Bob Kennedy called it "a helluva story . . . one that nobody knows because it never was told before." He was right. It *is* a helluva story about the Indians' playoff game against the Boston Red Sox for the pennant in 1948.

"Listen to me now, this will be interesting," he said, as we recalled that season of 50 years ago, and again, he was right.

"We're on the train, going to Boston to play the Red Sox the next afternoon, and I get in my berth and go to sleep. After a while (Joe) Gordon comes by and says, 'Bob, you asleep?' I said, 'Well, yeah, I was until now.' He says, 'I thought you'd want to know . . . you're playing tomorrow.'

"I said, 'That's great. I'm glad to hear that.' He says, 'I'm gonna take a sleeping pill, you want one?' I said I'd never had one, but since I was awake, I thought it would help me get back to sleep, so I told him to bring me one.

"Next thing I know it's morning and it's quiet, real quiet. I pulled the curtain back and leaned out of my berth and I don't see anybody. I looked down the aisle and saw Gordon, and a little farther down there was (Bob) Feller. But nobody else.

"I wondered where the hell was everybody? I looked at my watch and it was eleven o'clock. Eleven o'clock in the morning, and the game was at one o'clock.

"And, no, before you ask, I wasn't drinking. Maybe Gordon had a couple, but I didn't, and neither did Feller, as far as I know.

"The train was parked in the yard and everybody was gone. Everybody but Gordon, Feller and me.

"So, Judas Priest, we get dressed, run like a son of a gun and catch a cab to Fenway Park. On the way Joe told the cabbie to stop at one of those little lunch stands.

"He ran in, got three milkshakes with a couple of eggs in each of them, and jumped back in the cab. When we got to the park and walked in the clubhouse, (Manager Lou) Boudreau looked at us and started to say something, but Joe put his hand over his mouth and said to Lou, 'Not now . . . later.'

"We went out and took a couple swings in batting practice and, for whatever reason, maybe because we slept so well, the pitches looked like beach balls."

They didn't exactly look like beach balls to Kennedy during the game—he flied out, grounded out and sacrifice bunted twice against Denny Galehouse—but the Indians prevailed, 8-3, to win the pennant.

"Can you believe I almost missed the greatest game . . . the most *important* game of my career?" asked Kennedy,

After the victory over the Red Sox in the playoff game Kennedy said he walked back to the Kenmore Hotel in Boston, "But, I swear, my feet never touched the ground."

Bob Kennedy

And when the World Series against the Boston Braves began two days later, Kennedy acknowledged that "some of our guys were hung over—especially Bearden." But, as he also said, "We were all pretty relaxed because there had been so much pressure on us to win the playoff."

Kennedy's action in the World Series was limited; he was 1-for-2 as a defensive replacement in three games.

Now retired since 1992 and living in Mesa, Arizona, Kennedy chuckled often as we reminisced, though his smile faded when we talked about his family.

Kennedy's wife Claire died in September 1994 while undergoing major heart surgery. She was 73. They would have been married 50 years on June 9, 1995.

"The doctors said she needed to have two valves repaired, but they were confident it would be successful because she was in pretty good health," said Kennedy. "We were told the odds were 95 percent in her favor."

However, "30 or 40 minutes after the operation they called me and (son) Terry and said she'd passed away."

Terry is one of Kennedy's five children, along with Kathleen, Colleen, Christine and Bob Jr.

Both sons also played professional baseball, though only Terry made it to the major leagues. In fact, he and Bob Sr. comprise one of four father-son duos of which both members played in the World Series.

Terry, a catcher who was born in 1956, played in the major leagues from 1978-91 for St. Louis, San Diego, Baltimore and San Francisco. He appeared in the 1984 and 1989 World Series for the Padres and Giants, respectively. After retiring as a player, Terry coached and managed in the minor leagues for several organizations, and currently works for the Chicago Cubs. Bob Jr. was a minor league pitcher for the Cardinals.

The elder Kennedy's major league career began with the Chicago White Sox in 1939 and continued through 1957. It was twice interrupted for service in the Marine Corps from 1943-45 in World War II and again in 1952 during the Korean War as a fighter pilot and instructor.

"I volunteered in November 1942 for the Navy's V-5, Naval Aviation (college) program," Kennedy said. "I wanted to learn to fly and at the same time get the best education possible. Otherwise I probably would have been drafted." He returned to the White Sox in 1946 and was traded to the Indians on June 2, 1948.

Discharged with the rank of captain after the Korean War (during which he served with another Marine reservist, Ted Williams), Kennedy played for the Indians (from June 2, 1948-April 17, 1954), Baltimore, Detroit and the then-Brooklyn Dodgers, as well as with the White Sox from 1955-57 before hanging up his spikes at the end of the 1957 season.

Kennedy managed the Cubs from 1963 until he was replaced after 58 games in 1965, scouted for the Cubs the remainder of 1965, coached for Atlanta in 1967, and managed Oakland in 1968. He also worked in the front offices of the Indians, St. Louis, Chicago Cubs, Houston and San Francisco.

Prior to that "greatest" game he almost missed because of Gordon's sleeping pill, Kennedy said, "I was very nervous, but it was good nervous, if you know what I mean. If somebody had snapped his fingers before we got started, I probably would have jumped 20 feet in the air."

And while the Indians were pledged to secrecy that Gene Bearden would pitch for them, "We didn't believe Galehouse was going to start for the Red Sox," said Kennedy. "We thought they'd come up with two lineup cards, and that (Mel) Parnell was really going to pitch.

In fact, Louie (Boudreau) sent our traveling secretary (Spud Goldstein) around the park, even outside the park, to see if Parnell was warming up somewhere out of sight.

"When we found out it definitely was Galehouse, we felt there's no way he was going to beat us.

"That's the way that (1948) team was. Confident. Always confident. And close. Very close," said Kennedy. "We did things together that teams nowadays don't do . . . and few did back then.

"And because we were so close, I think I learned more baseball in 1948 with the Indians than I did my whole career.

"When we'd go on the road, a couple of guys would get kitchenettes in the hotel, we'd pick up some cold cuts and maybe a few bottles of beer and some pop, and we'd get together after games to chew the fat about what happened. You know, replay the game and get on each other about why we did this or that, or why somebody didn't do something. We knew we had a good club, but we also knew that (winning the pennant) wouldn't be easy.

"I'd have to say that (Joe) Gordon and (Bob) Lemon were the two main guys, the guys who got it started and kept it going.

"Usually there'd be nine or ten of us, maybe a dozen or so. It was very good. I know it helped me, and I've got to believe it helped all of us have the kind of season we did. When we walked on the field that season everybody knew what everybody else was going to do all the time."

It also helped Larry Doby and Satchel Paige, the two black players on the team. The 1948 season was only the second since the color barrier was broken in 1947 by, first, Jackie Robinson in the National League, and then, eleven weeks later, by Doby in the American League.

Kennedy said he had great respect for both Doby and Paige. "They were good players and first-class guys," he said, while also pointing out their personalities were drastically different.

"Doby was very serious, very intense and, while I don't fault him for it, he had a tendency to brood when he didn't do well. Paige was just the opposite. Loosey-goosey, you know. Not too much bothered old Satch, which I think was a big reason he was so good.

Bob Kennedy as a San Francisco Giants executive.

"In fact, if Larry would have had Satch's temperament, or if he'd been as easy going as Luke Easter (who joined the Indians a year later) there's no telling what Doby would have done . . . maybe be in the Hall of Fame today.

"But I'll say this about Larry Doby. After he got his feet on the ground he was one of the best ball players I knew, a guy who could carry the whole club by himself. When he was hot he never hit a single, he hit doubles, triples, homers . . . I mean, he did *everything*."

Interestingly, Kennedy was playing for the White Sox when Doby made his major league debut as a pinch hitter for the Indians in Chicago on July 5, 1947. The next day, in the second game of a doubleheader, Doby played first base and batted fifth, getting one hit in four at-bats.

"I remember it very well," said Kennedy. "After Larry reached first base he went to steal second and the next batter hit a long fly to the center fielder, who made a good play.

Larry didn't know the ball was caught and rounded second. The (Indians') third base coach was hollering, 'Get back! Get back! He caught the ball! Get back!'

"Well, Larry was already past the shortstop by then, so he just turned and ran across the pitcher's mound to first base, not realizing he had to re-tag second, and was called out.

"It's funny now, though it wasn't so funny to Larry when it happened."

Not only was it not funny, it also did not help Doby in terms of the way he was treated by opposing players his first few years in the league.

"I don't know about his experiences off the field, but on the field we did whatever we could to help him," said Kennedy.

"We made damn sure nobody got on him, and we also included him whenever we could, like going out to eat, things like that, although sometimes he wanted to be by himself because, you know, he was uncomfortable being the only black guy."

And what about Paige?

"Well, first, he was a helluva pitcher, I don't care how old he was, or how old people thought he was. He was a major league pitcher, period, and should have been pitching in the major leagues a long time before he did."

Paige was signed by Bill Veeck on July 7, 1948, the sixth black player in the major leagues. He made his debut two days later in a relief role against the St. Louis Browns, recorded his first victory on July 15 against the Philadelphia Athletics, and wound up the season with a 6-1 won-lost record and 2.48 earned run average in 21 games, seven as a starter.

"Some people thought Satch was a clown, but don't let anybody kid you, he was a doggone good pitcher and a very smart baseball man," said Kennedy. "We used to play catch a lot, warm up on the side, and he loved to put a handkerchief on the ground—a *folded up* handkerchief —and bet us quarters he could throw all of his pitches right over that handkerchief for strikes.

"Not only did he win a lot (of quarters), he'd throw 25, 30, 35 pitches in a row right over that folded up handkerchief. He had ungodly control with all of his pitches. He was a gawky-looking guy when he walked out to the mound, but when he wound up and threw the ball, he was poetry in motion.

"Don't let anybody tell you that Satch was a clown, or that he wasn't a good pitcher," Kennedy said again.

And what was he like off the field?

Kennedy laughed and said, "Well, most of the time he'd come to the ball park in a big limousine accompanied by a lady, and when we asked who she was, he'd say, "That's my wife.'

"I'll tell you this, there sure were a lot of Mrs. Paiges in the American League that year."

Kennedy, who batted .301 in 66 games in 1948, was acquired by the Indians in a trade with the White Sox.

Then a third baseman-outfielder, Kennedy had been a high school star in Chicago, having grown up in that city, and after rejecting an offer from the Boston Red Sox, he signed with the White Sox on June 23, 1937, two months before his 17th birthday.

"I was playing summer ball on an American Legion team, the Duffy Florals, and I got a phone call from a fellow who says to me, 'This is Herb Pennock of the Boston Red Sox . . . ,' and before he could say anything more, I hung up the phone. I figured somebody was pulling my leg."

Pennock was a former major leaguer who played 22 years and pitched in five World Series.

"My mother asked, 'Bobby, who was that?' and I told her it was somebody pulling a prank on me. With that, the phone rang again and this time she answered it. Again the fellow identified himself as Herb Pennock, and my mother said to me, 'You take this call and apologize to the man for hanging up on him.'

"I did and he asked me to meet him at a downtown hotel so he could talk to me about playing for the Red Sox. He told me to take a cab, that the doorman would pay for it. I still wasn't sure it really was Herb Pennock, but I put on some clean clothes and went to the hotel.

"When I got there, sure enough, it's Herb Pennock. We sat down in the lobby and who comes walking by but Jimmie Foxx and a couple other Red Sox players. Pennock told me, if I signed with the Red Sox, they'd keep me with them, that I wouldn't go to the minor leagues.

"This was in 1937 and I was only 16. I wasn't sure I'd ever get a chance to play, that I'd be stuck on the bench. Besides, I felt an obligation to a coach named Billy Webb, who'd let me go down to Comiskey Park to work out with the White Sox, which is how the Red Sox saw me in the first place.

"So I told Pennock that I'd call him, but I never did," said Kennedy.

"Did I make a mistake? I don't know. But if I had my life to live over, one of the things I'd change is that I'd get some advice, ask more questions of guys who have been around and knew more than I did."

After three years in the minor leagues, at Vicksburg (Mississippi), Dallas, Longview (Texas), and Shreveport (Louisiana), Kennedy was promoted to the White Sox for the final month of the 1939 season. He played for them through 1942 when the war interrupted his career.

Despite the fact that he was born and raised in Chicago, Kennedy was pleased to go to the Indians after 30 games with the White Sox in 1948.

As reported in *The Cleveland Press* after the trade, "Kennedy was exuberant, so tickled that he phoned Boudreau and said, 'It's the best break of my career.'"

"And it was," he confirmed during our interview. "Sure, Chicago was my hometown, but, hey, I went from last place to first place overnight. Why shouldn't I have been happy?"

At the time of the deal, the White Sox were 15 games behind the Indians, who were tied with Philadelphia at the top of the American League, four games ahead of New York.

Kennedy also was pleased to be joining Boudreau, whom he'd read about in the Chicago papers. "Louie's a little older (three years) than I am, but he was from Harvey (Illinois, a suburb of Chicago) and I'd heard a lot about him when I was growing up.

"It was great to be playing with Boudreau. I think he had the best season I ever saw a player have, both in the field as a shortstop, and at the plate. He was amazing.

"And so were the fans. We'd come out to the ball park and it got so that we knew many of them, just about everybody who sat in the field level boxes because they were there for almost every game.

"It was a great time to be an Indian."

The Indians also were pleased to get Kennedy, though "exuberant" would not have been an accurate characterization of their sentiments. At least not initially. Many observers—including players, fans and members of the media—were concerned that the price Veeck paid for Kennedy was too high and, some thought, too much of a gamble.

Sent to the White Sox for Kennedy were Pat Seerey, a powerful, long ball-hitting outfielder for whom expectations were high, and Al Gettel, a right-handed pitcher whose record was 11-10 in 1947, and who, it had been hoped, could fill the then-vacant No. 3 spot in the Indians' rotation in 1948.

The only established starters at the time of the deal were Bob Feller, who was struggling with a 4-4 record, and Bob Lemon.

As it turned out, Seerey, while hitting 19 homers that year—including four in one game for the White Sox—batted .231 in 1948 and was finished as a major league player after only four games in 1949.

Gettel won only 12 games while losing 19 for the White Sox and three other major league teams the next eight seasons, from 1948-55.

It wasn't only—or even primarily—Kennedy's bat the Indians sought when they traded Seerey and Gettel to get him. They also wanted him for defense, specifically, Kennedy's right arm, then one of the strongest and most accurate in baseball.

It was Kennedy's offense *and* defense that helped the Indians beat the Washington Senators, 7-6, in 11 innings on July 19, without which they would not have finished in a tie with the Red Sox—although, obviously, the same could be said about every game they won that season.

Kennedy calls that game "one of the best, maybe *the* best I ever played."

And of that victory over the Senators, played in Washington, *The Plain Dealer* reported the next day:

"Frank Merriwell came to life (last night). He came to life in the form of Bob Kennedy, a previously rather obscure character. But his dramatic exploits wrote a happy ending to a storybook ball game that unfolded before 18,035 incredulous customers at Griffith Stadium.

"Kennedy starred in a dual role, in the field and at bat . . . that kept the Tribe cemented in first place.

"The young outfielder . . . threw out a runner at the plate in the 10th inning with a bullet-like peg from right field, and in the 11th he drove in the winning run with a timely single."

Kennedy talked about what he did that night—especially the throw he made to prolong the game until his hit with Larry Doby on second scored the run that broke the tie.

"Actually, I didn't make that throw, I swear I didn't. God made it. He must have made it because I don't remember doing it," said Kennedy.

"Louie (Boudreau) put me and Doby in the game at the same time, in the bottom of the tenth with the bases loaded and one out. Doby went to center field in place of Walt Judnich, and I went to right in place of Allie Clark.

"I was playing a little close for a chance to cut what would have been the winning run down at the plate. As it turned out, the batter (Al Kozar) hit the ball back, over my head.

"I didn't know if I had a chance to get the runner trying to score, but I ran back, you know, past where the ball would come down, then turned around and came in so I made the catch on the run.

"I got the throw off, but honestly, that's all I remember, which is why I said God must have thrown that ball for me."

Whatever—or whoever threw the ball—it skipped on one bounce into the glove of catcher Jim Hegan, who tagged the runner, Ed Stewart, to complete a double play and send the game into the 11th inning for Kennedy to win it with his bat.

He singled through the hole at shortstop off Tom Ferrick, and Steve Gromek and Bearden held the Senators scoreless in the bottom of the 11th for the victory. It was credited to Gromek and enabled the Indians to cling to first place with a one-game lead over Philadelphia.

Kennedy was in and out of the lineup the rest of the season; as he said, "I was a role player . . . Louie used me mostly as a defensive replacement, as a pinch hitter, and sometimes platooned me against left- handed pitchers.

"I knew my role and I felt like I did a good job, but my best season came later, probably 1950, when I played (right field) all the time."

Kennedy batted .276 in 1949, when the Indians fell into third place, and .291 in 146 games the following season, when they finished fourth.

It was in 1950 that Kennedy made the most money in his 16-year major league playing career—all of $17,500—but not without a drawn- out contract hassle with Hank Greenberg and Rudie Schaffer, who was then business manager of the Indians.

"First, let me make it clear that I liked Hank, I got along well with him, most of the time, anyway," said Kennedy.

But not during the winter of 1949-50.

"I wanted $1,000 more than Hank was offering, but he didn't want to give it to me and was bickering about it when Schaffer came into the office. He sat there listening to me argue with Greenberg, then said, 'Hank, I wouldn't give it to him,' which really ticked me off.

"I yelled at Greenberg, 'Get that Jew sonofabitch out of here before I deck him.' Greenberg said, 'Rudie, you'd better go,' and he did.

"What makes the whole thing so funny is that Rudie Schaffer was German, not Jewish, and Greenberg was Jewish. I should not have said what I did . . . I was just upset at Schaffer."

But apparently Greenberg did not take offense to Kennedy's remark.

"When I asked Hank, 'How can I earn an extra $1,000?' He said, 'Play 100 games and you've got it.' I said, 'You've got a deal,' though we didn't even put it in writing.

"So, in July, the next season (1950), I've played 80 games and we're going on a road trip and Hank comes down to the clubhouse and tells me, 'When you get back from the trip, come up and see me.' I didn't know why he wanted to see me, but I said I would.

"When I did, he said, 'Here's your $1,000.' That was the only problem I ever had with Hank Greenberg.

"As I said, I liked the man . . . most of the time."

It raised the subject of baseball players' salaries today.

"What the hell," said Kennedy. "Nobody is putting a gun to the owners' heads, are they? If you're a player, you're going to take what they're willing to give you, aren't you?

"The only thing that bothers me is players always wanting more and more. I mean, how the hell much money do you need to live on? What's really the difference between, say, three million dollars and four million dollars?"

Kennedy's average fell to .246 in 1951 as a part-timer under then-new manager Al Lopez; he hit an even .300 while playing only 22 games after returning from the Korean War in 1952; .236 in 100 games in 1953, and asked to be traded in 1954.

"I wasn't angry . . . but I wanted to go somewhere to play," he said. Lopez complied. Four games into the season, after Kennedy had batted only once, he was traded to Baltimore for outfielder-third baseman Jim Dyck on April 17.

"Funny thing," Kennedy recalled his playing career. "My first big league game was in 1939 with the White Sox in Philadelphia against the (then Philadelphia) Athletics at old Shibe Park, when I also got my first big league hit.

"And I played my last big league game with the (then Brooklyn) Dodgers, and got my last big league hit, also at Shibe Park in Philadelphia, in 1957 against the Phillies.

"I also made the last out of the game (in the Dodgers' 2-1 loss to the Phillies), which also was the last out of the Brooklyn Dodgers . . . they became the Los Angeles Dodgers in 1958."

Kennedy's 16-year major league career batting average was .254 in 1,483 games, 821 as an outfielder and 540 as a third baseman (primarily with the White Sox before joining the Indians). He also occasionally played first and second base.

In the fall of 1957, Kennedy called Frank Lane, then general manager of the Indians, and asked for a job. "He told me, 'C'mon over, we'll see what we've got.'"

Lane hired Kennedy as a scout, which launched a new career for the former outfielder, then 37.

Two years later Kennedy became assistant farm director under Hoot Evers and it was in that capacity, in 1959, that he scouted and signed two left-handed pitchers who,

everyone thought, were destined for greatness—Sam McDowell and Tommy John.

As it turned out, McDowell, by his own admission, drank himself out of baseball while compiling a 15-year major league won-lost record of 141-134.

John did much better. He won 288 games and lost 231 in a 26 year career.

"We used to get the sports sections from newspapers in different cities and I kept reading about this kid in Pittsburgh throwing no-hitters," recalled Kennedy, talking about McDowell, who was 17 at the time.

"Our scout's reports on McDowell were not very good, that he had a bad attitude, or something, but I told Hoot that we couldn't afford to not check out the kid ourselves.

"So we did. We went to his last high school game and he was pitching a no-hitter for six or seven innings. He went behind the backstop to get a drink of water, so I followed him, and a bunch of younger kids were squirting water and horsing around.

"McDowell walked up to them, tapped a couple on the shoulder, excused himself and got a drink. Some of them began pushing McDowell and, you know, fooling around with him, but it didn't faze Sam. He just got his drink and walked away.

"I remember thinking to myself, 'That's pretty good temperament.' If that's me and I'm pitching a no-hitter, no way could I handle it the way he did. I was really impressed.

"On our way back to Cleveland, Hoot asked me how high I thought we should go to sign McDowell, and I told him, 'It's going to take a lot . . . probably about seventy,' meaning $70,000.

"Hoot said I was crazy, but that's what I told Nate Dolin (then an Indians vice president). Dolin said, 'OK, if you like (McDowell) that much, go a little higher if you have to.'"

They didn't have to . . . Kennedy and Evers returned to Pittsburgh, and met with McDowell's parents, who accepted the Indians' offer of $70,000.

"I later found out from Charlie Fox (then a scout for San Francisco) that the Giants would have gone as high as $100,000 for McDowell," said Kennedy.

A year later Kennedy heard about another left-handed pitcher, John, who was then an 18-year-old star in Terre Haute, Indiana.

"I really liked his action," Kennedy remembered the first time he saw John. "He wasn't overpowering, but he had good control, good rhythm, good command of his pitches. I knew we had to act fast because the Phillies were trying to sign him and were offering $30,000 or $35,000, and were waiting for an answer.

"I told one of our employees to take Tommy and his dad out to dinner. I cautioned him, 'Don't let them get to a phone, and keep them out late, I don't care what you have to do. Then pick them up the next morning at eight o'clock and take them out to a driving range because they love to hit golf balls.'

"The guy (employee) tells me, 'But I don't play golf, I don't hit golf balls,' and I told him, 'You're going to hit some tomorrow.'

"That's what happened. When Tommy and his dad got to the ball park the next day about two o'clock, I asked them, 'Did you make your phone call (to the Phillies)?' Tommy's father said, 'No, we didn't have a chance. We were out too late last night, and we were at the driving range hitting golf balls all morning.'

"Which is exactly what I wanted. So I said to Tommy's father, 'I've got an offer right here. I'll give Tommy $40,000 if you sign right now with the Indians.' He looked at Tommy and asked, 'What do you think?' Tommy said, 'Dad, I really like it here,' and the father says, 'OK, you've got a deal.'

"I picked up an old scorecard that was lying there and wrote out the details, spreading the money out over five years. Tommy's father signed it and I sent it up to the office to be typed.

"That's how we signed Tommy John . . . how we got him before the Phillies did," said Kennedy, smiling broadly again.

Kennedy left the Indians in 1962 before he ever saw his two phenoms, McDowell and John, pitch in the major leagues. He accepted a job as manager of Salt Lake City in the (Class AAA) Pacific Coast League.

"Gabe Paul, who was the general manager of the Indians then, said I was crazy to leave a major league job for one in the minors, but I wanted to manage one time to see what it was like . . . to see if I liked it," said Kennedy.

Salt Lake City finished second with an 81-73 record in 1962, and the next two-plus seasons Kennedy managed the Chicago Cubs, though not with the same degree of success. The Cubs under Kennedy were seventh in 1963, eighth in 1964, and when their record fell to 24-32 in June 1965, he was replaced.

Kennedy managed the Athletics in 1968, their first season in Oakland, finishing sixth with an 82-80 record. Later, he was general manager of the Cubs (1977-81), and worked under former teammate Al Rosen as vice president of baseball operations with both the Houston Astros (1981-85) and San Francisco Giants (1985-92).

But it was Kennedy's years in Cleveland that were the best of his career.

"My wife used to say that, when we were in Cleveland, it was like being in Camelot," he said.

"She was right. Especially in 1948."

DOUBLE PLAY COMBO-LOU BOUDREAU (L) AND JOE GORDON (R)

CHAPTER SIXTEEN

Allie Clark

"Don't you dare throw over here and try to pick somebody off first base."

Allie Clark wasn't sure how long he'd be able to talk about "the best team and the best bunch of guys I ever played with," as well as "the best year of my career," as he called the Indians of a half century ago.

"I've got cancer in the larynx and I don't know how long my mouth and throat will hold out, but I'll go as long as I can," said Clark, who still lives in South Amboy, New Jersey, where he was an ironworker for 29 years after his retirement from baseball.

"I got it (cancer) from cigars and chewing tobacco. Two and a half years ago (1995) the doctors at Sloan-Kettering (Cancer Center) in New York cut out part of my jaw. I've had 38 radiation treatments and I have to go back every two and a half months to get checked out. As far as I know, I'm doing fine, as long as it doesn't spread."

Clark's cancer is similar—though not as bad, he said—to that suffered by Bill Tuttle, another former American League outfielder who lost part of his jaw to the disease, and who visits professional baseball training camps every spring lecturing against the use of tobacco.

"With Bill, it's really a shame," said Clark. "His jaw, taste buds . . . so much is gone because of the cancer. Compared to him, I guess I was lucky. I only have an indentation on the left side of my neck that you can see, where they cut out part of my jaw."

Clark also referred to Brett Butler, the former Indians and Los Angeles Dodgers outfielder who had a cancerous tonsil removed in 1995 and retired after the 1997 season. "I have to carry a bottle of water with me every time I leave the house because my mouth and throat get so dry, the same as Butler," said Clark.

Even before his battle with cancer, Clark underwent coronary bypass surgery in 1991. "I didn't have a heart attack, but my breathing was bad. They found that I had five arteries that were all screwed up (blocked), I guess from too much good food all my life. I was pretty lucky then, too," he said.

"But I'm doing OK. Hey, I'm 74 (75 on June 16, 1998) and I've had some good times, some good years."

A handsome, dark haired, six-foot, 195-pound outfielder when he was traded to the Indians by the New York Yankees for pitcher Red Embree on December 11, 1947, Clark was a central figure in the playoff game against the Boston Red Sox in 1948.

Manager Lou Boudreau, wanting to take advantage of Clark's right-handed bat in Fenway Park, assigned him to play first base—even though Clark had never before played the position.

Not only did it result in a heated disagreement between Boudreau and his two bosses, owner Bill Veeck and Hank

Allie Clark

Greenberg, then vice president of the Indians, it also created a problem for the manager with Eddie Robinson, then the team's regular first baseman, who reportedly was upset about being benched.

"I don't know how Boudreau decided to play me at first base," said Clark. "After we lost that last game (to Detroit, 7-1, in Cleveland), we showered, got dressed, went to the station and rode the train all night to Boston.

"Lou never said anything to me, and when I got to the clubhouse (at Fenway Park), there was a first baseman's glove in my locker. I don't know whose it was. Maybe it was Boudreau's because he could play any position.

"I took it and went into Boudreau's office and asked him, 'Lou, is this right?' He said, 'Yeah, you're playing first base.' That's all. So I did.

"I know Eddie was disappointed . . . who could blame him? If I'd been in his shoes, I probably would have felt the same way. But it was nothing that I did, or could do about it."

Later, according to Gene Bearden, who pitched for the Indians, Clark went to him and said, "Don't you dare throw over here and try to pick somebody off first base. Remember, I never played here before."

Clark chuckled at the memory, and said, "Sure I was scared. Hey, the Red Sox had a guy named Ted Williams, and a couple other pretty good left-handed hitters in their lineup. I didn't know nothing about playing first base."

And Don Fitzpatrick, who was the visiting team batboy at Fenway Park in 1948, also recalled that, "Clark was so stressed out, so uptight, that he couldn't even sit down between innings. A couple of times Boudreau sent him down in the runway leading to the clubhouse because he made everybody else so nervous."

Clark didn't deny Fitzpatrick's comment. As he said, "I was the happiest guy in the world when Boudreau took me out and put in Robinson (after the Indians had taken a 5-1 lead in the fourth inning). Actually, I guess I did OK. I went 0-for-2, but I fielded one grounder and took four throws without doing anything wrong.

"Looking back at it, the amazing thing about it, if I had done anything to lose the game, I wouldn't have been blamed . . . you know who would have gotten the blame?"

Boudreau? "Right," said Clark. "That's the kind of manager he was. Boudreau would play his hunches, he'd do anything he thought would help win a game. I thought he was a helluva manager and, especially, a helluva player."

In the World Series that followed the Indians' victory over the Red Sox in the playoff for the pennant, Clark played right field in the second game, going 0-for-3, as Bob Lemon beat the Boston Braves, 4-1.

Clark was a good player, too, although, "I would have been a lot better if I had a better (throwing) arm. But it was my own fault that I didn't," he said.

"The biggest mistake I made in my life was having an operation on my elbow (in the winter of 1946-47). Back then doctors didn't know what the hell they were doing. They said there were some tissues or something tightening up in there, and thought they could fix it. I don't know why I listened to them and got it done.

"It didn't help, it ruined my whole career," Clark said of the surgery on his elbow, "and to this day I still feel soreness. It never got any better. Never.

"I didn't have a real strong arm to begin with, but the operation made it worse. I'd play five or six innings and they'd take me out because they were worried about my arm not being good enough.

"That's why the Yankees traded me to Cleveland. I was always a good hitter, but they thought I couldn't throw."

While the 1948 Indians were the "best team" and the "best bunch of guys" Clark said he ever played with, the Yankees were his boyhood favorites.

Growing up in South Amboy, he idolized Joe Gordon, who was a rookie second baseman for the Yankees when Clark was a 15-year-old sophomore in high school.

"Then the most amazing thing happened after the Indians got me," said Clark. "Who do you think I roomed with?"

Without waiting for a guess, Clark answered his own question: "Joe Gordon! My idol. That was really amazing!" he said again. "But I never told him. I figured it probably would make him feel too old, though he only had six or seven years on me."

Clark batted .310 while playing 81 games for the Indians in 1948, 65 in the outfield, five at third base and, of course, one at first base. Included in his statistics were nine homers and 38 runs batted in, though they weren't good enough to guarantee him regular employment.

The next season, 1949, Clark was up and down between Cleveland and the Indians' top farm club, San Diego of the (Class AAA) Pacific Coast League.

Clark hit only .176 in 35 games with the Indians, then lost his place on the roster to Luke Easter, who had been burning up the Pacific Coast League and was a favorite of Greenberg.

"They needed to make room for Luke and I was the one to go down," said Clark, who returned to the Indians in 1950, but didn't fare much better. He played 59 games in Cleveland that season, but hit only .215.

Al Lopez replaced Boudreau as manager in 1951 and, after only three games, Clark was traded, along with infielder Lou Klein, to the Philadelphia Athletics for outfielder Sam Chapman on May 10.

"I was sorry to leave the Indians because there were some wonderful people over there. But I thought it would be good for my career because I'd get a chance to play more in Philadelphia," said Clark.

He didn't, at least not much more. Clark went on to hit .251 in 59 games (18 as a pinch hitter) in 1951, and .274 in 71 games (21 as a pinch hitter) for the Athletics in 1952.

A year later, Clark's career took another turn for the worse as he was sold for the $10,000 waiver price to the Chicago White Sox. He batted .180 in 29 games that season with the Athletics and White Sox, and after being sent to Rochester of the (Class AAA) International League, Clark hit .328 in 80 games.

Shortly thereafter Clark was out of baseball. "Paul Richards (then general manager of the Baltimore Orioles) wanted me in 1954, but Rochester wouldn't let me go, and I hung it up . . . I became an ironworker," said Clark.

Clark's baseball career held much promise when it began back in 1941.

He was signed for a $250 bonus by the Yankees and worked his way up through the minors, from Easton, Maryland of the (Class D) Eastern Shore League and Amsterdam, New York of the (Class C) Canadian-American League that first season, then to Norfolk, Virginia of the (Class B) Piedmont League in 1942 and, briefly, to Newark, New Jersey of the (Class AA) International League in 1943, when Uncle Sam beckoned.

Clark spent the next three years in the Army medical corps. After serving in England, France, Luxembourg and Germany for eight months, he was discharged in February 1946 and immediately headed for Florida for spring training with the Yankees minor leaguers.

It was that season, at Newark, that Clark established impressive credentials with a .344 average, 14 homers and 70 RBIs.

Only one player in the league hit for a higher average than Clark —by only .005 percentage points—a rookie with Montreal named Jackie Robinson, who batted .349, but hit 11 fewer homers and drove in four fewer runs.

"I was impressed by (Robinson), and I was glad to see him make the majors," said Clark. "I thought I was on my way, too."

Which he was, though not as promptly, nor as successfully as Robinson.

Clark started the 1947 season at Newark, as the Yankees were well stocked with outstanding players, including outfielders Joe DiMaggio, Charlie "King Kong" Keller and Tommy Henrich.

However, at mid-season when DiMaggio and Keller were sidelined with injuries, the Yankees promoted Clark.

"That was the highlight of my career, the first time I walked into the clubhouse at Yankee Stadium. It was only 28 miles from where I grew up. As a kid I always dreamed about playing for the Yankees," said Clark, "and the feeling I had that day was something I'll never forget."

He appeared in 24 games, batting .373, though it wasn't good enough to keep him with the Yankees. When DiMaggio and Keller returned to action, Clark was sent back to Newark and again came close to winning the International League batting championship.

This time his .334 average (with 23 homers and 86 RBI) was third to the .337 mark compiled by Vernal "Nippy" Jones, and Hank Sauer, with .336. Both Jones and Sauer went on to productive seasons in the National League.

Clark was recalled by the Yankees in September and was issued uniform No. 3, making him one of the last players to wear Babe Ruth's number before it was retired in 1948.

Another distinction of which Clark is particularly proud was that he delivered a key run-producing single in the sixth inning of the seventh and deciding game in New York's 5-2 victory over Brooklyn in the 1947 World Series.

"I batted for Yogi Berra and I've been told that was the only time anybody ever pinch hit for him," said Clark. "I kid Yogi about it every time I see him."

Clark went to the plate with the Yankees leading, 3-2, with two runners aboard and two out, after left hander Joe

Allie Clark

"To me, the two best guys on the team were Gordon and Clark."

To Clark, "Everybody on that (1948 Indians) team was great. I liked 'em all. We didn't have any problems. None at all."

Of Larry Doby, who joined the Indians as major league baseball's second black player in 1947, and Satchel Paige, who was signed by the Indians a year later, Clark said:

"I never heard too much (abuse) aimed at Larry, and whatever there was, he handled it well. (Doby) was very quiet, but he didn't seem to be nervous or bothered by what was going on. He mixed in with all of us. Nobody on the team, that I knew of, caused him trouble and he did a helluva good job."

And Paige? "Well, Ol' Satch was a piece of work, but not a bad guy . . . a comical guy to be around. I'll never forget the time we went into Chicago (August 13-15) the first time after he was signed. The place (Comiskey Park) was sold out, but the (black) fans didn't care. They wanted to see Satch pitch and they broke the turnstiles to get in."

That was Paige's second major league start on August 13 and became his fourth victory as he pitched a complete game five hitter to beat the White Sox, 5-0.

As reported by Harry Jones in the *Cleveland Plain Dealer* the next day:

"A mob of 51,013 fanatics, one of the largest crowds in Chicago's baseball history, elbowed their way into Comiskey Park . . . to see the fabulous Satchel Paige pitch, and the old boy didn't disappoint them.

"Making a grand entrance as a major leaguer in a city in which he sparkled for years as the greatest Negro flinger of them all, Satchel hurled the Indians back into the American league lead. Paige's superlative efforts enabled the Indians to sneak back into the lead by virtue of a half game over the Philadelphia Athletics.

"Thousands were turned away from the gates and thousands more clogged the aisles as the ancient Alabaman made his second big league start a successful one, permitting only one White Sox runner to reach third base, and only two others to advance as far as second."

Clark said, "From then on, everybody wanted to see Satch pitch. Veeck was a great promoter, and signing Paige proved it. Not only because (Paige) pitched well for us, but

Hatten replaced Hank Behrman on the mound for the Dodgers. Clark's single scored Phil Rizzuto with the Yankees' fourth run.

Two months later he was traded to the Indians.

"Sure, the Yankees were my favorite team . . . my uncle used to take me to Yankee Stadium to see them play, and I was there the day Lou Gehrig made his 'luckiest man on the face of the earth' (retirement) speech in 1939. But I figured that going to Cleveland would be good for me," said Clark.

"I mean, how much of a chance would a young guy get to play on a team that has DiMaggio, Keller and Henrich, not to mention (Johnny) Lindell, in the outfield? So, all things considered, I was glad to go to Cleveland.

"The Yankees were a great team (in 1947), but I still think the Indians (of 1948) were best. Besides, they had Gordon (who had been acquired from the Yankees a year earlier), which really made it great for me," said Clark.

Interestingly, Steve Gromek, one of the Indians pitchers in 1948, said when he was interviewed for this book, also because he attracted a lot of fans everywhere we played."

Now, though he is battling the debilitating effects of cancer, Clark, who has been retired as an ironworker for 14 years, reflects often on his career, as well as the direction major league baseball has taken since the advent of free agency in 1976.

"The most I ever made was $12,500 in 1949, which was right after we won the World Series, and I got a $1,000 (a year) raise," he said. "The way I look at it, more power to the guys who are getting big money now.

"When I was playing, the (owners) told us to do this or take that. They had all the power, all the control. Now it's different, although I think some of the big name players and their agents are going overboard. That's the only thing I worry about. I hope they don't overprice themselves."

Clark and his wife Frances, whom he married in 1944, raised six children—Alfred, Eugene, Maureen, Susan, Kathy and Denise—and have 13 grandchildren, all of whom live in the area. "We're lucky, we see a lot of them all," said Clark.

And with that, the interview ended as Clark's voice began to weaken. "I guess I've done enough talking," he said.

CHAPTER SEVENTEEN

Mel Harder

"Bearden sure proved us wrong, and once he did . . . that's when I started to believe."

" I don't want to take anything away from those guys, but I never thought we had a chance in 1948, at least, not in the beginning," said Mel Harder, who became a coach for the Indians that season after a 20-year career as a pitcher—a very good pitcher.

"I knew it was a pretty good club, with some good veteran players. But you have to have pitching to win a pennant, and all we had were (Bob) Feller and (Bob) Lemon, and we weren't even sure about Lemon. We were only *hoping* he'd come through, and remember, it also was Feller's twelfth year or so.

"We went a long time, into May as I recall, looking for a third starter, and it wasn't until then that (Gene) Bearden even got a chance to pitch. Once he did, he was great. But my early evaluation of him was that, because his best pitch was a knuckleball, I didn't think of him as a starter.

"Bearden didn't have much of a curveball, and his fastball was just average. I figured he might be able to help us out of the bullpen, maybe as a middle man. I think we all felt that way; (Manager Lou) Boudreau and the other coaches, Bill McKechnie and Muddy Ruel.

"But Bearden sure proved us wrong, and once he did, I guess that's when I started to believe (we had a chance to win the pennant)," added Harder, who compiled a 223-186

won-lost record for the Indians from 1928-47 and—in the opinion of many—belongs in the Hall of Fame.

Something else that made the Indians a pennant contender in 1948, Harder said, "Was when Boudreau moved Larry Doby from right field to center (replacing Thurman Tucker). That changed our ball club.

"Tucker was a good outfielder, but he was just an average hitter. Doby became a great outfielder, covered a lot of ground, and kept improving as a hitter. Then we got Bob Kennedy from the White Sox (on June 2, 1948) which improved our defense even more, and the club really started playing well after that."

Harder said that McKechnie, who was then 61 years old and had managed for 25 years, winning four National League pennants before joining the Indians, was Boudreau's primary confidante and advisor.

"That's why Bill Veeck hired McKechnie (in 1947), because he felt Boudreau needed someone with more experience," said Harder.

Veeck also added Muddy Ruel to Boudreau's staff in 1948. Ruel, then 52, had managed the St. Louis Browns the previous season.

McKechnie and Ruel replaced Oscar Mellilo and George Susce, both close personal friends of Boudreau who

Mel Harder as an Indians pitcher in 1930.

has made no secret of the fact that he was angered when Veeck replaced them.

Harder was the first base coach in 1948, then served as the Indians' pitching coach from 1949-63. He said he was approached by Veeck midway through the 1947 season, when his record was 6-4—"I was lucky to have won that many," he said—with a 4.50 earned run average in 15 games.

"We weren't going anywhere and, sometime in June, Veeck and Boudreau talked to me about working with Lemon and (Steve) Gromek," said Harder. "I knew my (pitching) career was about over, so it didn't make any difference to me.

"I was a player-coach the second half of the season, and I was supposed to work with the minor league pitchers in 1948, which I did in spring training. But right after the season started, they called me back to Cleveland and made me the first base coach. Ruel, who had been Walter Johnson's catcher (1923-27), worked with the pitchers."

Still, it was Harder's influence on Lemon that helped make him a big winner—culminating in Lemon's election to the Hall of Fame in 1976. Harder also is credited with helping develop other Indians pitchers who came along later, most notably among them Early Wynn, Mike Garcia and Herb Score.

"Lemon's conversion to pitching was simple because he had such a terrific natural sinker," said Harder. "The main thing I did was to help Lemon improve his curveball, and to give him a little idea of what pitching was all about, that it was more than just throwing the ball.

"When he first started to pitch, he had the idea he had to throw as hard as he could, throw the ball by the batter all the time. But his sinker didn't work if he tried to overthrow it, and the main thing was that he had to get it over for strikes. Once he did, he was very good. He had a good arm and picked up pitching very fast.

"Seeing Lemon develop from a third baseman-outfielder to a pitcher was a source of much satisfaction to me," said Harder

Lemon, whose record was 11-5 in 1947, his first full year on the mound, blossomed in 1948 to 20-14. It was his first of three consecutive 20 victory seasons and seven in his 15-year major league career, during which he compiled a 207-128 won-lost record.

"I also had a natural sinker," said Harder. "I think, from the time I was about eight years old, I'd throw a ball

and it would sink. All I had to do was turn it over a little to make it sink.

"It was the same with Lemon. When he played third base (in the minor leagues (1938-42) and fielded a ball, he'd throw it six or seven feet high and by the time it got to first base it would be down low. After he was switched to center field (and played there briefly in 1946 and 1947), he'd catch a fly ball and have to throw it high to the plate because it would sink so much by the time it got to the catcher.

"That's the reason they made Lemon a pitcher. He had a natural sinker."

Harder also worked with Gromek, and helped Feller refine his curveball which, it was said, became an even more effective pitch than his famed fastball.

"When you throw a curveball," said Harder, "you don't throw it as hard as a fastball. The speeds must be different. If you try to put too much on a curveball, you won't get the spin that's necessary.

"For example, if you throw a 90 m.p.h. fastball, you should throw your curveball about 82 or 83 (m.p.h.) to make it bite. You've got to give the spin time to take effect, to get a bigger break on the ball."

All of which Harder preached to Lemon, as well as Gromek and Feller and other Indians pitchers who came along later.

Harder said he was "neither confident nor concerned" when the Indians were forced into a playoff game for the pennant. After Feller lost to Detroit and Hal Newhouser in the final regular game of the season, and Boston beat New York, the Indians and Red Sox each was left with a 96-58 record.

"I just hoped and prayed we had somebody to pitch a good game" said Harder, admitting, "I thought it would be Lemon" that Boudreau would pick to start against the Red Sox in Fenway Park.

"I was surprised . . . I think a lot of guys probably were (surprised), but everybody accepted it . . . nobody argued with Boudreau that I can recall.

"The only thing along that line that I remember is that Joe Gordon said that Boudreau had been making the decisions all year and got us that far, and that he for one was satisfied to let Boudreau do it for one more game.

"It's possible that McKechnie had some input (in the decision to start Bearden), and maybe Boudreau went to him and asked for his advice, I don't know. All I know is that Boudreau told us Bearden was going to pitch, and that was that," said Harder.

"How did I feel about it?" Harder repeated the next question. "I thought it was good because Bearden had been pitching good ball. He was good against both right-handed and left-handed hitters, and the fact that he threw mainly knuckleballs didn't take much out of his arm."

After an overnight train trip to Boston, the Indians went directly to Fenway Park for the afternoon game the next day. "Boudreau didn't have anything to say before the game, we didn't have a meeting or anything, we just went out on the field and played," said Harder.

And beat the Red Sox, 8-3.

Harder said he also was glad that Joe McCarthy, the Red Sox manager, chose Denny Galehouse, not Mel Parnell to pitch for Boston.

"Galehouse had done a good job against us in relief earlier in the season (July 30) which probably was the reason McCarthy picked him," said Harder.

Galehouse's record against the Indians going into the playoff game was 1-1, and Parnell's was 3-2.

"The way it turned out, I'm glad it was Galehouse and not Parnell," added Harder.

Beating the Red Sox vaulted the Indians into the World Series, and Harder, ever the connoisseur of pitching, said he was worried about the Boston Braves, primarily because of their two aces, Johnny Sain and Warren Spahn.

They had combined to win 39 games that season, inspiring the Braves' battle cry, "Spahn and Sain and two days of rain!" meaning each could pitch effectively with only two days between starts.

But still, the fact there was no day off—the so-called "travel day" —scheduled between any of the World Series games in 1948, probably helped the Indians.

Harder called Sain's 1-0 victory over Feller in the opener "well deserved," even though the Braves' run was tainted, the result of a blown call by second base umpire Bill Stewart on an attempted pickoff play by Feller and Boudreau in the eighth inning.

"No doubt about it, the runner (Phil Masi) was out . . . he was out by two or three feet," said Harder. "Everybody in the park saw it, except the guy who made the call (Stewart). Sure, it upset our guys, but there was nothing we could do about it. Sain was very good." He allowed four singles, struck out five and didn't issue a walk.

Sain also was effective the next time he pitched, three days later, in the fourth game, but so was Gromek, who "pitched probably his best game of the year, and Doby won it for him," said Harder. Gromek tossed a seven hitter and Doby hit a home run that provided the margin of victory.

"I felt bad for Feller, we all did, getting beat the way he did in the first game, and he didn't have anything (in the fifth game, an 11-5 loss to the Braves). But that's the way it goes for pitchers sometimes," said Harder.

The Indians won the Series as Bearden saved Lemon's 4-3 victory in the sixth game, and everybody expected they'd repeat in 1949.

But it didn't happen. They fell to third place, eight games behind the Yankees, who won the pennant, and seven behind Boston, which finished second.

Bearden, the biggest hero in 1948, became the biggest disappointment in 1949 as his record fell to 8-8.

According to Bearden, it was a hamstring injury he suffered in spring training that hampered him all season, causing his ineffectiveness—though that revelation came as a surprise to Harder.

"Gene never said anything to me about his leg bothering him, and I don't know if he ever said anything to Boudreau," said Harder. "I was surprised when I heard about it, after (Bearden) left the club (in 1950).

"The only thing I could figure was that he had trouble controlling his knuckleball. He had trouble getting it down in the strike zone."

That theory was in accordance with a report that previously had been attributed to Casey Stengel, who'd been Bearden's minor league manager. Stengel allegedly had advised his players on the Yankees, and others around the league to lay off Bearden's knuckleball, and make him come in with his below-average fastball and curve.

Harder, who was Stengel's pitching coach with the New York Mets in 1964, said, "Casey never admitted that to me, but it makes sense . . . Bearden was having control trouble (in 1949)."

After Boudreau was fired in November 1950, Harder remained as the Indians pitching coach under Lopez (1951-56), Kerby Farrell (1957), Bobby Bragan (1958), Joe Gordon (1958-60), Jimmie Dykes (1960-61), Mel McGaha (1962), and Birdie Tebbetts (1963).

As a coach under Lopez, Harder was involved in another World Series, in 1954 which the Indians lost to the then-New York Giants in four games.

"It's a shame that Feller didn't get a chance to pitch one of those games, but we had to go with our best, and he wasn't one of our best that season," said Harder. Lemon started twice, and Wynn and Garcia once each.

It was in 1957 that Harder witnessed the worst injury he'd ever seen in baseball. "I was in the bullpen, but I could see that Herb (Score) was really hurt," Harder talked about the night, May 7, Score was hit in the eye by a line drive off the bat of the Yankees Gil McDougald.

"I was afraid he'd lose his eye . . . we didn't know if he'd ever pitch again," said Harder. "When he did come back (in 1958), Bragan was the manager and we took it easy with Herb, we never pushed him."

Score pitched 12 games that season, five as a starter, and had a 2-3 record.

It was during one of those games that he hurt his arm—Score has said it was a torn tendon in his elbow—and it was that injury, not being hit in the eye the previous season, that he insists all but ruined his career.

"Only the Lord knows how good he could have been if he had not been injured, either his eye or his elbow, whatever it was," said Harder.

After his eye injury, Score won only 17 games and lost 26 the next five seasons, and went into broadcasting in 1964.

From 1957-61, Harder also worked under Frank Lane, then the Indians general manager who was credited (should that be *blamed*?) for making 49 deals involving 108 players in fewer than five seasons.

"He was a wild man," Harder said of Lane. "He couldn't go to sleep at night without dreaming up a trade. He was always up to something, and we never knew what it was until after he did it. I can't say what kind of an effect Lane had on the team, except that I know the players didn't like him.

"And, of course, they especially didn't like it when he traded Rocky Colavito (to Detroit for Harvey Kuenn on April 17, 1960).

"Rocky was at the top of his game at the time and guys on the team were really disgusted. It might have had an effect on what we did that season (finished fourth with a 76-78 record)," said Harder.

Of all the Indians managers with whom Harder worked, there's no doubt he held Lopez in the highest regard.

"Al was great," said Harder. "He could manage guys and he knew what he was doing on the field. He didn't make a big deal about anything, he just went about his job and made sure everybody else did, too."

And the others?

"Well, Kerby (Farrell) might have been overwhelmed," said Harder. "He might have been a good minor league manager, but . . .," and that which he left unsaid spoke volumes.

"Bragan was a pretty good manager, but he did too many things people didn't like."

People? "People like Frank Lane. (Bragan) was a good talker, but . . . ," and again Harder's voice trailed off, leaving much unsaid, though clearly understood.

"The players liked Gordon. They played hard for him, and what more could you want? I thought he made good moves, and ran a good game. It's just that things went bad for Joe, which was too bad.

"The same could be said for Dykes. He had some good years as a manager, and some bad years as a manager. He was, more or less, like Gordon. A player's manager, if you know what I mean."

McGaha? "Well, we were good friends. But he might have been overwhelmed, too. He also was a good minor league manager, but . . . ," and again Harder left unsaid what he thought.

And Tebbetts? "I don't know if he liked me or not. Birdie did things that other managers wouldn't do."

Like what? "Well, he knew his baseball and he always let you know that he did, but I'll let it go at that."

What about Boudreau? "Well, I was surprised when (Indians owner) Alva Bradley gave him the job (in November 1941). I was surprised because Lou was so young (then 24). Once he got some experience, he was OK.

"One thing about Boudreau, he was a real gambler. I don't mean that he gambled money, I mean he gambled on the field. He played hunches. He thought he could handle every situation that way. Sometimes got him in trouble, but a lot of times it was good. Like it was in the playoff game against the Red Sox when he started Bearden and played Allie Clark at first base. That was typical of the things he'd do.

"But I've got to say, too, that he thought about things, he was always ahead of things, hitting and everything. A lot of times he gave signs to the catcher as to what pitch to call for, especially if he had an idea it was time to throw a certain pitch, a curveball or a change up. He was always thinking ahead."

It was Gabe Paul who fired Harder as pitching coach at the end of the 1963 season. "That was OK, it was Gabe's prerogative as general manager. But the way he let me go is what burned me up. He called me on the phone a couple of days after the end of the season. I don't know why he couldn't have told me right away."

"He told me they were going to make a change. He didn't give me a reason. Nothing. Just that they were going to make a change.

"I told him, 'OK, Gabe.' That's all. Why should I have said anything more to him?"

Harder joined the Mets, under Stengel, when he was replaced by Early Wynn, one of the pitchers he'd tutored—one of the pitchers he'd helped get into the Hall of Fame.

However, one season in New York was all Harder could handle, and he resigned when the 1964 season ended.

"Casey wanted to know whether he did anything wrong," said Harder. "I told him he didn't, that he was the only reason I liked it (with the Mets), which was the truth. I loved Casey, but I hated New York.

"And don't let anybody kid you. Casey was not a clown. He knew what he was doing, what he was talking about—even if some of you guys (in the media) didn't."

Upon leaving Stengel and the Mets, Harder wasn't out of work for long. The following season, 1965, he joined the Chicago Cubs, then managed by Kennedy who'd played for the Indians in 1948.

But when Leo Durocher replaced Kennedy in 1966, he fired all the coaches and Harder went to the Cincinnati Reds as pitching coach, first under then-manager Don Heffner, and later Dave Bristol through the 1968.

In 1969, Harder rejoined another former member of the 1948 Indians, Gordon, who was then managing the Kansas City Royals.

At the end of the season Harder, then 60, hung up his uniform and retired, ending a 42-year career in major league baseball.

And though Harder said he never had any managerial aspirations, he is credited with a perfect 3-0 record as an interim manager of the Indians on two different occasions.

Coach Mel Harder with radio broadcaster Jimmy Dudley.

He led them to an 8-5 victory over the then-Los Angeles Angels on October 1, 1961, after Dykes was fired, and to a sweep of a double header over the Angels on September 30, 1962, after McGaha was dismissed.

Harder faced some of baseball's all-time greats in his career— Babe Ruth, Lou Gehrig, Ty Cobb, Jimmie Foxx, Joe Cronin, Mickey Cochrane, Al Simmons, Charley Gehringer, Joe DiMaggio and Ted Williams, among many others—and it was Williams, in fact, who once called Harder the toughest pitcher he ever faced.

It did not, however, open the door to the Hall of Fame for Harder, even though Williams is a member of the Veterans Committee which elects oldtimers for the honor coveted by all professional baseball players.

"I don't know what they think about, what the standards are (for election to the Hall of Fame)," Harder said when he was bypassed again in 1997.

"Sure, I was disappointed. Anyone would be. People in Cleveland bring it up to me often, my family, everybody.

(But) What can I say? I'm not making a big deal out of it. I don't let it bother me. I won't let it get me down. Maybe some day I'll make it, but for now, well, that's it," and again Harder's voice trails off, leaving his thoughts unstated.

When he's asked if he believes he deserves to be in the Hall of Fame, Harder replied, "I do, because (my statistics) compare with some of the others who are in the Hall of Fame."

The fact is, Harder won more games than 18 of the 56 pitchers enshrined in the Hall of Fame (through 1997).

Also relevant is the fact that Harder never pitched for an Indians team that won a pennant—the closest was in 1940 when they lost by one game to the Tigers—and in six of Harder's 20 seasons with the Indians their won-lost record was below .500.

There were five high points of Harder's career, he said. "They were the four All-Star games (in which he pitched), and pitching the opener in Cleveland in 1932 (the first game in the Stadium against the Philadelphia Athletics) . . . they're all tied at the top."

Harder did not allow a run in the 13 innings he pitched in those four All-Star appearances in 1934, 1935, 1936 and 1937. Those 13 scoreless innings are the most by any pitcher in All-Star competition.

It was in the 1934 game, in which Carl Hubbell of the National League gained lasting fame by striking out five future Hall of Famers in succession (Babe Ruth, Lou Gehrig, Jimmie Foxx, Al Simmons and Joe Cronin) before Harder took over for the American League and pitched five scoreless innings, allowing one hit.

Then, in 1935, Harder blanked the National League over the final three innings to earn a save in the 4-1 victory credited to Lefty Gomez.

As for pitching the Stadium opener on July 31, 1932 in front of a crowd of 80,184, Harder scattered six hits, but lost, 1-0, to Hall of Famer Lefty Grove, who tossed a four hitter to beat the Indians.

Of that game, Harder said, "I wasn't supposed to pitch, Wes Ferrell was, but when he got to the park he said his arm was stiff so Peck (Indians manager Roger Peckinpaugh) gave me the ball. It was the biggest thrill of my career, until then, to pitch that game. I would have liked to win but I wasn't any more disappointed than for any game I lost."

The toughest batter he ever faced, Harder said, "Probably was Gehrig. It was hard to fool him and, unlike Ruth, Gehrig would hit the ball where it was pitched. If it was away from him, he'd take it to left field. If it was in on him, he pulled it to right field.

"Ruth was different. He'd pull everything, going for a home run. But everything he hit was a rocket, like a golf ball.

"Pitching against either one of those guys, Gehrig or Ruth, was no easy job. You couldn't throw the ball down the middle to either one, you had to work the corners, go outside, inside, and keep it low. If you wanted to go up, you'd go inside, maybe chest high inside.

"And you had to change up on them once in awhile. You couldn't keep showing them the same speed all the time, otherwise they'd kill you."

As for Williams and DiMaggio, Harder said: "I had pretty good luck against both of them. I pitched both of them the way I pitched most guys. I moved the ball in and out, stayed away from the middle of the plate, and used all my pitches, my sinker, curveball and change up. They were just like Ruth and Gehrig; they'd kill you if you gave them a fat pitch down the middle."

And what about Cobb? "I only faced him once, in 1928, my first year and his last," said Harder. "It was a big thrill, although maybe it shouldn't be. Not what happened, anyway."

What happened, according to Harder, was this: "It was my first trip to Philadelphia (where Cobb and former Indians great Tris Speaker were then playing for the Athletics), and I went to Shibe Park early to watch them hit.

"Roger Peckinpaugh, our manager then, took me over to the Philadelphia dugout and introduced me to (Athletics owner and manager) Connie Mack, and then to Speaker and Cobb. That's what was so thrilling to me.

"When the game started, I was in the bullpen, as I was pitching relief then, and Peckinpaugh told me to warm up early in the game with the Athletics ahead something like 7-2 though I don't remember the exact score (it was 6-1).

"Peckinpaugh called me into the game in the bottom of the second and I got out of it OK, and again in the third, but not the fourth. I don't remember the first batter I faced (it was Max Bishop), but I walked him and then Cobb was up. I got behind on the count and had to come in with a pitch and he hit it over the right field wall.

"It was the first (major league) home run I gave up, and the last one of Cobb's career, as well as the only one he hit that season, as both he and Speaker retired when it ended.

Coaches Mel Harder (left) and Bill McKechnie (center) hug second baseman Joe Gordon after the Indians beat the Boston Red Sox, 8-3, in a one-game playoff to win the 1948 American League pennant. Pitcher Bob Lemon is directly behind Gordon, and pitcher Russ Christopher is at the right.

We lost that game big (15-2), though I wasn't the loser." Jake Miller was.

Harder faced Cobb one more time that season, again in relief on June 15 in a game at League Park, and walked him as the Athletics prevailed, 12-5. Thus, Cobb's career batting average against Harder was 1.000 (1-for-1).

"Some years later, when (the Indians) trained in Arizona, Cobb, who then lived in Scottsdale, came out to the park one day and looked me up. We sat in the dugout together and talked for ten or fifteen minutes. I remember him telling me that he remembered the home run he hit off me.

"I heard tell that Cobb was a pretty tough guy when he was young, when he was playing, but he was very good with me the few times I had anything to do with him," said Harder.

And who, in Harder's opinion, was the best pitcher? "I never saw Walter Johnson because he retired (in 1927) the year before I got to the big leagues. But from everything I heard, he must have been the best, although my favorite was Ted Lyons," who pitched for the White Sox from 1923-46.

"Lyons threw in the 85 to 90 m.p.h. range, but he had five pitches —fastball, curveball, knuckleball, change up

on his fastball, and change up on his curveball—and, I think, was the smartest pitcher I ever saw. I never took my eyes off him, anytime he pitched against us."

Where did Feller rank among the best pitchers in baseball? "I hate to say it, but Feller was not as good as I heard Johnson was, and in my opinion, Lefty Grove was second, with Feller behind both of them."

The worst time of Harder's career probably was the 1940 season, the year of the infamous "Cleveland Cry Babies," when the Indians staged a rebellion against then manager Oscar Vitt.

A dozen players, including Harder as spokesman, delivered, on June 13, a petition to Alva Bradley, the team owner, requesting that Vitt be fired.

According to Harder in a 1964 interview, "(Vitt) lost the respect of the players . . . it all started with the way he operated. He would pat you on the back one minute and then criticize you the next minute to somebody else. It was the sort of two-faced way of doing things that finally got to some of the players.

"We had a good ball club that year—Bob Feller, Hal Trosky, Jeff Heath, Lou Boudreau, Ken Keltner and a lot more—and they all thought we had a good chance to win the pennant. But they didn't feel we could do it with Vitt managing.

"(Pitcher) Johnny Allen and I tried to calm the thing down. The players wanted to go to Mr. Bradley right away. We tried to talk them out of it. Allen and I wanted to go to Mr. Bradley just by ourselves, since this wouldn't cause any publicity. Nobody would know about it.

"The way it finally happened was that a group of us went down there, and everybody who saw us walk into Mr. Bradley's office knew there was something going on. So that's how it started.

"But Vitt was kept on and we wound up losing the pennant to Detroit by one game," when Detroit rookie, Floyd Giebell, beat Feller, 2-0, at the Stadium on the third to last game of the season. The Indians won the next two, but the Tigers finished one game ahead.

On October 8, nine days after the season ended, Bradley fired Vitt, saying he was sorry he didn't do it sooner.

As he was still active as a player in 1947, Harder was present on July 5, when Doby was signed by Veeck as the first black player in the American League, and introduced by Boudreau to his new teammates when the Indians were in Chicago to play the White Sox.

"I remember that day very well," said Harder. "I was there, in the clubhouse, when Boudreau brought Doby around to meet everybody." He acknowledged there were "three or four players" who refused to shake hands with Doby. When asked who they were, Harder said, "Mostly southerners," but wouldn't otherwise identify them.

"I don't want to say," he said. "I don't want to get into that. They were guys who were southerners, guys who were brought up that way."

Southerners on the Indians roster when Doby joined them in 1947 were Jack Conway, Les Fleming, Eddie Robinson and Les Willis from Texas; Al Gettel, Virginia; Al Lopez, Florida; Dale Mitchell, Oklahoma; and Pat Seerey, Arkansas.

Harder said "just a few players" among the Indians showed any animosity toward Doby, that "they did their own way" and that "Larry took it all pretty good, too."

Otherwise, Harder said, "I don't know about the bench jockeys on other teams, but I do know Larry had a lot of trouble with hotels, he couldn't stay with us everywhere we played. It was especially tough for him in spring training (in Tucson, Arizona), and when we played exhibition games in the south. It was terrible, I felt sorry for him.

"(Doby) was able to handle things a little better in 1948, probably because he had gained some confidence in himself and was playing every day, and playing well, especially after Boudreau switched him to center field. I think that made a big difference in him. You could see that he was going to be very good."

Harder said he was taken completely by surprise when Veeck signed Satchel Paige. "We were all surprised. Nobody knew anything about it until after it happened," said Harder. "I had no idea how we were going to use him, whether as a reliever or starter. I had seen Satch in the Negro League, but that was some time before he joined us."

And when he saw Paige throw for the Indians? "I could see that the old guy knew how to pitch, and that good control was his best asset; he could hit the corners (of the plate) consistently, and he'd give you side-arm, three-quarters and overhand deliveries, and a lot of different pitches, which helped him.

"But he wasn't as fast, he didn't throw as hard with us as I'd remembered seeing him throw (in the Negro League)," said Harder.

When asked to compare the 1948 Paige with the one he'd seen a few years earlier, Harder said, "If he was a ten in the Negro League, he probably was a five with us . . . but he did a good job for us, as a reliever and when he started.

"Satch was a good guy, though he did his own thing and rules didn't mean too much to him. I don't think anybody (on the team) resented what he did, or got away with, everybody just kind of put up with it, although, if somebody else did what he did, I don't think they would have gotten away with it.

"But Satch . . . well, we all kind of got a kick out of him and his shenanigans, you know? Generally, Boudreau was a pretty laid back manager, except when somebody went beyond the limit."

Baseball has undergone many changes since Harder broke in as a fuzzy-cheeked rookie in 1928 under Peckinpaugh, and as he said, not all of the changes have been for the better.

"I'm glad to see players making more money—my peak salary was $18,000 in 1935 and again in 1936—but in many cases salaries have gotten out of hand," said Harder.

"Sometimes too much money changes a guy. I can't imagine anybody, in baseball or any other line of work, being worth $11 million a year (as Albert Belle was being paid by the White Sox at the time of this interview). And it keeps getting worse. A guy hits .260 and gets $1.5 million or $2 million. That's crazy. I worry about where it's going to end.

"It's got to change. It can't continue the way it's going. The players union has too much power. Clubs can't do anything without first going through the union. The same with agents. You can't do anything without talking to a player's agent.

"And, when clubs—not just in baseball, but in all professional sports—run out of money they just pick up and move somewhere else. But one of these days there won't be any more places to go."

On the other hand, there have been changes for the better, as Harder also pointed out. "The pension plan that players have won is wonderful. And travel is much better than it was in my day, although there were some advantages in traveling by train, as we did, instead of flying, as teams do now.

"We were able to get closer to each other, to know our teammates better, and there's a lot to be said for that. But now, (teams) fly from one city to another in a matter of a few hours, and the players hardly have a chance to say hello to each other."

As for the game itself, Harder chuckled as he said, "It seems strange to me when I read about teams having five-man pitching rotations and each guy getting four days off between starts. In my day we worked with three days' rest and never thought a thing about it. I did that for 20 years.

"And relief pitching is different, too. Now, as soon as a starter gets by the fifth inning, he's practically through and a relief 'specialist' comes in, first, either a middle man or a set-up man, then the closer. When I pitched, the relief pitchers were guys who weren't good enough to be starters."

When Harder was asked if he wished he could be pitching today, he replied, unequivocally, "No . . . because when you get around to the sixth inning and you give up a hit or two, you're gone.

"In a way, pitchers' records are tainted because everybody goes by the number of games a guy wins. How many innings a pitcher pitches doesn't seem to mean anything. If a guy wins ten games he'll make $500,000 and get a three-year contract. That's just for winning ten games!

Mel Harder

"Even the media is different, and that's not all good either," continued Harder. "Now the reporters go into the clubhouse after a game and get a couple of quotes from two or three players and one from the manager, then write their stories without really saying what happened in the game.

"They didn't operate like that in my day. They wrote their stories about what happened in the game and seldom came into the clubhouse. We never saw Cobby (Gordon Cobbledick, former sports editor of the *Cleveland Plain Dealer*), or Whitey (Franklin Lewis, former sports editor of the *Cleveland Press*) in the clubhouse."

In comparing players of the 1930s and 1940s with those who have come along since then, Harder said, "There were more true big leaguers in those years and fewer average players because expansion has watered down the talent. Many of the players who were stuck in the minor leagues (Class AAA) then were better than a lot of big leaguers today.

"But I also will say this: If you take the best players of each era and compare them, in my opinion I think you'd find some who are playing now are better than the best who played when I did, and vice versa.

Now living in Chardon, Ohio, about 35 miles east of Cleveland, Harder is in good health except for a problem with his legs. It prevents him from continuing one of his favorite pastimes, playing golf, which he did regularly until 1994 with two other former Indians pitchers, Harry Eisenstat and Al Milnar, both of whom also live in the area.

"Actually, the problem with my legs involves the muscles and nerves in my feet," said Harder. "I don't have any pain, but it affects my balance. I can't walk like I did when I was young and, when I sit for a while, I have to push myself up and it takes me a little time to get going again.

"I get around all right, though not like I used to, but otherwise I feel fine," said Harder whose wife of 54 years, Sandy, died in 1986. They raised two daughters, Kathryn (who was nicknamed Gay), who was born in 1934 and died in 1994, and Penny, born in 1943. Harder has five grandchildren and seven great grandchildren.

The Indians retired Harder's uniform number—18—in 1989, an honor that was well deserved.

Another honor that is equally well deserved would be Harder's election to the Hall of Fame.

Hopefully, it will be forthcoming.

Mel Harder

——— *BILL VEECK, 1914-87* ———

CHAPTER EIGHTEEN
. . . .

Gone But Not Forgotten

The final roster of the Boys of the Summer of '48 in cluded 38 players, though only 28 made substantial contributions to what was the greatest season in Cleveland Indians history, and 12 of them remain, along with coach Mel Harder.

The 16 who are deceased: Johnny Berardino, Don Black, Russ Christopher, Hank Edwards, Joe Gordon, Jim Hegan, Walt Judnich, Ken Keltner, Ed Klieman, Dale Mitchell, Bob Muncrief, Satchel Paige, Hal Peck, Joe Tipton, Thurman Tucker and Sam Zoldak.

Coaches Bill McKechnie and Muddy Ruel also are deceased.

Johnny Berardino

A utility infielder whose best position probably was second base, Johnny Berardino played in 66 games for the Indians in 1948. Though he batted only .190, Berardino did a good job of filling in for Joe Gordon 20 times, Eddie Robinson 18 times, Lou Boudreau 12 times, and Ken Keltner three times, as well as serving as a pinch hitter and pinch runner.

Berardino was acquired from the St. Louis Browns on December 9, 1947, after he'd initially been traded to Washington, but refused to report to the Senators. Veeck said he made the trade primarily to keep Detroit from getting

Berardino, who had threatened to quit baseball to continue an acting career, which he'd started as a child in the "Our Gang" comedies.

Berardino's primary distinction—though only temporarily—was that he cost the Indians "in excess of $50,000," making it the largest cash outlay in club history until then.

Indians outfielder George Metkovich was included in the trade for Berardino, but couldn't play for the Browns because of a broken finger and was returned to Cleveland, requiring Veeck to pay St. Louis an additional $15,000 for the utility infielder.

Never one to pass up an opportunity for publicity, Veeck capitalized on Berardino's acting aspirations by taking out—and making sure it was appropriately ballyhooed—an insurance policy on the infielder's face.

"We thought it prudent to protect John's future," Veeck said in his autobiography, *Veeck As In Wreck*. "If Berardino had been hit in the face by a batted ball . . . and was left so disfigured that he was no longer able to pursue his career as an actor, he would have been compensated to the amount of one million dollars."

The policy, Veeck subsequently admitted, cost the Indians "something like 78 cents a month . . . but, as I always say, nothing is too good for one of my boys."

Johnny Berardino

Don Black

On July 10, 1947, Don Black reached the zenith of his career, pitching a no-hitter—the first in the 15-year history of the Cleveland Municipal Stadium—against the Philadelphia Athletics, beating them, 3-0, in front of 47,871 fans in the first game of a twi-night double header.

Fourteen months later, Black, who should have been at the peak of his career at age 32, suffered a near-fatal brain hemorrhage during a game on September 13, 1948.

The injury happened while Black was batting in the second inning against the St. Louis Browns and his former teammate, Bill Kennedy. Black fouled off a pitch from Kennedy, then staggered away from the plate. Black turned to umpire Bill Summers and said, "My God, Bill, what happened?"

Summers bent over Black and asked what was wrong, and the pitcher replied, "It started on that last pitch I made to (Eddie) Pellagrini," the last St. Louis batter in the top of the second inning.

According to a newspaper account, "It was a curveball for a third strike and the physical effort expended on that pitch to Pellagrini, plus the full-bodied swing at the plate taken by Black a few minutes later, triggered an aneurysm.

"Blood flooded Black's brain and spinal cord, and he was rushed to the hospital. Surgery was considered but dismissed because Black's condition was too serious. Doctors gave Black only a 50-50 chance to live."

Black survived, but he never pitched again.

It was a drinking problem that drove Black out of Philadelphia when his contract was sold by the Athletics to the Indians on October 2, 1945. Black started the 1946 season with the Indians and posted a 1-2 record in 18 games, but in mid-July was optioned to Milwaukee of the (Class AAA) American Association where he had an 0-5 record and never got back to Cleveland that year.

After joining Alcoholics Anonymous at the insistence of Bill Veeck, Black seemed to have turned his career around, going 10-12 with a 3.92 earned run average in 1947, but was inconsistent again in 1948. Failing to win a job in the starting rotation, Black's record fell to 2-2 in 17 appear-

Berardino remained with the Indians in 1949 and was released after four games in 1950, after which he played for Pittsburgh and the Browns. He returned to the Indians briefly in 1952, and ended his baseball career with the Pirates later that season.

Berardino's best year was 1941 when he hit .271 and drove in 89 runs in 128 games for St. Louis. His lifetime batting average in 11 major league seasons with three clubs was .249 in 912 games. He was one of the few men—perhaps the only man—to play for three different major league teams twice.

After hanging up his spikes, Berardino dropped the second "r" from his name, making it "Beradino," as his acting career flourished. As "Dr. Steve Hardy," Beradino was a regular on "General Hospital," one of the longest-running soap operas on television, from 1963-93. Before retiring from the show, Beradino was honored with a star on the Hollywood "Walk of Fame."

Beradino died at age 79 on May 19, 1996, in Los Angeles.

Don Black

Russ Christopher

Originally a starter, Russ Christopher became a reliever—and one of the best in baseball—in 1947 because he was weakened by a congenital heart ailment that prevented him from pitching more than a couple of innings at a time.

And it was that heart problem, resulting from a childhood case of rheumatic fever, that led to Christopher's contract being sold to the Indians for $25,000 on April 3, 1948.

Christopher made 45 relief appearances for the Indians that season with a 3-2 won-lost record and 2.90 earned run average. He was credited with a league-leading 17 saves (though the save rule was not an official statistic then and was different from what it is now).

The acquisition of Christopher speaks highly for the baseball acumen of Bill Veeck, based on his negotiations in the acquisition of Christopher, as related in his autobiography, *Veeck As In Wreck*:

"Mr. (Connie) Mack told me he couldn't sell Christopher to me because of his bad heart. I told (Mack) I knew all about that. 'But he's in bed with pneumonia,' Mr. Mack said. 'I'm afraid this may be the final blow to the poor boy.'

ances as a spot starter-reliever, prior to suffering the aneurysm.

On September 22, nine days after Black was stricken, Veeck staged a "Don Black Night" at the Stadium, and all proceeds—approximately $40,000—from the crowd of 76,772, were donated to the pitcher.

In his no-hitter, the ninth in the history of the Indians, Black walked six, including the first two batters he faced on eight consecutive pitches, and had to wait out a 45-minute rain delay in the middle of the second inning.

He was aided by four outstanding defensive plays, the first by Joe Gordon, who raced into short right field to snare a pop fly off the bat of Elmer Valo in the third inning, another by George Metkovich, who made a long running catch in deep center field to take a hit away from Buddy Rosar in the fourth, and two by Ken Keltner on grounders by Sam Chapman and Eddie Joost.

Black died at age 42 on April 21, 1959, in Cuyahoga Falls, Ohio.

Russ Christopher

"'I'll give you twenty-five for him,' I said, 'if I can talk to him first.'

"Mr. Mack was shocked. 'That would be a terrible thing for me to do to you. He's a sick man. He can't play.'

"'That's not your problem, Mr. Mack. I'm willing to give you the $25,000 if you'll give me permission to talk to him.'

"Russ was lying in bed, with his head peeking out from a mountain of blankets. At best, Russ was gaunt and hollow cheeked. Sick as he was, he was all nose and ears. Around his eyes there was that sickly bluish cast. I hadn't expected him to look as if he could run a marathon, but to be truthful, the sight of him gave me pause.

"'Hey, Russ,' I said cheerfully. 'Do you think you can pitch?'

"He was so weak he could hardly talk. 'I don't know,' he whispered.

"'Do you want to?'

"'Sure I want to. I'm a pitcher, and I want to pitch. But I don't know. Look at me.'

"'I'm going to go down and buy your contract,' I told him. 'I'll take a gamble on you.'

"'Bill,' he said, 'I think you're crazy but you have my word on one thing. I'll do the best I can for you.'"

Which Christopher did, and which was very good. He's another about whom it could be said that the Indians would not have won the pennant in 1948 without his contributions.

Christopher was a starter for the Athletics from 1942, when he made his major league debut, through 1946, winning in double figures in 1944 (14-14) and 1945 (13-13). In 1947, Christopher's first year as a reliever, he went 10-7 with a 2.90 ERA in 44 appearances.

After the 1948 season, Christopher retired and took a non-strenuous job with an aircraft manufacturer in San Diego. He underwent heart surgery in 1951.

Christopher died at age 37 on December 5, 1954, in Richmond, California.

Hank Edwards

Big things were expected of Hank Edwards, based on his minor league credentials and his competitive zeal from the time he broke into professional baseball in 1939 and hit .395 at Mansfield, Ohio to win the batting championship of the (Class D) Ohio State League.

In 1941, Edwards led the (Class B) Three-I League with a .364 average at Cedar Rapids, Iowa.

Unfortunately, for the Indians as well as Edwards, it was his fierce competitiveness that shortened, and perhaps even cost him a promising career.

In the first game of a double header on August 1, 1948, Edwards suffered a severely dislocated right shoulder making a spectacular leaping catch against the right field fence at the Stadium. It finished him for the season after only 55 games, in which he batted .269, and, of course, kept him out of the World Series. He was never a regular thereafter.

Edwards also suffered a series of injuries that sidelined him for much of 1947, when he hit .260 with 15 homers after a break-through season in 1946. Then, returning from two years in the Army during World War II, Edwards batted .301 and led the American League with 16 triples.

Had he been less competitive, less determined, Edwards probably would have gone on to a much more productive career.

As it was, the Indians sold Edwards to the Chicago Cubs on May 7, 1949, and four years later, the tough luck outfielder's career was finished after he went from the Cubs to Brooklyn and then to Cincinnati, the Chicago White Sox and St. Louis Browns. Edwards retired after the 1953 season with an 11 year major league batting average of .280.

Edwards at age 69 on June 22, 1988, in Santa Ana, California.

Joe Gordon

When Joe Gordon returned in 1946 to the New York Yankees from the Army and World War II, he hit a career low .210 with only 11 home runs in 112 games. It proved to be a great thing for the Indians.

Yes, the Indians.

Because of Gordon's sub-par statistics—in six previous seasons his career average was .278 with 142 homers, and he was the American League's Most Valuable Player in 1942—the Yankees figured he was washed up and traded him to the Indians.

As it was, New York made a good deal for Gordon (and infielder Eddie Bockman), receiving pitcher Allie Reynolds in exchange, on October 19, 1946.

But so did the Indians.

Gordon bounced back to hit .272 with 29 homers and 93 RBIs in 1947, and without the veteran second baseman the Indians would not have won the pennant in 1948.

Gordon, who became a close confidante of player-manager Lou Boudreau and was, in his own right, a team leader, strengthened the Indians' defense up the middle and hit .280 with career highs of 32 homers and 124 RBIs in 1948.

In his four seasons with the Indians, Gordon hammered 100 homers and was named to the American League All-Star team three times, from 1947-49, and from 1939-43 and 1946 with the Yankees.

As a rookie in 1938, Gordon replaced Hall of Famer Tony Lazzeri and, in his seven seasons with the Yankees, played exactly 1,000 games and made exactly 1,000 hits. He participated in five World Series with the Yankees.

Upon retiring after the 1950 season, when he hit .236 with 19 homers and 57 RBIs, Gordon managed in the minor leagues, and on June 26, 1958, replaced Bobby Bragan as manager of the Indians.

Under Gordon the Indians went 46-40 the rest of the season, finishing in fourth place, and were in contention for the pennant in 1959 until the final three weeks, when their final record was 89-65, second best to Chicago.

But it was a season of travail and, with seven games left, Gordon announced his intention to resign. However, General Manager Frank Lane, unable to hire Leo Durocher, convinced Gordon to return in 1960, which he did—though he didn't stay long.

On August 3, with 59 games remaining and the Indians in fourth place with a 49-46 record, seven games behind the league-leading Yankees, Lane and Bill DeWitt, then-general manager of the Detroit Tigers, pulled off an unprecedented trade of managers.

Lane sent Gordon to the Tigers in exchange for Jimmy Dykes. The Indians went on to win 26 and lose 32 under Dykes, while the Tigers were 26-31 under Gordon.

Gordon was not rehired by Detroit, but surfaced in 1961 to manage the Kansas City Athletics the first 60 games of the season, and also managed the Kansas City Royals in 1969.

Gordon died at age 63 on April 14, 1978, in Sacramento, California.

Jim Hegan

His lifetime batting average was only .228, but nobody belittled Jim Hegan when he was the Indians' regular catcher from 1946-56. As Hall of Famer Bill Dickey said, "When you can catch like Hegan, you don't have to hit."

And, as another catcher, Joe Tipton, said of his teammate, "When batters strike out against the Indians, they cuss out Hegan."

Or, as yet another former catcher and manager, Birdie Tebbetts said, "You start and end any discussion of catchers with Jim Hegan. Of all the things a catcher has to do—catch, throw, call a game—Hegan was the best I ever saw."

Hegan made everything look easy, from catching a 100 m.p.h. fast ball, to blocking a wicked breaking curve in the dirt, to throwing a base stealer out at second, to camping under a twisting foul ball, to tagging a runner out at the plate.

An American League All-Star five times (1947, 1949-52), Hegan began his career with the Indians in 1941, spent three years (1943-45) in the Navy during World War II,

Joe Gordon

Catcher Jim Hegan with young son Mike, who grew up to become a major league first baseman and is now a radio and television broadcaster for the Indians.

Walt Judnich

When Walt Judnich started in professional baseball in 1935 as a farmhand of the New York Yankees at Akron, Ohio of the (Class C) Middle Atlantic League, he was called by one observer "a left-handed hitting Joe DiMaggio," which spoke highly of the young center fielder's ability.

And, for the next four years, as Judnich progressed through the Yankees' minor league system, he continued to draw rave reviews. He batted .316 at Oakland of the (Class AA) Pacific Coast League in 1937, and drove in 209 runs the next two seasons at Kansas City of the (Class AA) American Association in 1938, and Newark of the (Class AA) International League in 1939.

But DiMaggio was still in his prime, and the Yankees also had great young outfielders in Tommy Henrich and Charlie Keller, so they sold Judnich to the St. Louis Browns.

From 1940-42, before going into the Air Force for three years during World War II, Judnich continued to live up to his advance notices. He hit .303, .284 and .313 with a total of 55 homers in his three seasons with the Browns.

But soon thereafter, nobody was talking about Judnich being another DiMaggio. After returning from the war his average fell to .262 in 1946, and to .258 in 1947. "I don't know what happened . . . I just never got untracked," Judnich said after he was acquired by the Indians in a five-player trade on November 20, 1947.

Pitcher Bob Muncrief accompanied Judnich to the Indians, and St. Louis received pitcher Bryan Stephens and outfielders Dick Kokos and Joe Frazier and $25,000.

With the Indians, Judnich was expected to take over center field in 1948, which he did, but only temporarily. He was displaced by Thurman Tucker, then was used as a first baseman as well as in the outfield and batted .257 in 79 games. His home run production also dropped drastically, from 18 with the Browns in 1947, to two with the Indians in 1948.

When the season ended, the Indians sold Judnich to Pittsburgh for the waiver price of $10,000, and he was cut loose by the Pirates in 1949 after playing in only ten games.

Judnich at age 54 on July 12, 1971, in Glendale, California.

returned to Cleveland in 1946, and continued with the Indians through 1957 when he was traded to Detroit and then to the Philadelphia Phillies in 1958. His contract was sold to San Francisco in 1959, and Hegan retired after playing for the Chicago Cubs in 1960.

In his 17-year major league career, Hegan was behind the plate for 1,629 games, and caught 20-game winners Bob Feller, Bob Lemon, Early Wynn, Mike Garcia, Herb Score and Gene Bearden, and no-hitters by Don Black, Lemon and Feller.

Despite the praise that invariably was directed his way, Hegan always preferred to talk about his pitcher-teammates. "They threw the ball, I only caught it," he always said.

Hegan, whose son was a major league first baseman-outfielder for 12 seasons and is now a television broadcaster of Indians games, was a coach with the New York Yankees from 1960-73, the Tigers from 1974-78, and the Yankees again in 1979 and 1980.

Hegan died at age 63 on June 17, 1984, in Swampscott, Massachusetts.

Walt Judnich

DiMaggio didn't, primarily because of Keltner, who made two outstanding, back-handed plays behind third base to retire the famed "Yankee Clipper." DiMaggio went hitless for the first time since May 14. In two other trips to the plate that night, DiMaggio walked and bounced into a double play in the eighth inning, as the Yankees won, 4-3.

"I wasn't thinking about DiMaggio's streak when I made those plays," Keltner said. "All I was concerned about was winning the game because we still had a chance (in the pennant race)."

Nicknamed "Benny Beltner" by his roommate, Gene Bearden, Keltner was a rollicking, fun-loving athlete who had as many good times after the games as he did during them. It has been said by those who were there, that nobody—absolutely, not anybody—celebrated more thoroughly after the Indians won the World Series in 1948.

Keltner got his start in professional baseball in 1936 at Fieldale, Virginia of the (Class D) Bi-State League where he hit .360 with 33 homers and 116 RBI.

A .310 average and 27 homers for Milwaukee of the (Class AA) American Association the following season got

Ken Keltner

Though he played more than 1,500 games in the major leagues, two stand out above all others in the 13-year career of Ken Keltner, who was one of the best third basemen the Indians ever had.

Keltner's best game, because it was most important to the Indians, was the October 4, 1948 playoff for the pennant against the Boston Red Sox in Fenway Park.

Keltner, who hit .297 with 31 home runs and a career-high 119 RBI that season, hammered a three-run homer in the fourth inning of that pressure-filled game. It broke a 1-1 tie and gave the Indians a lead that was never jeopardized. He also singled and doubled as the Indians beat the Red Sox, 8-3, to win the pennant.

The other game that shares top billing with that performance by Keltner in Boston took place seven years earlier, on July 17, 1941, to be exact.

It was against the New York Yankees and Joe DiMaggio, who had hit safely in 56 consecutive games and was at the Stadium trying to extend the streak to 57, in front of a then-record night game crowd of 67,468.

Ken Keltner

Keltner to Cleveland where he was the Indians' third baseman from 1938-49 (though he spent 1945 in the Navy during World War II).

The best of Keltner's many good seasons for the Indians was 1939 when he batted .325. He was a member of the American League all-star team from 1940-44, 1946 and 1948. After being released following the 1949 season, Keltner ended his career in Boston in 13 games in 1950.

Keltner died at age 75 on December 12, 1991, in New Berlin, Wisconsin.

Ed Klieman

As was the case with many pitchers of his era, Ed Klieman became a reliever—and a very good one—because he was inconsistent as a starter, which he had been from 1937, when he entered professional baseball, through 1946.

Actually, Klieman started in baseball as an outfielder, but switched to pitching, he said, "because my eyes were so bad I couldn't see well enough from out there," although another factor was that he always had a strong arm.

Klieman's poor eyesight kept him out of the service during World War II, and it was in 1943, while pitching for Baltimore of the (Class AA) International League that he became a 20-game winner, earning a promotion to Cleveland.

After going 11-13 as a rookie with the Indians in 1944, Klieman's record slumped to 5-8 in 1945, and he was demoted to Indianapolis, Indiana of the (Class AAA) American Association in 1946.

Given another opportunity with the Indians in 1947, Klieman blossomed as a reliever, making 58 appearances and was credited with a league-leading 17 saves, with a 3.03 earned run average.

"I don't know what happened, I guess it was just a matter of experience," Klieman tried to explain his success as a reliever."

Klieman's best pitch was a sinker that he learned from a fan while he was pitching for Cedar Rapids, Iowa of the (Class B) Three-I League in 1942.

"An old fellow who came to all our games asked me one night if I wanted to learn how to throw a sinker. I thought he was kidding, but I went along with him," Klieman was quoted in a 1948 newspaper article.

"He came down out of the stands and told me to hold the ball a certain way, and to snap my wrist when I threw it.

When I did, darned if the ball didn't do tricks. It was amazing. By the middle of the season I was going great with my new pitch."

Klieman's record that year was 17-7, and earned him the promotion to Baltimore where he was 23-11 in 1943.

While Russ Christopher was the Indians' ace reliever in 1948, Klieman also was dependable out of the bullpen, making 44 appearances in what is now called a "set-up" role.

That winter, on December 14, 1948, Klieman figured in one of the Indians' best-ever trades; he was packaged with first baseman Eddie Robinson and pitcher Joe Haynes (who'd been obtained from the Chicago White Sox) and sent to the Washington Senators for pitcher Early Wynn and first baseman Mickey Vernon.

Klieman never regained the sharpness that he enjoyed previously, going only 2-0 with three saves in 20 games with Washington and the Chicago White Sox in 1949, and after being traded to the Philadelphia Athletics, pitched in five games in 1950 and was released.

Klieman died at age 61 on November 15, 1979, in Homosassa, Florida.

Ed Klieman

Dale Mitchell

Hank Greenberg and Lou Boudreau had differences of opinion on many subjects during the time they were together with the Indians, from 1948-50, and one of them—a major disagreement—concerned Dale Mitchell, the team's left fielder from 1946-56.

It was Greenberg who chided Mitchell in 1948 for being what he called "a slap hitter." Greenberg, who slugged his way into the Hall of Fame, told Mitchell, in an attempt to motivate him, "Singles hitters drive Fords, home run hitters drive Cadillacs."

But Boudreau obviously was satisfied with the way Mitchell played the game—he was one of the American League's leading hitters midway through that 1948 season—when the manager was quoted in the *Cleveland News* as saying, "If any Indian of our time bats .400, his name will be Dale Mitchell."

Mitchell did hit .432 for the Indians in 1946 when he was promoted from Oklahoma City of the (Class AA) Texas League and played 11 games in September, but never came close to fulfilling Boudreau's prediction.

Dale Mitchell

But he did hit .300 or better six times, with a career-high .336 in 1948, led the American League with 203 hits and 23 triples in 1949, was named to the all-star team in 1949 and 1952, and finished his 11-year major league career in 1956 with the Brooklyn Dodgers with a lifetime average of .312.

Equally impressive was that, in 3,984 plate appearance, Mitchell struck out 346 times, an average of only once every 11.5 times at bat.

Unfortunately and unfairly, Mitchell probably is best remembered by most fans for being called out on strikes as the last batter to face Don Larsen in his perfect game, 2-0, victory for the New York Yankees over the Dodgers in the fifth game of the 1956 World Series.

He was a pinch hitter for Sal Maglie and, until the day he died, Mitchell maintained (and many observers agreed) that Larsen's final pitch, which umpire Babe Pinelli called strike three, was wide of the plate and should have been called ball two.

Though he hit only 41 home runs in his career, including a high of 13 in 1953, Mitchell's last homer (and the only one he hit in 1954) accounted for the deciding run in Early Wynn's 3-2 victory over Detroit on September 18 that clinched the pennant for the Indians.

Mitchell, who became the Indians' regular left fielder in only his second year (1947) of professional baseball, was sold to the Dodgers on July 29, 1956, after he'd lost his position to Al Smith, and retired at the end of that season.

Mitchell died at age 65 on January 5, 1987, in Tulsa, Oklahoma.

Bob Muncrief

The Indians had high hopes that Bob Muncrief could join Bob Feller and Bob Lemon in the starting rotation when they obtained him (with outfielder Walt Judnich) in a five-player deal with the St. Louis Browns on November 20, 1947.

Muncrief had been a consistent, if not greatly successful pitcher for the hapless Browns, whose manager in 1947 was Muddy Ruel, an Indians coach in 1948.

But Muncrief, who was coming off arm surgery that winter, never lived up to expectations. In 21 games, nine as a starter, he compiled a 5-4 record with a 3.98 earned run average which, in a way, was something of a blessing in disguise for the Indians.

Because of Muncrief's inability to pitch well in his starting assignments, the Indians tried Gene Bearden, who had been tabbed as a reliever, and he responded with an outstanding, 20-7 record, winning the playoff game for the pennant, and Game Three in the World Series against the Boston Braves.

Before coming to the Indians with Judnich, in exchange for outfielders Dick Kokos and Joe Frazier, pitcher Bryan Stephens and $25,000, Muncrief was a regular in the Browns' rotation from 1941-47, with an overall 69-67 won-lost record and 3.66 ERA. His best season was 1945, when the Browns finished third and his record was 13-4. Muncrief also won 13 games in 1941, 1943 and 1944.

The Indians sold Muncrief's contract to Pittsburgh on November 20, 1948, and he spent the 1949 season with the Pirates and Chicago Cubs, combining for a 6-11 record. In 1950, Muncrief pitched for the Los Angeles Angels in the (Class AAA) Pacific Coast League where his record was 15-17. He was drafted by the New York Yankees on November 16, 1950. He appeared in only two games for the Yankees in 1951 and was released.

Muncrief died at age 80 on February 6, 1996, in Duncanville, Texas.

Satchel Paige

It is regrettable that Satchel Paige didn't get a chance to pitch in the major leagues until 1948, when—by his admission, he was "about 40 years old, pretty soon," though some believed he was closer to 50— Bill Veeck purchased his contract from the Kansas City Monarchs.

The legendary Negro League star joined the Indians on July 7 and, not only did he prove that he could still pitch and win, Paige also attracted huge crowds whenever he was scheduled to take the mound.

Despite his age, and the fact that he began his career in the Negro Leagues in 1926, Paige still had good stuff, excellent control, despite a wild, windmill delivery, and a variety of distinctive pitches such as the "two-hump blooper," which was a moving change up; "Little Tom," a medium fastball; "Long Tom," his hard fastball; and a "hesitation pitch," in which he momentarily stopped his delivery to throw off a batter's timing.

According to him, the seventh of eleven children, he was born in Mobile, Alabama when accurate birth records were not always kept, which again, he said, accounted for the uncertainty of his age, though it was later believed that he was born in 1906.

His given name was Leroy Robert Paige, but "Satchel" stuck because he had earned money as a youth carrying suitcases at the Mobile train station. Records also show that, in 1918 when he was thought to be 12, Paige was sent to the Alabama Industrial School for Negro Children for five years after being arrested for shoplifting.

It was during his career in the Negro Leagues that Paige barnstormed in the off season with major league stars, including Bob Feller, and also played winter ball in Mexico, Venezuela and the Dominican Republic, drawing huge crowds everywhere.

Paige made his first appearance with the Indians in relief on July 9 when he pitched two scoreless innings (yielding two hits and striking out one) in a 5-3 loss to St. Louis, as 34,780 fans in the Stadium witnessed the historic occasion.

Five days later, on July 15, Paige was credited with his first major league victory when he held the Philadelphia Athletics to three hits in 3 1/3 innings after replacing Bob Lemon with two out in the sixth inning of the second game of a twi-night double header and the Indians rallied for four runs to win, 8-5.

Paige made his first start on August 3 in front of a then-record crowd of 72,434 at the Stadium and pitched seven innings, giving up three runs on seven hits, to win, 5-3, with relief help from Ed Klieman.

Paige went on to win six games while losing one, with 2.48 earned run average, in 21 games, seven as a starter in 1948, and made a brief appearance in the fifth game of the World Series, facing and retiring the only two batters he faced in the seventh inning of the Indians 11-5 loss to the Boston Braves.

Two of his victories in 1948 were shutouts, both against the White Sox, 5-0 in Chicago on August 13, and 1-0 in Cleveland (in front 78,382, the largest night game crowd in baseball history at that time) on August 20.

In 1949, Paige pitched in 31 games with a 4-7 record, and was released at the end of the season when Veeck sold the Indians, only to be signed by Veeck again for the 1951 St. Louis Browns, for whom he pitched through 1953 winning 18 games and losing 23 (including a 12-10 record with ten saves and eight victories in relief in 1952).

Paige resumed barnstorming in 1955, and also pitched in the minor leagues into the 1960s, and was signed for one

Leroy "Satchel" Paige

last hurrah in 1965 by Charley Finley, who owned the Kansas City Athletics. Paige made one appearance for the Athletics, a three-inning starting stint in which he gave up one hit and struck out one batter against Boston on September 25.

He was given a job as a coach for Atlanta in 1968 and 1969 to help him gain a pension, and in 1971 was elected to the Hall of Fame by the Negro Leagues Committee.

"Satch was the most unusual man I've ever known," said veteran sportswriter-columnist Hal Lebovitz, who covered the Indians for the *Cleveland News* and wrote *Pitchin' Man, Satchel Paige's Own Story* in 1948.

"He went by his own drummer . . . he was unusual in all sorts of ways," said Lebovitz. "Schedules and times meant nothing to Satch because he was his own guy, he was in another world. I'd make a date with him and more times than not I couldn't find him. I discovered that the best place to get him was on the trainer's table at the ball park."

Paige also was indifferent to team rules, which created problems for Indians Manager Lou Boudreau, and did nothing to help the pitcher's late-blooming major league career.

When Paige joined the Indians, one of the reasons given for his acquisition was that he could pair up with Larry Doby, the young, often sensitive outfielder who was the first black player in the American League.

That rationale proved to be a fallacy. "They (Paige and Doby) were too much different," said Lebovitz. "Larry was quiet, introverted, and Satch was just the opposite. Very outgoing. As I said, he was his own man. Did his own thing.

"But he could still pitch. No doubt about that. Oh, he didn't have his outstanding fastball anymore, but he had a bunch of other pitches, some of them 'trick pitches,' and he had great control. Nobody could have better control than Satchel did."

Veeck would agree that Paige was "unusual." As he wrote in *Veeck As In Wreck*, "Sometimes Satch would write (on team questionnaires) that he was married, other times that he wasn't. Every day, though, he was leaving a ticket at the box office for Mrs. Paige, and every day a different woman was picking it up. At length, we cited this phenomenon to him to try to get his marital status straightened out for our records.

"'Well,' he said, 'it's like this. I'm not married, but I'm in great demand.'"

Paige died at (the approximate) age of 76 on June 8, 1982, in Kansas City, Missouri.

Hal Peck

A hunting accident cost Hal Peck two toes on his left foot, and a weak throwing arm also kept the left-handed hitting outfielder from reaching the potential many, including Bill Veeck, had predicted for him.

But Peck always was one of Veeck's favorites—the Indians owner called him "my old good luck charm"—and despite his shortcomings, Peck proved to be a valuable commodity, leading the American League with eight pinch hits in 1948.

Veeck and Peck went back a long way together, beginning in 1940 when Veeck owned the Milwaukee Brewers, then in the (Class AA) American Association, and Peck was their right fielder and batted .294 in his third professional baseball season.

Peck played for Veeck and the Brewers through 1944—and, in fact, Veeck was at Peck's bedside when the outfielder shot off his toes on September 3, 1942.

Hal Peck

After Peck came back strong to hit .345 for Milwaukee in 1944, his contract was purchased by the Philadelphia Athletics, for whom he played in 1945 and 1946, then was sold to the New York Yankees who traded him to Cleveland on December 6, 1946

The deal involved five players and turned out to be very good for the Indians, though not only because they acquired Peck. In addition, they received pitchers Al Gettel and a hitherto obscure southpaw knuckleballer named Gene Bearden, in exchange for second baseman Ray Mack and catcher Sherman Lollar.

While Lollar turned out to be an outstanding player for the Chicago White Sox, who got him from the Yankees, the Indians probably would not have won the 1948 pennant without Bearden.

As for Peck, he batted .293 in 114 games for the Indians in 1947, and the following season appeared in only 45 games, nine in the outfield and 30 as a pinch hitter. His playing time was cut to 33 games (only two in the field) when he hit .310, in 1949, his last year in the major leagues.

Peck died at age 78 on April 13, 1995, in Milwaukee, Wisconsin.

Joe Tipton

The presence in spring training of rookie catcher Joe Tipton, whose minor league credentials were outstanding, led to the expectation that Jim Hegan, an excellent receiver whose offensive ability was suspect, would be traded before the 1948 season would start.

Bill Veeck made no secret of the fact that he was exploring opportunities to deal for a starting pitcher, with Hegan being dangled as part of the bait.

But, to the Indians' good fortune, Veeck could not get what he wanted for Hegan, who went on to an excellent career with the Indians. Tipton remained as the second string catcher until he, instead of Hegan, was traded on November 22, 1948 in a deal that led to the acquisition of future Hall of Fame pitcher Early Wynn.

It happened this way: after Tipton appeared 47 games (40 behind the plate) and hit .289, Veeck shipped him to the Chicago White Sox for pitcher Joe Haynes, the son-in-law of Washington Senators owner Clark Griffith.

Then, three weeks later, on December 14, Veeck packaged Haynes with relief pitcher Ed Klieman and first baseman Eddie Robinson and sent them to the Senators for Wynn and first baseman Mickey Vernon.

Tipton, despite his minor league statistics—in four seasons (1941-42, 1946-47) before and after he spent three years in the military service during World War II he never hit less than .313—he was a substitute catcher the rest of his major league career, with the White Sox in 1949, Philadelphia Athletics from 1950-52, the Indians again from 1952-53, and the Senators in 1954.

After leaving the Indians in 1948, Tipton's best season was 1950 when he batted .266 in 64 games for the Athletics, and his seven-year major league career average was .236.

Tipton died at age 72 on March 1, 1994, in Birmingham, Alabama.

Thurman Tucker

Before the Indians were sure that Larry Doby could play the outfield, Bill Veeck dealt for veteran center fielder Thurman Tucker, a light hitting but outstanding defensive player who had spent four of the five previous seasons (1943-47) with the Chicago White Sox.

After a year in the Navy during World War II, Tucker hit .288 in 121 games in 1946 and, though he slumped to .236 in 1947, the Indians liked his glove and speed on the

Thurman Tucker

bases. They got him for minor league catcher Ralph Weigel in a trade on January 27, 1948.

A softspoken, quiet man about whom Franklin Lewis wrote in the *Cleveland Press*: "You never knew Tucker was on the ball club except when he was playing and you saw his name in the lineup . . . (which is) a virtue in baseball, believe me."

Tucker just did his job, whenever he was asked to do so, which he was in the sixth game of the World Series when he made two splendid catches in the outfield, the second to steal what probably would have been a game tying extra base hit off the bat of Clint Conatser. It preserved Bob Lemon's 4-3 victory that won the World Championship for the Indians.

Nicknamed "Joe E." because of his facial resemblance to one of the most popular movie star-comedians at the time, Joe E. Brown, Tucker opened the season as the Indians' center fielder and leadoff batter, with Doby stationed in right.

However, by late June, Tucker was replaced by Walt Judnich and, in mid-July, Doby was installed in center field where he remained for eight seasons.

Judnich was sold to Pittsburgh during the winter of 1948-49, while Tucker remained as a substitute outfielder-pinch hitter-pinch runner until May 7, 1951 when his contract was sold to San Diego of the (Class AAA) Pacific Coast League, ending his major league career with a .255 average in 701 games over nine years.

Tucker died at age 75 on May 7, 1993, in Oklahoma City, Oklahoma.

Sam Zoldak

At one time Sam Zoldak represented the largest cash outlay— more than $100,000—ever paid for a professional baseball player, and turned out to be worth every penny of it.

A left-handed pitcher, Zoldak was dealt to the Indians for that amount and rookie pitcher Bill Kennedy, by the St. Louis Browns on June 15, 1948.

Bill Veeck was the first to admit the price he paid for Zoldak was exorbitant, but said, "If he helps us win the pennant, he's worth three times what we gave to get him."

Which was true. Zoldak won nine games for the Indians that season, losing six, as a spot starter-reliever, though his overall record (including 2-4 with the Browns) was 11-10, the only time in his nine-year major league career he won in double figures.

Zoldak also acknowledged his pricetag had been inflated, as Veeck related in his autobiography, *Veeck As In Wreck*:

"After we won the playoff game in Boston, I threw a gala victory party for the players at the Kenmore Hotel. The champagne flowed like Burgundy, and the Burgundy flowed like champagne. As the evening was coming to an end, I toasted each of the 25 players individually, with a passing mention of their more remarkable attributes and contributions. When I got to Zoldak, I lifted my glass and said, 'And here's to our $100,000 pitcher.'

"Big, round tears began to topple down Sam's chubby face—remember, we were all pretty well along by that time. He threw his arms around me and still sobbing, he said, 'Bill, this is the nicest thing that ever happened to me.

"'But I've got to tell you something, Bill. I'm not really worth $100,000.'"

Sam Zoldak

Pitcher **Mike Garcia**, who went 19-16 at Oklahoma City of the (Class AA) Texas League in 1948, and pitched two innings in one game for the Indians after his late-season promotion (in 1949 he began a 14-year major league career in which he won 142 games and lost 97).

Garcia died at age 62 on January 13, 1986, in Fairview Park, Ohio.

Pitcher **Al Gettel**, who was 11-10 for the Indians in 1947, but failed to win a job in the starting rotation in 1948, losing his only decision in five starts and was traded on June 2, 1948, with outfielder Pat Seerey to the Chicago White Sox for outfielder Bob Kennedy.

Gettel, who will be 81 on September 17, 1998, resides in Virginia Beach, Virginia.

Pitcher **Ernie Groth**, who received a late-season trial with the Indians in 1948 after winning a promotion from Baltimore of the (Class AAA) International League, and on December 2, 1948, was traded with pitcher Bob Kuzava to the Chicago White Sox for pitcher Frank Papish.

Groth, who will be 76 on May 3, 1998, resides in Beaver Falls, Pennsylvania.

Zoldak wasn't in 1949 when, in 27 appearances, all in relief, his record was 1-2 with a 4.25 ERA, and when he went 4-2 in 1950, Zoldak was traded to the Philadelphia Athletics on April 30, 1951. In the three-team deal, Zoldak and catcher Ray Murray went to the Athletics, outfielder Minnie Minoso wound up with the Chicago White Sox, and the Indians got relief pitcher Lou Brissie.

On July 15, 1951, Zoldak pitched the best game of his career, beating the White Sox, 5-0, with a one hitter in the second game of a double header.

But that was his only distinction. After leaving the Indians, Zoldak went 6-10 and 0-6 the next two seasons, giving him a 43-53, nine-year major league career record.

Zoldak died at age 47 on August 25, 1966, in New Hyde Park, New York.

Pitcher **Bill Kennedy**, who appeared in six games, three of them as a starter with a 1-0 record for the Indians in 1948, was traded (with $100,000) to the St. Louis Browns for Sam Zoldak on June 15.

Kennedy died at age 62 on April 9, 1983, in Seattle, Washington.

Pitcher **Bob Kuzava**, an Indians farmhand who was in spring training in 1948 but didn't survive the final cut and was returned to the minor leagues, and on December 2, 1948, was traded with pitcher Ernie Groth to the Chicago White Sox for pitcher Frank Papish.

Kuzava, who will be 75 on May 28, 1998, resides in Wyandotte, Michigan.

Others who were on the Indians roster in 1948, but played only sparingly, if at all:

Pitcher **Lyman Linde**, who'd been a big winner in the Indians farm system, pitched 10 innings in three games for the Indians in 1948, and was returned to the minor leagues.

Hank Ruszkowski

Pitcher **Les Webber** was signed as a free agent after five seasons in the National League with Brooklyn, and pitched two-thirds of an inning in one game for the Indians in 1948, and was released.

Webber died at age 71 on November 13, 1986, in Santa Maria, California.

Pitcher **Charlie Wensloff**, a successful wartime pitcher for the New York Yankees was given a trial by the Indians and appeared in one game in relief and was charged with a loss, and was released.

Wensloff, who will be 83 on December 3, 1998, resides in Mills Valley, California.

Four other players were listed on the Indians roster as published by *The Sporting News* on March 31, but did not make it through spring training: Pitchers **Cal Dorsett**, who died at age 57 on October 22, 1970, in Elk City, Oklahoma, and **Dick Rozek**, who will be 71 on March 27, 1998, and resides in Cedar Rapids, Iowa; first baseman **Elbie Fletcher**, who died at age 78 on March 9, 1994, in Milton, Massachusetts; and shortstop **Len Ratto**, who will be 78 on July 13, 1998, and resides in Concord, California.

Linde died at age 75 on October 24, 1995, in Beaver Dam, Wisconsin.

Catcher **Hank Ruszkowski**, who'd been the Indians opening day catcher in 1945 when he batted .204 in 14 games before going into the Army during World War II, returned to hit .259 in 23 games in Cleveland in 1947, but didn't make the team in 1948.

Ruszkowski, 73 on November 10, 1998, resides in Cleveland, Ohio.

Outfielder **Pat Seerey**, a slugger who could hit baseballs great distances but struck out too often, played for the Indians from 1943-47, and 10 games in 1948 (when he went 6-for-23 .261) before being traded on June 2 to the Chicago White Sox with pitcher Al Gettel for outfielder Bob Kennedy.

Seerey died at age 63 on April 28, 1986, in Jennings, Missouri.

Pat Seerey

Bill McKechnie, the Indians' third base coach from 1947-49, was a successful manager in the National League for the Pittsburgh Pirates from 1922-26, the St. Louis Cardinals from 1927-28, the Boston Braves from 1930-37, and the Cincinnati Reds from 1938-46. His teams won four pennants and the World Series twice.

McKechnie died at age 79 on October 29, 1965, in Bradenton, Florida.

Muddy Ruel, the Indians' bullpen and pitching coach from 1948-50, was Walter Johnson's catcher with the Washington Senators from 1923-27, played for six major league teams from 1915-34; and was manager of the St. Louis Browns in 1947.

Ruel died at age 67 on November 13, 1963, in Palo Alto, California.

Bill McKechnie

EPILOGUE

It was supposed to be the start of a dynasty for the World Champion Cleveland Indians—the Boys of the Summer of '48—whose owner, Bill Veeck, was the reigning "Executive of the Year," whose on-the-field leader, Lou Boudreau, was the American League's Most Valuable Player, and whose pitching staff featured three of the best in all of baseball—Bob Lemon, Gene Bearden and Bob Feller.

It was a team that had faced the most oppressive pressure possible and prevailed, a team that had fought back time after time when the odds against it were the longest, and a team that had been supported in record numbers by a legion of fans who literally idolized virtually every player.

Veeck, who had tried to get rid of Boudreau 12 months earlier, was so happy and *expectant* of even greater things in 1949—he extended the contract of the shortstop-manager through 1950 at a substantial increase in salary, strengthened the pitching staff with the acquisition of Early Wynn, and flatly predicted at the annual "Ribs 'n Roasts" awards dinner that the Indians would win again in 1949.

"We have a better ball club and we should have an easier time (because) we have a pitching staff that is good for another five years," he said.

Even Hollywood expressed its brand of optimism by contracting with Veeck to make a movie, "The Kid From Cleveland," about the Indians, starring George Brent, Lynn Bari and Rusty Tamblyn.

Tamblyn was featured as a juvenile delinquent who reformed because he wanted to be a major league baseball player like his hero, Boudreau. Brent was a sportswriter whose girlfriend was Bari. And the advance publicity called it "the story of a kid, a city and thirty godfathers."

Those "godfathers" were the Indians, and even Veeck, Hank Greenberg and trainer Lefty Weisman had roles in the film.

Initially, everybody was flattered, including—perhaps especially—Boudreau.

But in retrospect, he admitted that the movie was a distraction because of the demands made on the team by the production company, Republic Pictures.

When the Indians were playing in Cleveland, filming would begin about nine in the morning at League Park. After breaking for lunch, Boudreau and the players would shower and go home, then report to the Stadium later in the afternoon for a game that night. The shooting continued into early June.

As Boudreau later said, "It was like being on the road every day. It was more than tiring; it also was a great distraction. I know it hurt me and there's no doubt it had a negative effect on the whole team. Though Veeck never admitted it, I've got to believe he was sorry that he let us go ahead with it."

Whatever the reason—overconfidence, a letdown or, as Boudreau lamented, the lack of concentration caused by their involvement in the movie—the Indians of 1949 fell with a thud from their lofty perch as America's favored team.

And instead of a dynasty, a litany of unsuccessful seasons ensued.

Oh, the Indians won their third pennant six years later, but were swept in the 1954 World Series by the then-New York Giants, came close to winning in 1959, and did win American League championships in 1995 and 1997.

But they still haven't won another World Championship in half a century of trying.

The Indians' failure in 1949, when they plummeted into third place, was capped by Veeck's decision to sell control of the Indians to a group headed by Cleveland insurance executive Ellis W. Ryan.

When the deal was consummated on November 21, 1949, Veeck was quoted by Gordon Cobbledick in *The Plain Dealer*: "I want to get married. I want to take a good long rest. After that—believe me, I haven't the faintest idea what comes after that."

The Indians' fall from grace also cost Boudreau his job, though his departure didn't come until after another season of frustration in 1950.

When the Indians dropped into fourth place behind New York, Detroit and Boston, Boudreau was fired by Greenberg, who had taken over as vice president and general manager and hired Al Lopez to manage the team.

And when the Indians opened under Lopez in 1951, only eight of those who had made significant contributions to the success of the Boys of the Summer of '48, were still key members of the team—Feller, Lemon, Steve Gromek, Larry Doby, Jim Hegan, Bob Kennedy and Dale Mitchell.

Lou Boudreau, (center) Cleveland's shortstop-manager, was all smiles as he congratulates pitcher Bob Feller (left) and Ken Keltner.

What happened in 1949 to bring down the best team in baseball in 1948?

The answers—and there were many—are painfully obvious, though it would be unfair to point a finger at any one as the primary cause.

Bearden, arguably the best pitcher in the American League a year earlier, slumped from 13 victories over .500 to an 8-8 record with a bloated 5.10 earned run average; Feller, on the downside of his remarkable career, won only 15 games while losing 14; Wynn fell short of expectations, compiling an 11-7 record after starting the season with a sore arm; Joe Gordon slumped from .280 with 32 homers and 124 RBI to .251, 20 and 84, and at the age of 34 was on the way out; Ken Keltner, able to play only 80 games because of injuries, hit .232 with eight homers and 30 RBI; and Boudreau himself, coming off his greatest season as baseball's premier clutch hitter, batted 71 points below his 1948 average of .355, his home run production dropped from 18 to four, and his RBIs from 106 to 60.

The Indians started poorly, struggled most of the season and never spent even one day in first place. They lost 17 of their first 29 games, three each by Feller and Bearden, falling into seventh place for three weeks in late May and early June.

It was so bad that, on May 27, Veeck staged a "second opening day," replete with ceremonies and the mayor throwing out a ceremonial first pitch, hoping it would revive the floundering Indians.

But they didn't recover a semblance of satisfaction until the All-Star break, July 11-13, climbing into second place with a 44-32 record, though they were still 51/2 games behind New York. On August 4 the Indians were within 21/2 games of first place, but never got closer and were behind by 11 as late as September 24.

The Yankees, under the direction of new manager Casey Stengel, led the league most of the season, but had to defeat Boston in the final game to win the pennant.

Lou Boudreau with pitcher Bob Lemon.

Bill Veeck

It was Stengel's presence that was considered by many, including Veeck, to have been significant in the downfall of Bearden. The Indians' hero of 1948 never again won in double figures, nor did he even win more games than he lost in any season the rest of his major league career, which ended in 1953.

As Veeck wrote in his book, *Veeck As In Wreck*, Stengel who previously had been Bearden's manager at Oakland, advised his players to lay off Bearden's knuckleball, which usually dropped out of the strike zone, until after there were two strikes against them.

That, Stengel theorized, would force Bearden to come in with a fast ball or curve, both of which were "very ordinary," Veeck said, or start his knuckeball high, making it easier to hit. The information "got around the league with the speed of light, and Bearden was through," Veeck wrote.

Bearden scoffed at Veeck's contention, claiming his trouble in 1949 was due to a severe hamstring injury he suffered in spring training which bothered him all season.

Whatever, as said by Hal Lebovitz, a sportswriter for the *Cleveland News* at that time. "The 1949 Bearden wasn't the 1948 Bearden anymore ... not even close."

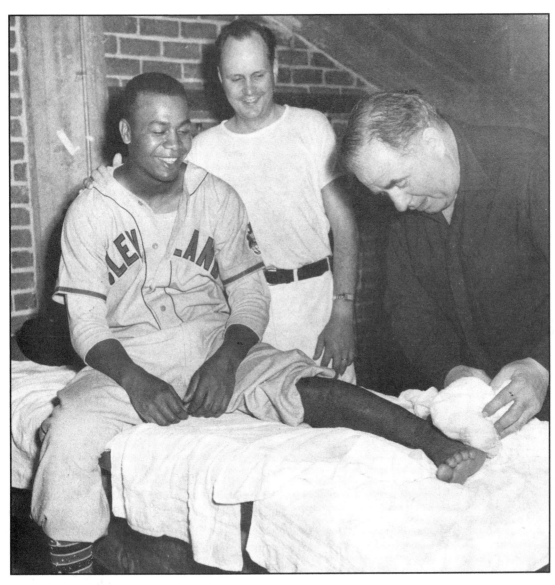

Larry Doby with trainers Wally Bock (center) and Lefty Weisman in 1949.

On September 23, with the Indians in fourth place, eleven games behind the Yankees, Veeck capitulated, holding a mock funeral at the Stadium prior to the game that night against Detroit.

The pennant won by the Boys of the Summer of '48 was brought in by a horse-drawn hearse and buried behind the center field fence.

Then, with 29,646 "mourners" in the stands, the Indians lost again, 5-0.

And two months later, Veeck sold the Indians for $2.2 million.

Greenberg wasted no time making over the Indians in 1950. Keltner was released, Gordon would be replaced at second base by Bobby Avila, and Ray Boone took over as the regular shortstop with Boudreau filling the role of utility infielder.

But it made no difference. By early September, with the Indians mired in fourth place, all but mathetmatically out of the pennant race and attendance declining, Greenberg publicly criticized Boudreau and the players.

"We may lose (the pennant) again in 1951, but not with this team," he said.

Greenberg lived up to his threat. Boudreau was fired, several key roster changes were made, and the Indians didn't win the pennant again.

And though they did in 1954, and in 1995 and 1997, there has not been a World Series Championship in Cleveland in half-a-century—or a season that compares with that which was achieved by the Boys of the Summer of '48.

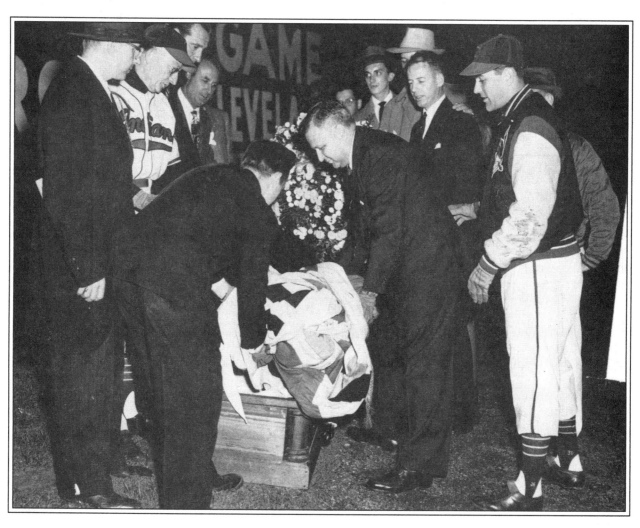

MOCK BURIAL SERVICES FOR THE 1948 PENNANT.

1948 Cleveland Indians Pitching/Batting Statistics

	W	L	G	GS	CG	IP	H	BB	SO	ERA
Gene Bearden	20	7	37	29	15	229 2/3	187	106	80	2.43
Don Black	2	2	18	10	1	52	57	40	16	5.37
Russ Christopher	3	2	45	0	0	59	55	27	14	2.90
Bob Feller	19	15	44	38	18	280 1/3	255	116	164	3.56
Mike Garcia	0	0	1	0	0	2	3	0	1	0.00
Al Gettel	0	1	5	2	0	7 2/3	15	10	4	17.61
Steve Gromek	9	3	38	9	4	130	109	51	50	2.84
Ernie Groth	0	0	1	0	0	1	1	2	0	9.00
Bill Kennedy	1	0	6	3	0	11 1/3	16	13	12	11.12
Eddie Klieman	3	2	44	0	0	79 2/3	62	46	18	2.60
Bob Lemon	20	14	43	37	20	293 2/3	231	129	147	2.82
Lyman Linde	0	0	3	0	0	10	9	4	0	5.40
Bob Muncrief	5	4	21	9	1	72 1/3	76	31	24	3.98
Satchel Paige	6	1	21	7	3	72 2/3	61	25	45	2.48
Les Webber	0	0	1	0	0	2/3	3	1	1	40.50
Charlie Wensloff	0	1	1	0	0	1 2/3	2	3	2	10.80
Sam Zoldak	9	6	23	12	4	105 2/3	104	24	17	2.81
	97	58		156	66	1,4091/3	1,246	628	595	3.22

	G	AB	R	H	2B	3B	HR	RBI	SB	AVG.
Johnny Berardino	66	147	19	28	5	1	2	10	0	.190
Ray Boone	6	5	0	2	1	0	0	1	0	.400
Lou Boudreau	152	560	116	199	34	6	18	106	3	.355
Allie Clark	81	271	43	84	5	2	9	38	0	.310
Larry Doby	121	439	83	132	23	9	14	66	9	.301
Hank Edwards	55	160	27	43	9	2	3	18	1	.269
Joe Gordon	144	550	96	154	21	4	32	124	5	.280
Jim Hegan	144	472	60	117	21	6	14	61	6	.248
Walt Judnich	79	218	36	56	13	3	2	29	2	.257
Ken Keltner	153	558	91	166	24	4	31	119	2	.297
Bob Kennedy	66	73	10	22	3	2	0	5	0	.301
Dale Mitchell	141	608	82	204	30	8	4	56	13	.336
Ray Murray	4	4	0	0	0	0	0	0	0	.000
Hal Peck	45	63	12	18	3	0	0	8	1	.286

	G	AB	R	H	2B	3B	HR	RBI	SB	AVG.
Eddie Robinson	134	493	53	125	18	5	16	83	1	.254
Al Rosen	5	5	0	1	0	0	0	0	0	.200
Pat Seerey	10	23	7	6	0	0	1	6	0	.261
Joe Tipton	47	90	11	26	3	0	1	13	0	.289
Thurman Tucker	83	242	52	63	13	2	1	19	11	.260
		5,446	840	1,534	242	54	155	802	54	.282

OTHER TITLES PUBLISHED BY SPORTS PUBLISHING INC. INCLUDE:

Lou Boudreau: Covering All the Bases
by Lou Boudreau with Russell Schneider

Lou Boudreau: Covering All the Bases is the personal history of one of the most extraordinary men in baseball history. While leading the Indians to the 1948 World Series victory, he invented the "Ted Williams' shift", and became the only player/manager ever to win the American League MVP award. Voted to the Hall of Fame in 1970, Boudreau also managed the Kansas City Athletics, Boston Red Sox, and Chicago Cubs and served as a Cubs broadcaster for 30 years. $24.95

Lou Boudreau: Covering All the Bases
Limited leatherbound edition.

Leatherbound edition signed by Hall of Famers Boudreau and Bob Feller. Limited to 500 copies. $59.95.

Just Call Me Minnie: My Six Decades in Baseball
by Minnie Minoso with Herb Fagen

On May 1, 1951, a legend was born. Newly acquired Orestes Minoso, the first African-American to play major league baseball in Chicago, stepped into the batter's box for his first at bat in a White Sox uniform. Minnie tells of his boyhood in the sugar fields of Cuba, racial discrimination in Cuban society, and feelings of betrayal upon being traded from the Cleveland Indians to the Chicago White Sox in 1951. $19.95.

New Release!

All the Way to The Top: The 30th Anniversary of the 1968 Ohio State National Champion Football Team
by Steve Greenburg and Larry Zelina

Celebrate the 30th anniversary of the last undisputed Big Ten National Champion football team with *All the Way to the Top*, scheduled for release in Fall 1998. The 10-0-0 Buckeyes featured a star-studded cast with players like Brockingham, Otis, Tatum, Hayden, Worden, Mayes, Jankowski and many more. Get the inside scoop on the team that defeated O.J. Simpson's Southern Cal team for the national championship. $29.95.

Bob Huggins: Pressed for Success
by Bob Huggins with Mike Bass

Since taking over an embattled basketball program at the University of Cincinnati in 1989, Bob Huggins has inspired almost as many debates as victories. He has returned the team to its heritage of being a national program, taken the school to the Final Four and Elite Eight, and earned enough respect that he was almost swept away by the Miami Heat. $22.95.

Bob Huggins: Pressed for Success
by Bob Huggins with Mike Bass

Leatherbound edition signed by Huggins.
Limited to 500 copies. $49.95.

AVAILABLE IN ALL FINE BOOKSTORES
or to order any of these titles *call* 1(800)327-5557,
fax (217)359-5975, *e-mail* us at
SportsPublishingInc.com
or *send* orders to Sports Publishing Inc.,
804 North Neil Street, Suite 100, Champaign, IL 61820.